Blood 'n' Thunder's Cliffhanger Classics Volume 2

Blood 'N' Thunder's Cliffhanger Classics Volume 2

Ed Hulse

MURANIA PRESS

DOVER, NEW JERSEY

Copyright © 2017 by Murania Press

ISBN-13: 978-1546881032
ISBN-10: 1546881034

Most of the essays herein were originally published in *Blood 'n' Thunder* magazine and are copyright © their respective years of publication (2012-2017) by Murania Press. Other essays have been reprinted from the book *Handsome Heroes and Vicious Villains* and are copyright © 2016 by Murania Press.

All rights reserved. No part of this publication may be reproduced, stored in a retrieval system, or transmitted in any form by any means—electronic, mechanical, photocopying, audio recording, or otherwise—without the written permission of the copyright holder. Inquiries can be addressed to muraniapress@yahoo.com.

Special thanks to Sam Sherman and Packy Smith for contributing scans of rare stills from their collections.

Murania Press
Dover, New Jersey
muraniapress.com

Book Design and Layout: Ed Hulse
Cover Design and Execution: Chris Kalb

Printed in the United States of America

FIRST EDITION

10 9 8 7 6 5 4 3 2 1

Contents

7 Preface

9 Introduction to Volume One

15 The Perils of Pauline

28 The Million Dollar Mystery

44 The Diamond from the Sky

58 The First Serial Team: Ford and Cunard

84 The Riddle Rider: William Desmond

97 Gallery 1

115 Tarzan the Fearless

130 Chandu the Magician: A Brief History

155 The Lost City

164 Radio Patrol

175 Red Barry

187 Gallery 2

205 Hawk of the Wildnerness

215 The Spider, Master of Men

231 Adventures of Red Ryder

247 Anatomy of a Serial: The Making of Spy Smasher

269 Secret Service in Darkest Africa

280 Gallery 3

Preface

THE FIRST VOLUME of *Blood 'n' Thunder's Cliffhanger Classics* was published in the summer of 2012 and quickly became a reliable seller in the Murania Press catalog. Since "Cliffhanger Classics" remained a popular department in *Blood 'n' Thunder* until I ceased publication of the magazine in 2016, it seemed like a good idea to bring out a second collection.

Volume One's coverage was divided more or less equally between silent and sound serials. It also featured essays from multiple contributors, including Rex Layton, Daniel Neyer, and Brian Taves. This time around the articles are all mine, with one-third devoted to silent-era chapter plays and two-thirds to those of the talkie years. Although the early titles are unavailable for screening (with the exception of *The Perils of Pauline*, about half of which exists and is accessible), the sound serials covered in these pages can be seen without much difficulty. Some are commercially available on DVD; others were released on VHS and laserdisc, and still can be tracked down in those formats; and several more are easily viewed on streaming-video websites.

For this book I've decided to reprint my introduction to Volume One. It offers historical background I would otherwise have to recapitulate, and, frankly, I doubt I could say it any better. The single thing worth repeating is that I've always taken chapter plays seriously, unlike many film historians, and have scrupulously avoided rehashing the work of others. Wherever possible I've obtained first-hand information and recollections from those who actually made the serials: actors, writers, stuntmen, producers, and directors. To aid with documentation I've consulted primary source materials—original scripts, studio records, trade-journal reviews and news stories—rather than rely solely on the memories of elderly Hollywood veterans.

One essay included herein warrants special mention. "Anatomy of a Serial: The Making of *Spy Smasher*," written specifically for this book, is my attempt to chronicle production of a well-regarded chapter play from beginning to end. Over the years I've gleaned a great deal of information about *Spy Smasher* from director William Witney, stuntmen Dave Sharpe and Tom Steele, leading lady Marguerite Chapman, and action heavies Tris Coffin and George J. Lewis. But the essay could not have been possible without the pioneering work of Republic Pictures superfan Jack Mathis, whose fine books *Republic Confidential* and *Valley of the Cliffhangers* set a new standard for Hollywood studio histories.

I never met Jack personally, but we spoke by phone several times and he was always generous with his time. He was also happy to authenticate my findings and offer additional facts—taken straight from Republic records, to which he had unlimited access—that filled gaps in my own research. Much of the hard information in the *Spy Smasher* essay, including budget items and location details, came from Jack. Some of it he gave to me over the phone, the rest can be found scattered throughout his books. But I couldn't have written my own account of this classic serial's production without his help.

Ed Hulse
June 2017

Introduction

I LOVE SERIALS. Always have, always will.

As a middle-aged man who remains enthusiastic about a cinematic form that generally targeted juvenile audiences, I've often found it difficult to explain my fondness for the chapter play and, frankly, have given up trying. The old maxim comes to mind: "For those who understand, no explanation is necessary. For those who *don't* understand, no explanation is possible."

My love affair with movie serials began in 1962, when I was nine years old. Growing up in northern New Jersey, I watched television stations that broadcasted from New York City. One of them, WPIX, ran an afternoon kiddie show hosted by a local celebrity who dressed like a cop and called himself Officer Joe Bolton. His daily program, which aired in the late afternoon just as kids were arriving home from school, offered cartoons, Three Stooges comedies, and serial chapters.

One day, having visited a friend's house to consummate a comic-book trade, I stayed long enough to see *Officer Joe's Funhouse* for the first time. The genial host's avuncular patter didn't particularly impress me, but the serial chapter—from Republic's 1952 epic, *Zombies of the Stratosphere*—gripped me from beginning to end. The hero, a guy named Larry Martin (played by Judd Holdren, as I later learned), was prosecuting a war against alien invaders using little more than his "rocket suit" and a ray-gun or two. Of course, the bullet-shaped helmet and leather-jacket rocket pack had been developed several years earlier for *King of the Rocket Men*, but I had no way of knowing that at the time. Nor did I have any idea that the episode's cliffhanging ending, in which an unconscious Martin lay slumped in the front seat of his speedboat while it sailed over the crest of a waterfall to plunge into the churning rapids below, was stock footage from *G-Men vs. the Black Dragon* (1943).

No, what really grabbed me was the mingling of frustration and anticipation I felt when the final shot cut to black and Officer Joe's beaming countenance once again filled the small screen. To found out what happened to Larry Martin, he explained, we'd have to turn in tomorrow at the same time. In those days, to avoid confusing young viewers, WPIX cut away after the cliffhanger ending, just before the end-title card that said "At This Theater Next Week." Instead, Officer Joe spelled out the next chapter title in a simple alphabetical code. That was the tease; once you'd decoded something along the lines of "Death Rides the Rails" or "Plunge to Oblivion," there was no way you were going to miss the following episode.

After seeing a few more chapters of *Zombies*, I was hooked. It was followed by *Radar Men from the Moon*, which brought back the rocket suit, now owned by a bland-looking fellow who called himself Commando Cody. At the time I didn't know that *Radar Men* had preceded *Zombies*, but it didn't matter. I was enthralled just the same.

Officer Joe's "Funhouse" ran Republic serials from the Fifties, and over the next year I saw them all. Other WPIX programs presented older serials, especially the Flash Gordons, which were on the air almost continuously, in one time slot or another, for the entire decade. During one glorious summer—it was either 1965 or '66—the station ran classic chapter plays every weekday morning: *The Phantom Empire* on Mondays, *Tim Tyler's Luck* on Tuesdays, *The Masked Marvel* on Wednesdays, and so on. They all delighted me, to varying degrees.

The fall of 1966 saw competing station WOR launch a Saturday-afternoon program titled "Action Theater" or something along those lines. In two-hour time slots it ran the 100-minute feature versions of 26 Republic serials, hastily prepared by National Telefilm Associates (owners of the Republic film library) to capitalize on the success of the *Batman* TV show and the recent theatrical release of the 1943 *Batman* serial produced by Columbia. WOR's director of film programming, Chris Steinbrunner, was a serial fan from way back, but he didn't have to sell station management on the wisdom of leasing the NTA package. They offered no resistance. In those days the hip pop-culture trend was "high camp," and what could possibly be more campy than those old "cliffhangers," right? Meanwhile, I looked down my 13-year-old nose at the erstwhile hipsters who sneered and chuckled at serials. What did *they* know?

By this time I had practically memorized every word in every issue of *Screen Thrills Illustrated*, a short-lived companion magazine to Forrest J. Ackerman's *Famous Monsters of Filmland*. Publisher Jim Warren saw *Screen Thrills* as another catalog for the motley assortment of mail-order products he sold as "Captain Company." But editors Sam Sherman and Bob Price were determined to make the new zine a haven for serial lovers like me. They reprinted rare photos, wrote perfunctory articles on chapter plays, and occasionally interviewed old serial stars; every one of *Screen Thrills'* ten issues offered something new to me.

Around this time I also discovered Alan G. Barbour, a Queens, New York resident who self-published his own magazines, targeted even more narrowly to hard-core film buffs. His chapbook-sized *The Serials of Republic* was indispensable to me because it listed casts and credits. By comparing character names to performer names while watching chapter plays, I was soon able to identify my favorite players and stuntmen by sight.

What I didn't know at the time was that all these people—Alan Barbour, Chris Steinbrunner, Sam Sherman, Bob Price—were friends and film collectors who assembled at various places (most often Alan's Queens apartment) to watch old 16mm prints of the classic cliffhangers. In fact, there existed in New York City an entire underground network of movie buffs, many of whom congregated at a tenement-basement "clubhouse" every weekend to screen old serials, Westerns, and "B" mysteries.

I met Chris Steinbrunner at the 1972 New York Comic Con, where he handled the film programming; at that holiday-weekend convention I saw *Adventures of Captain Marvel* for the first time. Chris invited me to join the club, rather pretentiously called the Cooperative Film Society, and for the next ten years or so I could be found there more weekends than not. Joining this group of aficionados also persuaded me that I just *had* to start collecting 16mm—a decision that kept me broke but happy for a good many years. Prints were hideously expensive, especially compared to the later videotapes, videodiscs, and DVDs. Complete serials in 16mm cost hundreds of dollars.

Back in the early Seventies I resolved to see every extant sound serial—which is all but a handful of the 231 produced. It was an undertaking I finally completed in 2009 upon seeing the recently unearthed *Daredevils of the West* at the Lone Pine Film Festival. I still hold out hope that the few remaining "lost" serials, including *Tarzan the Fearless* and *Clancy of the Mounted*, will be found during my lifetime.

I began writing about episodic epics in 1966 with a series of articles published in *Photon*, a mimeographed fanzine devoted primarily to horror and science-fiction movies. The editor, Mark Frank, was not keen on covering serials, but I persuaded him to let me do so provided I draw some connection to fright-film icons. Hence my articles on *Shadow of Chinatown* and *The Return of Chandu* (both with Bela Lugosi) and *Captain America* (Lionel Atwill), among others.

The Seventies found me attending various nostalgia-themed film festivals where I met—and in some cases developed long-lasting friendships with—actors, stuntmen, writers, and directors who toiled on some of my favorite chapter plays. During this period I was intensively researching serials, and interviewing the people involved in their making filled many gaps in my knowledge.

When I started writing professionally in 1980, my knowledge of movies in general helped me secure a berth at the late, lamented *Video Review* magazine, which every month published hundreds of capsule reviews for the benefit of home tapers. At that time the major studios were just beginning to dip their toes into the video waters, and most titles they released on tape were relatively recent films. *Video Review* covered their product while also providing a valuable service to curious cinephiles who kept stocked up on blank tape. My first major article on serials ran in a 1981 issue.

As both a professional journalist and a film historian, I interviewed dozens of actors, actresses, writers, directors, and even stuntmen who worked in chapter plays. Being involved in the planning of such film festivals as Cinecon, an annual event celebrating silent and early-talkie movies, enabled me to meet even more "picture people." In 1991, *Captain Marvel*'s Frank Coghlan Jr. helped me arrange a 50th-anniversary reunion of that classic serial's surviving participants, including director William Witney and cast members Louise Currie and Billy Benedict. The following year, at my behest, *Hop Harrigan* star William Bakewell persuaded his old friend Sally Blane to appear at Cinecon.

At that same 1992 festival I was introduced to Kay Hughes, leading lady of Republic's *The Vigilantes Are Coming* and the first *Dick Tracy* chapter play. While working with *Entertainment Tonight*'s Leonard Maltin on a book project, I assisted him during the production of his Cliffhangers documentary for Republic Pictures Home Video. In that capacity I met and struck up a friendship with Barry Shipman, one-time head writer of Republic serials. More recently, as a moderator of panels at the annual Lone Pine Film Festival, I've interviewed distaff serial stars Noel Neill, Peggy Stewart, Lois Hall, and the late Ann Rutherford. All in all, I've gleaned valuable information from more than a hundred veterans of episodic thrillers.

Most of the essays in this book, which originally saw print in the pages of my journal *Blood 'n' Thunder* (you can check it out at muraniapress.com) include first-hand information gleaned during those many encounters with survivors of Hollywood's Golden Age. I've never been interested in writing gushy, fact-free, sentimental articles on these films. I've always believed serials worthy of study and documentation, no matter how unimportant they have seemed not only to film historians but also to the people who made them. Chances are, many of you reading this book are familiar with the chapter plays covered herein. But I'm willing to bet that you'll learn a great deal about them you never knew or even suspected. If you love serials as much as I do, you'll enjoy the 20 essays that follow. And if you don't . . . well, this book might just be the beginning of a beautiful friendship.

Ed Hulse
July 2012

The Perils of Pauline

(1914, Pathé / Eclectic Film Company)

MOVING PICTURES WERE an exciting novelty in 1896, when four French brothers—Charles, Jacques, Emile, and Theophile Pathé—founded a company they not surprisingly called Pathé Frères. The siblings began producing and exporting short films immediately, and that same year a Pathé "movie" was exhibited for the first time in America at Buffalo's Vitascope Theater. With Charles as the firm's driving force, Paris-based Pathé Frères expanded rapidly, acquiring the Lumiere brothers' camera patents in 1902 and opening branches in 18 foreign cities over the next two years. The New York City branch generated the most revenue due to America's enormous demand for filmed entertainment. By 1907 nearly two thirds of the 1,200 motion pictures released annually in the United States were still being made outside the country. Most came from France, and most of those were Pathé productions.

That situation changed as American nickelodeon owners and patrons gradually came to resent European-made films and began clamoring for domestically produced pictures reflecting our values and culture. Jacques A. Berst, general manager of Pathé's fast-growing American division, urged the brothers to let him establish a permanent studio in this country. The firm already maintained a processing plant in Bound Brook, New Jersey, and had just reached an accommodation with the Edison-led Motion Picture Patents Company, which essentially bullied Pathé into joining the trust. This was no time to alienate American theatergoers.

Berst acquired property in Jersey City, just across the river from Pathé's New York headquarters, and in 1910 had a studio built on the corner of Congress Street and Webster Avenue. The tops and sides of its two stages were made of small glass panes, greenhouse-style, to facilitate natural-light photography, but the studio was also outfitted with large arc lights and banks of Cooper-Hewitt mercury-vapor tubes for use during periods when sunlight wasn't sufficiently plentiful. Future Oscar-winning cinematographer Arthur Miller, at that time working for Pathé's newsreel division, remembered the studio at 1 Congress Street as "one of the most modern and well equipped of the time."

Enjoined from releasing too much product through the trust's distribution outlet, General Film Company, Pathé Freres sought other means of getting both its European- and American-made films into theaters. To this end a subsidiary, first called Cosmopolitan Films but almost immediately renamed Eclectic Film Company, was formed in late 1912 with Pathé employee Kurt W. Linn listed as "general agent." Pathé's ownership of the new firm was not publicized for fear of antagonizing the trust. Linn spent most of 1913 touring the country and renting space for exchanges in major cities. An anonymous squib in the Chicago-based trade paper *Motography* said of his activities, "[I]f we can read the signs, we are face to face with a new and powerful film factor that must be reckoned with, beginning now."

In early 1914, the prominent trades reported that Pathé had just aligned itself with the powerful Hearst newspaper chain, a development that would revolutionize the motion-picture business. It immediately resulted in what would become the most famous (if not the best) serial of them all.

By that time William Randolph Hearst's dominance of America's media culture was unquestionable. The 1912 acquisition of the *Atlanta Georgian*, his first Southern sheet, gave Hearst important daily newspapers in every region of the country and six major cities. That same year he bought *Harper's Bazaar*, adding it to his stable of prosperous slicks, which included *Good Housekeeping* and *Cosmopolitan*. The latter, with a circulation of some 750,000 copies, was his most successful magazine.

Hearst had put an indelible personal stamp on his newspapers by syndicating to them news, photographs, feature articles, gossip columns, comic strips, and a Sunday supplement. The creation and dissemination of this material was handled by a recently formed subsidiary, the International News Service (I.N.S.), which also established a wire service to transmit breaking news. With myriad sources of information at his disposal both here and abroad, the media magnate next turned his attention to motion pictures, enlisting the aid of Colonel William Selig to produce a weekly newsreel. Pathé and Vitagraph already marketed newsreels, but neither organization had the resources or news-gathering talent available to Hearst. The first *Hearst-Selig News Pictorial*, distributed by General Film Company, was released on February 17, 1914. By then "the Chief," as Hearst's employees called him, was already planning something new.

At that time millions of Americans purchased Hearst newspapers every Sunday. Just as the Hearst-Selig newsreel was getting underway, Edward A. McManus, by then working for the Chief, brokered a deal that would prove mutually beneficial to Pathé and the media tycoon. Although the plan's exact details remain murky—not even Hearst's several biographers were able to uncover them—they involved running prose versions of Pathé-released films in both the daily papers and the syndicated Sunday supplement, then edited by Morrill Goddard. Presumably Pathé committed to lucrative advertising contracts in exchange for what amounted to a full page of publicity every day.

"Boosting Pathé Pictures," a news story in the March 14, 1914 issue of *Moving Picture World*, quoted Pathé executive L. P. Bonvillain on the new alliance's merits. "From our reports," he stated, "we are led to believe that the scheme is bringing to the picture theaters a new clientele—a fresh class of people is becoming interested. We can now, through the medium of all these newspapers, which cover so large a portion of the more thickly settled sections of the country, tell the story of the picture in a satisfactorily complete form. We can do fully what the sub-titles try to do: We can make more intelligible all the happenings of the play; we can analyze character, explain motives—we can, if you will, amplify the action and set forth those things which cannot be shown on the screen."

Bonvillain went on to say that, from a commercial point of view, the newspaper fictionalizations would prove just as enticing to potential movie patrons as the large, colorful posters displayed outside theaters. "Instead of limiting the advertising of the picture to the very door of a theater, we are carrying it further. We are going into the whole city, into the whole of many cities, to try and bring customers to [the exhibitor], to attract them to his place."

World subscribers reading Bonvillain's words were probably unaware that Hearst had already taken advantage of the alliance with Pathé in a way none could have anticipated. No doubt mindful that the *Chicago Tribune*'s circulation had grown by 10 percent while publishing a prose version of Selig's chapter play, *The Adventures of Kathlyn*, the Chief decided to bring something similar to Pathé on a silver platter. He discussed the idea with numerous staffers and began scouting around for an author of note to write an original story. Morrill Goddard suggested his brother Charles, an accomplished playwright whose stage hits included *The Ghost Breaker* (1909) and *The Misleading Lady* (1913).

Although Charles W. Goddard had no previous experience writing screen stories or scenarios, he accepted the assignment and whipped up a 500-word synopsis that Morrill edited before they took it to Hearst, who asked questions and made suggestions. Reportedly the Chief himself came up with a title: *The Perils of Pauline*. After their meeting, on the way home, Charles suddenly realized they hadn't left a copy of the synopsis with Hearst. "Oh, he doesn't need a copy," Morrill said. "He has one in his memory." (This was not a facetious claim: months later, following the serial's completion, the tycoon good-naturedly chided Goddard for neglecting to tie up a loose end left dangling in the first chapter.)

Pathé readily agreed to undertake filming of *The Perils of Pauline*, which became the pet project of 38-year-old Louis J. Gasnier, a French theatrical director who started working for the company in France and emigrated to America in 1912. The serial was carefully planned, not only with regard to its physical production but also to promotion, advertising, and distribution. Prose versions of each chapter would appear in Sunday editions of Hearst newspapers (and others that chose to purchase it from the Newspaper Feature Service, forerunner of King Features Syndicate) with their celluloid counterparts exhibited in theaters on Mondays. Installments were released fortnightly—not weekly, as has often been reported—to maximize the impact of advertising placed during the intervening two weeks. As an inducement to get patrons into theaters for the first episode, Pathé announced a contest that offered a thousand dollars to some lucky spectator who correctly guessed the answer to a question—"What Did the Mummy Say?"—posed in a Chapter One sub-title. Participants were instructed to confine their answers to 200 words. The contest was extended for months, with Pathé promising to award a total of $25,000 in cash prizes.

As the serial's heroine, heiress Pauline Marvin, Gasnier cast 24-year-old Pearl White, a native of Springfield, Missouri. Of English and Scotch ancestry, born to descendants of early Puritan settlers, Pearl attended public school until the middle of her sophomore year in high school, when she succumbed the blandishments of the stage and began performing with the Springfield-based Diemer's Stock Company. Her father quickly put a stop to her budding career, which resumed after she turned 18 and left home to join another stock company touring throughout Missouri, Kansas, and Oklahoma. That same year she married one of her fellow troupers, Victor Sutherland, but the impetuously conceived union was not successful.

Pearl claimed later that her voice, never strong to begin with, gave out after several years of strenuous emoting in melodramas of the 10-20-30 type. In 1910 she abandoned stage work for silent films, working first for the New York-based Powers Film Company, then briefly at Lubin and Pathé, and finally with the Crystal Film Company, for which she appeared in nearly 100 productions, most of them one-reelers. Attractive and vivacious, Pearl built a loyal following among motion-picture fans, and while the Crystal films were not the sort to strain her histrionic ability, they proved her more than capable of essaying the leading role in a serial. On screen she was refreshingly natural and spontaneous, a winning combination.

The story devised by Charles W. Goddard was a simple one that allowed for a variety of subplots. Pauline Marvin, the ward of a recently deceased millionaire, was due to inherit half of the family fortune upon reaching the age of 21. Should anything happen to her before that time, the inheritance would go to the millionaire's faithful secretary, Raymond Owen. While Pauline, an aspiring writer, willingly courted danger to get sensational material for her stories, the greedy Owen plotted ways to have her killed in order to claim her share of Marvin's wealth. The old man's son, Harry, who loved Pauline and wanted to marry her, served as the girl's protector, but whether he would always be around to save his sweetheart from Owen and his henchmen was an open question. Matinee idol Crane Wilbur, a handsome young man with dark, wavy hair, played Pauline's suitor and German character actor Paul Panzer took the villain role.

Goddard provided each episode's story, which was adapted to scenario form by George B. Seitz, one of Pathé's top scriptwriters. Interiors were shot in the Jersey City studio, but for exteriors the *Pauline* unit visited numerous locations in New Jersey (including Fort Lee, Coytesville, and Englewood) and New York (including Saranac Lake and Ausable Chasm in the Adirondack mountains). The cinematography was handled by former newsreel cameraman Arthur Miller, not quite 19 years old, and his assistant Harry Wood.

Also among the crew were Joe Cuny, Frank Redman, and Charles "Pitch" Revada, who performed multiple functions in those pre-union days. Redman took charge of the props department; Cuny and Revada did everything from doubling Pearl White and leading man Crane Wilbur to lugging reflectors on location, to rigging automobiles with wooden platforms on which Miller perched while shooting "running inserts" during chase scenes. Later, 22-year-old Spencer Bennet joined the company; he did stunts and assisted director Donald MacKenzie, who replaced Gasnier approximately halfway through production. These men formed the nucleus of Pathé's New York serial unit and worked together on the company's East Coast chapter plays for years.

The most important aspect of *Perils of Pauline* was not its narrative. Most of the 20 episodes unfolded along the same lines: Against Harry's wishes, Pauline participates in an exciting but dangerous event. Owen arranges to have her imperiled or hires secondary villains to arrange an "accident" or kidnap the girl for killing at some future date. The basic set-up varied little from chapter to chapter.

What made Pauline's exploits thrilling was the employment of virtually every existing means of conveyance as a potential deathtrap. The adventure-loving girl shuttled from one peril to another via yacht, steamship, race car, express train, motorcycle, aeroplane, hydroplane, and hot-air balloon. The horse-and-buggy days were not that far in the past, and many moviegoers had never laid eyes aeroplanes or steamships.

Filming began in the early spring of 1914 and progressed at a leisurely pace, although inclement weather occasionally forced cast and crew to finish their allotted scenes for the day with more haste than Gasnier and MacKenzie would have liked. Hearst received regular progress reports and occasionally visited the company on location. The April 15 *New York Dramatic Mirror* carried a picture of the Chief watching the taking of a scene in the New Jersey Palisades.

Since thrills were the lifeblood of serials, chapter-play actors were frequently called upon to gamble their lives. In the form's earliest days, dangerous feats staged for the camera were thought of as "all in a day's work," and few actors insisted on stunt doubles, whatever their misgivings. "It took a brave guy to say 'I am afraid,'" confessed *Perils of Pauline* leading man Crane Wilbur nearly a half-century after making the serial. "The more cowardly way was to do the thing yourself."

Pearl White took particular pride in eschewing doubles for all but the most dangerous feats, and she certainly suffered for her art. A manhandling by Chinese extras left her badly bruised. She sustained minor burns during the staging of a fire scene. What seemed at the time to be a relatively minor tumble was actually the cause of her chronic back pain in later years. She explained the mishap in an interview conducted by Mabel Condon for publication in *Motography*'s August 22, 1914 number:

> In *The Perils of Pauline*, the most risky things I've had to do have been the most successful. But do you remember that [episode] in which I was being carried up the stairs with my hands bound? That picture should have been the most harmless of any. Yet, when the man who was carrying me got as far as the seventh step—only the seventh!—he stubbed his toe and I was thrown to the floor on my head. As my arms were tied, I couldn't break the fall so my head and spine got the full force of it. I couldn't do a thing for weeks afterward. . . .
>
> Then another instance of my "small time" jinx happened in the Chinese [episode] when Owen and the Chinamen hid me in a secret room of the Chinese restaurant. The door through which they took me was a low one and the Chinamen carrying me neglected to lower me sufficiently, when we were going through, and it nearly took the top of my head right off.
>
> But anything as really dangerous as that runaway balloon—and it was the most dangerous peril of any, so far— or being chased down the hill by a big boulder, or coming down from Execution lighthouse in a breeches-buoy—and

that was not at all easy though it looked to be—all these were safe ventures compared to the risk I'd run if I attempted to walk around the block.

Additionally, Pearl made headlines in New York and New Jersey papers when she was accidentally cast adrift in a hot-air balloon while shooting a sequence for the sixth episode. She floated across the Garden State for hours before the balloon's owner, riding in the box with her, released enough gas to enable a safe landing. But she had far more harrowing experiences as well. *Perils of Pauline* cinematographer Arthur Miller related one of Pearl's narrow escapes in his 1967 memoir:

> I remember a stunt from one of the early episodes that was not considered to be dangerous—just the transfer from the running board of one moving automobile to another, also in motion. The cars didn't have to move very fast, as under-cranking the camera created the illusion of high speed for both cars. Pearl struggled free of her captors, got out on the running board of the car, but as she reached for the other automobile traveling alongside that was to rescue her, she somehow lost her footing and fell between the moving cars. Only the quick thinking of the two drivers—who turned their cars out and apart—prevented a serious accident.

Over the course of 20 two-reel episodes Pauline was imperiled by spies, gypsies, pirates, gangsters, and even Sioux Indians, all recruited by Owen or his henchmen to bedevil the vivacious heiress. She was bound and left to die in burning houses and flooded cellars, embroiled in elaborate schemes designed to put her out of the way for good while leaving the villainous secretary in the clear.

During production of the serial Pearl endeared herself to cast and crew alike. She remained enthusiastic about the enterprise even when it grew tedious, and in addition to being unfailingly cooperative she displayed a ribald sense of humor and delighted in making herself the butt of good-natured jokes.

The Perils of Pauline went into general release on March 29, 1914 with only a few episodes having been completed. Reviews were generally favorable, and even the toughest critics had good things to say. The *Moving Picture World*'s Hanford C. Judson wrote: "Miss White hasn't had so good a chance in a long while to show her art, and she plays this picture's ingenuous heroine with the truly wonderful naturalities that she has so surely at her command. Perhaps she doesn't always hit square in the center of the effect she desires; but she does it so often that she continually commands the heart-interest of the audience."

Hearst's top dramatic critic, the *New York American*'s "Alan Dale" (Alfred J. Cohen), was notorious for flippant and caustic comments that stabbed like daggers at the hearts of any works he disliked, but his tongue-in-cheek review of *Pauline* indicated a pulling of punches, more likely attributable to a desire not to offend his boss: "*The Perils of Pauline*, which is full of plot and incident and melodrama, 'gets over' capitally in 'movie' form. Nothing misses fire, and you can follow it all with the greatest facility. You don't even have to have an imagination—though I hope you have one, as it's a handy thing to have around the house. . . . The cast seemed to be an interesting one, and Pauline herself was awfully nice. . . . The nefarious ones kept well in the background, and their 'vile machinations' were not much in evidence. That was as it should be. *The Perils of Pauline* certainly affords big scope for incident. Never was girl in a more precarious plight. Never!"

Variety's "Mark," commenting on Chapter Two, opined: "In the second installment of the Pauline picture the [plot-to-character] connections were well made, the photography is immense, and the plot hangs so well that at the 23rd Street Theatre Tuesday night the picture made a big hit. . . . There's life to the picture and the excitement is well staged. It is holding its own as a feature."

One of the most persuasive trade-paper ads was a full-pager reproducing actual telegrams sent by Eclectic exchange managers to the home office in New York City; they demonstrated, better than any hyperbolic copy could have, just how popular the serial was. From the San Francisco branch: "Hurrah. *Pauline* the talk of the town. Everybody wants it. Biggest booking record ever. Demand growing together. Will have to have more prints of the second episode." From Atlanta: "Deluged with orders [for] *Pauline*. Wild excitement. Nothing ever like it before. Every good theater fighting for first release privileges." From Boston: "Must have more copies [of] *Pauline*. Don't have to work to book. Exhibitors chasing us hard for bookings. The papers have the public worked up as never before. Congratulations. Biggest thing ever put over."

Eclectic's bookings in New York City alone included all theaters in the prestigious Fox, Keith, and Proctor circuits, as well as such showplaces as Loew's Broadway. The serial's success extended to Europe, where France-based Pathé Freres had established a distribution network stretching across the continent. Within months of *Pauline*'s premiere Pearl White was an international star. No longer fearful of the Patents Company or General Film, Berst announced the "acquisition" of Eclectic exchanges and formally changed the company's name to Pathé Exchanges, Inc. Before Pauline had completed its initial playoff Pearl was rushed into a follow-up serial, *The Exploits of Elaine*, based on Arthur B. Reeve's Craig Kennedy detective stories appearing in *Hearst's Cosmopolitan* magazine. This chapter play, released at the end of 1914 in weekly increments, improved upon *Pauline* and was even more profitable, spawning two sequels produced and released back to back for a total of 36 episodes.

Pearl went on to make six more serials for Pathé before leaving the firm in 1920 to star in feature films for Fox Film Corporation. Although handsomely paid, she failed to duplicate the success of her serials and returned to Pathé in late 1922 for one last chapter play, *Plunder*, directed by her old friend George B. Seitz and released the following year. It earned a significant amount of money but was not the box-office sensation that her earlier starring vehicles were. Wisely sensing that her day in the sun had come and gone, Pearl White retired a wealthy woman in 1923. She moved to France, where she was still enormously popular, and returned to the United States only a few more times before dying in 1938 at the age of 49.

In the decades following its release, *The Perils of Pauline* acquired the reputation of being incomprehensible and amateurishly produced. This verdict was reached by critics who, invariably, based their judgments on screenings of washed-out 16mm dupe prints of a poorly reedited nine-chapter version that originated from European source material. In his 1967 memoir, Arthur Miller railed against film historians who took *Pauline* to task for its ragged continuity, apparently poor photography, and laughably illiterate sub-titles:

> In 1916 I tried for personal reasons to obtain a print of one of the episodes of *The Perils of Pauline* and was told by Louis Gasnier that the negative had been shipped to France. Even before that time, the serial had been a big hit in France, and Pearl White became as popular there as she was in America. After the disastrous fire that took the lives of 180 of the cream of French society in the early days of motion pictures, the French government had passed and strictly enforced a law providing that all projection machines must be enclosed in a fireproof booth. In 1912 the Lumiere brothers placed on the market what was known as "safety" film, and for showing this film a booth was not required. The film, 28mm in width, became known in France as the "educational" film size. *The Perils of Pauline* was in such demand that a dupe negative in 28mm size was made. No one knows how many prints were sold that were shown throughout the countryside in tent shows and other places. Of course, the English titles were translated by a Frenchman and naturally took on a French flavor.
>
> Several years after World War I, American film historians began to be interested in *The Perils of Pauline*, since it was the first American serial. [Miller was mistaken in this.] The original negative could no longer be found, and as no 35mm prints were located, it was therefore presumed that

they had been destroyed in order to retrieve whatever silver hadn't been removed during the original processing. The French, with their sharp eye for business, gathered some of the 28mm prints and retranslated the French-flavored titles back to what they considered was good English usage. It is true that the results often were funny, but everyone interested knew what had happened. Such prints as found their way back to the United States were again duped to 16mm film. In some instances, the duped negative was blown up to 35mm and reduction 16mm prints made, one of which I have. It is a wonder that anything could be salvaged after the many duping stages *The Perils of Pauline* went through.

Today, the crudely captioned French version, condensed to nine half-hour episodes that present major sequences out of their original order, is all that survives of Pathé's sensational first serial. It's small wonder that latter-day critics and historians have treated *Perils of Pauline* unkindly; what remains of the chapter play is barely comprehensible. Visible splices in conservation scenes indicate where important dialogue titles were removed, and the rewritten explanatory captions do not convey enough information to fully explain or contextualize the on-screen action. And the clumsy reediting results in the loss of *Pauline*'s most suspenseful episode ending: the Chapter Twelve finale in which the girl reaches into a basket of flowers without knowing that a poisonous snake lays coiled at the bottom.

The Perils of Pauline was a big grosser for Pathé, reportedly earning the French firm more than three quarters of a million dollars in American film rental alone. European rentals were equally impressive until World War I shut down many of the continent's most lucrative markets. Despite the serial's apparent crudity, it helped turn regular moviegoing into a habit for millions of Americans who previously regarded "fillums" as a novelty worthy of only occasional patronage. Moreover, along with *The Million Dollar Mystery*, it created an insatiable appetite for chapter plays.

The Million Dollar Mystery

(1914, Thanhouser Film Company)

COLONEL WILLIAM N. SELIG'S *The Adventures of Kathlyn* (1913), the first true serial, was a sensation both on film and in print. It was undertaken as a circulation stunt, linking a film to a newspaper by running a novelized version of the story in weekly increments printed in Sunday supplements. The prose version of *Kathlyn* garnered some 50,000 new readers for the *Chicago Tribune*, boosting the paper's circulation a full 10 percent, and the serial was still in playoff when Patterson and company started thinking about a follow-up.

In early 1914, with the Selig chapter play still underway in thousands of theaters, they engaged the prominent Nichols-Finn advertising agency to analyze *Kathlyn*'s success and devise a plan to duplicate it. Paul R. Kuhn, the agency's top merchandizing expert, was assigned to the project, and following a brief but intense period of market research he determined that a serial with a strong mystery element stood the best chance of sustaining audience interest and enthusiasm over a prolonged period. The *Tribune* accepted his recommendation and, with nary a word of story put to paper, decided on *The Million Dollar Mystery* as a marketable chapter-play title.

According to Terry Ramsaye in *A Million and One Nights*, his book-length history of the silent-film era, what happened next was a miracle of coincidence. While taking the Twentieth Century Limited from New York to Chicago, the agency's co-owner, Joseph Finn, engaged in a smoking-car conversation with Lloyd Lonergan, scenario supervisor for the Thanhouser Film Corporation. Lonergan was accompanied by the firm's president, Charles Hite, whom he lost no time introducing to Finn. Ramsaye claims that upon reaching Chicago the trio made a beeline for the *Tribune* offices to pitch Thanhouser as the producer of *Million Dollar Mystery*.

The Thanhouser Company, which at that time enjoyed a reputation as one of the classier independent film suppliers, was established in late 1909. Edwin Thanhouser, a Milwaukee theater owner and director of his own stock company, saw potential in moving picture production and applied to the Patents Company for a license. Refused admittance to the trust, he decided to go it alone and set up shop in New Rochelle, New York, a charming little town that was home to many Broadway writers, producers, and performers. He purchased a large building that had until recently housed a skating rink, and converted it to a studio with an adjoining laboratory for processing film. This original facility was destroyed by fire in January 1913, but the firm quickly acquired a building on Main Street and shortly thereafter purchased additional property overlooking Long Island Sound. That stretch of land encompassed a three-acre park used for exterior scenes.

With experienced stage actors at his disposal Thanhouser turned out one-reelers, primarily, but eschewed the sort of knockabout comedy and coarse melodrama in which most of his competitors specialized. His releases were applauded for their strong performances, solid production values, and relatively sophisticated storytelling technique. Initially they were distributed by the newly formed Motion Picture Distributing and Sales Company, a coalition of fractious independent producers dominated by one Carl Laemmle. Later the firm's output was handled by the Mutual

Film Corporation, an independent distribution entity founded in July 1912 by Harry E. Aitken and his brother Roy, along with John R. Freuler, their partner in a Wisconsin film exchange. Earlier that year, Thanhouser had sold his company to Mutual investor Charles J. Hite, an ambitious Chicago exchange owner and canny entrepreneur whose motion-picture career was blossoming.

Plans for *The Million Dollar Mystery* took shape in the early spring of 1914. John M. Burnham & Company, investment bankers from the Windy City, helped organize the Syndicate Film Corporation to finance the chapter play and direct the sales effort; James M. Sheldon was installed as president of the new concern. (Its assistant treasurer, 26-year-old W. Ray Johnston, would later play a significant role in serial history.) Offices were opened in Chicago and New York, at that time the twin hubs of the motion-picture industry. It was decided to promote *Mystery* with a contest, just as Pathé was doing with *The Perils of Pauline*. Viewers would be given a chance to solve the riddle of the missing million, with a $10,000 cash prize to be awarded for the best 100-word solution. Back at Thanhouser's New Rochelle headquarters, Lonergan began writing the scenario.

Thanhouser "teased" its upcoming serial in a full-page advertisement placed in early April issues of the leading trade papers. Headlined "Extraordinary Announcement to Motion Picture Exhibitors," it simply stated that *Adventures of Kathlyn* would be followed on theater screens by *The Million Dollar Mystery*, "the most stupendous feat in motion picture drama, with a fictionalized version of the chapter play appearing weekly in "200 leading newspapers in the United States." Harold MacGrath was listed as the story's author.

A follow-up ad published two weeks later featured a personal message from C. J. Hite to the exhibitors of America:

> Our recent announcement of the coming of the stupendous production, *The Million Dollar Mystery*, has so overwhelmed us with inquiries from exhibitors that I take this means of notifying theatre managers everywhere that

arrangements have been perfected for releasing even a greater number of reels that originally planned—I hope sufficient to take care of the tremendous demand.

The producing of *The Million Dollar Mystery* is, by far, the greatest task ever undertaken by any film manufacturer. You have, no doubt, heard that the *Chicago Tribune* and 200 other leading newspapers will print this remarkable story by Harold MacGrath (scenario by Lloyd Lonergan) simultaneously with its appearance in the theatres and that a capital prize of $10,000.00 in cash will be paid for the best solution of this mystery. *The Million Dollar Mystery* will succeed the *Kathlyn* series.

Lonergan's premise for the serial was deceptively simple. A young heiress, having recently lost her father, would spend months looking for the million dollars in cash he hid before apparently meeting death at the hands of a criminal organization he betrayed years before. The girl would be aided by a clever young reporter and the dedicated family butler. Unbeknownst to any of them, a supposedly loyal friend belonged to the secret society and fed inside information to the conspirators in a bid to recover the fortune before the heiress did.

Hite assigned leading roles to the company's most popular and personable stars: Florence La Badie, Marguerite Snow, and James Cruze. The latter, an erstwhile vaudevillian and one-time medicine-show performer, began his film career as a Pathé player and became Thanhouser's top male actor shortly after joining the company. Snow, who began working for Thanhouser in 1911 and married Cruze two years later, played good girls and bad girls with equal facility. A vivacious brunette, she proved the perfect counterpart to blonde, placidly beautiful La Badie, the perennial ingenue. Australian character actor Sidney Bracy, square-jawed Frank Farrington, and fluttery Lila Chester rounded out the principal players. In a brilliant stroke motivated purely by expediency, the members of the criminal combine "The Black Hundred" all wore masks when called upon to assemble for the plotting of their schemes. Facial coverings obviated the need for ensuring that all the same extras would be available during a production period expected to span five or more months. But masked conspirators added a fillip of intrigue to the proceedings and provided additional justification for the serial's title.

Lonergan's scenarios were forwarded to Harold MacGrath, who whipped up prose versions for publication in the *Tribune*, adding such details as needed to make the yarn more compelling. Reportedly he devised numerous situations that Lonergan interpolated into his scripts for the later chapters.

While the elaborate production was being readied for filming, the Nichols-Finn ad agency was trying to devise a scheme for generating early publicity. Brash promotional copywriter J. Casey "Jay" Cairns, dispatched to New Rochelle and given free reign, came up with a suitably outlandish idea implemented with all due haste. As Ramsaye recounted the story in *A Million and One Nights:*

> The shades of night were falling on the village when a very sober-faced, worried-looking young man with a Western manner, presented himself at the New Rochelle police station and asked private audience with the officer in charge.
>
> "A very serious thing has happened Miss Florence Gray millionaire's daughter, you know, has disappeared millions involved, and we suspect there may be foul play. Hate to call you into it, but I know you'll be careful, etc., etc."
>
> Cairns was reluctant and hesitated often. But under the pressure of police questioning he decided to give the officer a written statement on the affair, which he chanced to have with him. It was a neatly typed synopsis of the opening chapter of *The Million Dollar Mystery*. The names were those of the fictitious characters.
>
> It took the "missing heiress story" fully an hour to reach Park Row, New York City, and ten minutes more to get all over the United States. It was an otherwise dull night for news. The story flowed freely over the leased wires.

In the *Chicago Tribune* office that night as usual, E. S. Beck, the managing editor, was shrewdly scanning the telegraph news proofs as they arrived wet from the composing room. The "missing heiress" story brought him up with a start. He sniffed. There was something slightly familiar about that story, but he could not place it. It had something of the odor of fish.

The *Tribune* did not carry the missing heiress story. Nearly every other newspaper in the United States did, including the Chicago Hearst paper down Madison Street. And they continued to carry it. . . . On the third day Cairns reluctantly parted with "the only photograph in existence" of the missing heiress. It bore a striking similarity to publicity stills of Florence La Badie issued by the Thanhouser company.

Several days later the *Tribune* launched an ad campaign for *The Million Dollar Mystery* prepared by the Nichols-Finn agency, and outraged editors across the country realized they had been snookered by Jay Cairns. Ramsaye later characterized this coup as "the first of the great film press-agent hoaxes."

With early episodes completed, Thanhouser in May launched an ad campaign in the trade papers, exhorting exhibitors to "Get busy *now!* Book this stupendous series to pack your theater during the dull summer months. . . . You must act *quickly!* You can secure these films regardless of what program you may be using." At this time Hite's company offered "The Thanhouser Three-A-Week"—three one-reel subjects released to first-run houses every Tuesday, Friday, and Sunday. Occasionally the firm's weekly offerings included a two-reeler and a one-reeler, but subscribers to the Thanhouser program could count on receiving three reels of film every seven days. *The Million Dollar Mystery* was marketed as a special feature, independent of the Three-A-Week lineup.

Production of the 22 chapters consumed the spring and summer of 1914. Principal photography took place in and around Thanhouser's New Rochelle plant, with Charles Hite's palatial estate at 3 Meadow Lane (then valued at $200,000) standing in for the millionaire's residence. There were occasional location jaunts to New York City, New Jersey, and points south. One late chapter began with Cruze's character visiting Washington, justifying numerous shots of the Capitol and other D.C. landmarks. Additionally, Thanhouser's camera captured close-up views of such federal luminaries as vice president Thomas R. Marshall, House speaker Champ Clark, and the Secretaries of War and the Treasury.

An early May expedition undertaken for the serial is now recognized as having historical significance. Chapter Twelve was dominated by an underwater search for the missing million, believed to have been hidden in the ocean in a small chest. Brothers George and John Ernest Williamson had modified an invention of their father's—a collapsible submarine—to include a chamber, the Photosphere, that enabled underwater cinematography. The siblings had just finished a well-publicized documentary called *Thirty Leagues Under the Sea*, which they filmed in clear waters off the Bahamas.

After negotiating with the Williamsons for the use of their Photosphere, Thanhouser dispatched ace cinematographer Carl Gregory to Nassau to oversee the shooting of sequences in which divers plunged from a schooner into the sea and recovered the chest. Universal's 1916 adaptation of *20,000 Leagues Under the Sea* is often cited as the first fictional film to employ the Williamson process, but that honor actually belongs to *The Million Dollar Mystery*. The underwater photography lent verisimilitude to the episode and thrilled viewers seeing such footage for the first time.

As production continued over the next several months, the makers of Thanhouser's chapter play routinely shocked ordinary citizens who happened to observe unprecedented stunts being performed on location for the cameras. In July a reporter for *Motography* (or perhaps publicist Jay Cairns) described one such thrill, staged for Chapter Seven:

> Persons waiting for the Seacliffe ferry at New Rochelle were startled one day last week when an automobile

rushed toward the open draw[bridge] and plunged into Long Island Sound, carrying with it three men passengers. Just as the machine tottered on the edge of the draw another car raced up and out of it stepped a man holding a smoking revolver in his hand, and a daintily gowned woman.

The onlookers stood horrified until cameras ceased clicking and then realized that a new thrill had been written into *The Million Dollar Mystery*, Thanhouser's new serial. [English actor and acrobat] Albert Froome, formerly of the Hippodrome, and two other daredevils were the men who made the mad plunge, James Cruze was the man with the smoking revolver and Florence La Badie was his partner in the second auto.

It took two days to get this scene as the crowd that gathered on the first attempt made it impossible for the players to work.

That was not the only water-based feat of daring observed by members of the public during shooting of *Mystery*. Just a few weeks later, while filming the climax to Chapter Nine, Florence La Badie thrilled fellow passengers on the ocean liner *George Washington* by leaping from the deck into choppy waters off Sandy Hook, New Jersey. Director Howard Hansel and the cameraman caught the jump from a tugboat and watched anxiously as waves tossed their star about. Flo gamely plowed ahead but was nearly exhausted when a crew member finally tossed the actress a rope and pulled her aboard the tug.

A month or so after that, *Mystery*'s leading lady got another soaking as part of a spectacular sequence lensed for Chapter Fifteen. While shooting off the waters of Shippan Point, near Stamford, Connecticut, La Badie dove from a speeding hydroplane into the Atlantic. She was plucked out of the ocean by Cruze's character, who dropped from the sky in a seaplane to rescue her.

Previously such physical demands had not been placed on Thanhouser's stock company, but the players rallied around their director and pushed themselves far beyond their comfort levels to ensure that *Mystery* contained the visceral thrills associated with sensational melodrama of the "10-20-30" type. On occasion, after seeing developed footage, Hansel decided that the desired effect had not been achieved and insisted upon retakes. One trade paper reported that replacement scenes for the first episode were completed just days before scheduled preview screenings.

Chapter One opened with a brief prologue showing Charles Hite with Hansel, Lonergan, and the principal players, presumably celebrating the serial's release. Hite was shown brandishing the $10,000 certified check that would be presented to the picture patron submitting the best 100-word solution to the mystery. Following this half-reel of footage the story began to unfold....

One dark night Stanley Hargreave (Albert Norton) furtively approaches the Susan Farlow Select School for Girls and, after tenderly depositing his safely swaddled infant daughter on the veranda, raps on the window and retreats to a carriage waiting nearby. Miss Farlow (Lila Chester) opens the door to find the child, to whose clothing is pinned an envelope containing a note and half of a bracelet. "The name of this child is Florence Gray," reads the message."Take care of her and educate her. I shall provide liberally for her. The other half of the enclosed bracelet will identify me when I send for her."

Seventeen years pass. Florence (La Badie) grows up to young womanhood, her every material need provided by monthly checks sent to Susan Farlow as promised by the girl's unknown benefactor.

A flashback reveals that Hargreave took the unusual step of abandoning his daughter out of fear that both their lives were in danger. Twenty-five years before, as an adventure-seeking youth living in Russia, he had taken a vow of loyalty to a secret society known as the Black Hundred. Before long he realized his mistake: the Hundred was an organization of ruthless criminals. Wishing to break away and begin life anew, Hargreave fled to America, establishing himself as a reputable businessman and amassing a million dollars. But he has lived in constant fear that the merciless Black Hundred whose reach has spread to other countries will someday catch up to him. To avoid identification he has grown a thick mustache and a bushy beard.

One night while dining at a Broadway cafe with newspaper reporter Jimmy Norton (Cruze), Hargreave is introduced to a Russian countess named Olga Perigoff (Snow) and her escort, Leo Braine (Frank Farrington). Unbeknownst to him, they are members of the Black Hundred's New York chapter. After studying the millionaire at close quarters Braine and Countess Olga suspect that he is the traitor whose picture they have at the Hundred's secret headquarters.

At a hastily convened meeting of the group, Braine examines their carefully preserved photograph of Hargreave as a young man and decides that he and Olga have guessed correctly. The conspirators decide to send Hargreave a threatening note alerting him that the Black Hundred has found him at last and is prepared to wreak vengeance upon him.

Having just withdrawn his million dollars from the bank and arranged to have Florence brought to him preparatory to leaving the country, Hargreave abruptly changes his plans upon receiving the note. To begin with, he shaves off his facial hair, at which point a marked resemblance to his butler Jones (Sidney Bracy) becomes apparent. Then he hires balloonist A. Leo Stevens (himself) to sail toward the Hargreave mansion and hover nearby in the event a quick escape is necessary.

Around this time the audience is treated to a view of the library and a close-up of the safe therein. A hand unlocks the vault and removes packages of bills of high denomination. What becomes of the money is not revealed.

Soon thereafter Jones, carefully watching the grounds, warns his master that members of the Black Hundred are about to storm the house. Hargreave sets off a rocket signaling Stevens, who guides his airship above the mansion. The millionaire climbs out onto the roof and jumps into the wicker basket, at which point the craft drifts away. Braine's henchmen fire their guns toward Hargreave and a bullet punctures the balloon, which is seen to plunge into the Atlantic.

The conspirators break into the house, overpower Jones, and force him to lead them to the safe—which, to the surprise of all, is empty. Hargreave must have taken the money with him! At which point the audience sees the collapsed hot-air balloon floating on ocean waves, and Chapter One comes to an end.

Chapter Two begins with the bound butler freeing himself and calling the police. Braine and his associates make a quick and perfunctory search for the missing million and narrowly escape capture. Florence Gray, accompanied by Susan Farlow, arrives at the house and is heartbroken to learn that her long-lost father has disappeared. Jones produces the other half of the broken bracelet and presents the girl with a note from Hargreave. It informs her that the butler has been entrusted with enough money for her needs and can be trusted implicitly. She decides to stay at the mansion in the event her father is found.

Braine instructs Countess Olga to visit the Hargreave home and introduce herself to Florence as a family friend. By worming her way into the girl's confidence Olga hopes to gain some clue to the missing million. Not content to wait, Braine orders two henchmen to impersonate police detectives and conduct a more detailed search of the house. Jimmy Norton, assigned by his editor to interview Florence Gray, takes an immediate liking to the heiress and becomes her champion on the spot. He suspects the two "detectives" of being impostors and calls police headquarters to check up on them. Exposing the pretenders precipitates a huge fight in which Norton holds his own against the two heavies until real police arrive. The unsuspected Olga realizes that her pretense of friendship for Florence is the Hundred's best hope of securing the missing Hargreave fortune.

Meanwhile, as the second episode winds down, a newspaper dispatch mentions that two men have been taken aboard a ship that sailed near the wreckage of a hot-air balloon many miles out to sea. Hargreave is alive but did he have the million dollars with him? And if so, does it now rest on the ocean floor?

The basic plot and principal characters had been established. *The Million Dollar Mystery* was off and running.

The national release date for Chapter One was Monday, June 22. Some 200 newspapers in addition to the *Tribune*—among them the *Boston Globe*, *New York Globe*, *Cincinnati Enquirer*, and *Buffalo Courier*—had pre-purchased Harold MacGrath's fictionalized story for publication in their Sunday supplements, to begin immediately following completion of *The Adventures of Kathlyn*. Within two months that number had swelled to 300.

An anonymous critic for *Variety* attended a trade screening of the first two chapters and filed a favorable notice published in the June 26 issue. "The picture is full of thrills," he noted, "and is bound to have a big following as it goes along. The photography is clear and the interiors are well arranged. A great number of these weekly two-reel releases have been pushed upon the market but there has yet to be one that is on a par with this Thanhouser mysterious film story."

The New York Dramatic Mirror, one of the most respected theatrical trade papers, offered carefully measured praise:

> We had heard much of *The Million Dollar Mystery* and naturally awaited with interest our first glimpse of "the nine-mile serial" [a nickname referring to the chapter play's length in feet of film]. Taking the initial installment as a criterion, we are to expect nine miles of thrills, nine miles of conspiracies, captures and escapes; in a phrase, nine miles of unvarnished, old-fashioned melodrama. If the prescription may seem unduly large, it is but necessary to remember that the individual doses are exceedingly moderate and well calculated to suit the tastes of photoplay fans.
>
> The producer has aimed at two targets: the injection of mystery and the maintenance of the suspense created by that mystery through the introduction of thrill piling upon thrill. . . . The staging gives evidence of care, many of the interiors offering unusual depth. Photographically, the picture is entirely satisfactory. Each installment of the serial tells its own story, no time being given to recounting the events that have transpired before.

Howard Hansel's cast and crew worked diligently to stay ahead of schedule. Lloyd Lonergan's scenarios introduced many situations that would become chapter-play staples. Each episode was designed to provide at least one memorable thrill: There were death-defying leaps, fires and explosions, and crashes of aeroplanes, automobiles and locomotives. The schemes of Braine and Countess Olga became increasingly desperate, but Jimmy Norton and Jones the butler (who, contrary to the prevailing screen stereotype of manservants, showed himself to be a most efficient ally) proved eminently capable of beating them back.

It is impossible to overestimate the impact of *The Million Dollar Mystery* on 1914 moviegoers. The Syndicate Film Corporation's sales and marketing efforts reaped huge rewards as exhibitors nationwide reported extraordinary interest in the serial from their patrons. With each episode playing to standing-room-only crowds in first-run theaters, competing showmen in the same communities vied for second-run contracts knowing that their houses too were likely to be filled with customers frozen out of initial engagements. *The Perils of Pauline* today enjoys a reputation as the attraction that popularized motion-picture serials, but *The Million Dollar Mystery* was every bit as influential, and perhaps more so. In that transitional period when a program "feature" had not yet been established as a film with a running time of an hour or more, *Pauline* and *Mystery*—whose first-run playoffs overlapped—served as the primary lures to millions of Americans previously unaccustomed to visiting their local picture palaces on the same day every week.

In his invaluable "Harvesting the Serial," a chronicle of the chapter play published in *Photoplay*'s February 1917 issue, Alfred A. Cohn recalled that first-run exhibitors paid $25 a day for episodes of *Mystery*. Second-run bookings fetched $20 a day; subsequent rentals cost less, tapering to $5 per day six months after the June 22 national release.

Joe Gilday, manager of Kansas City's Broadmore Theater, one of the leading showplaces in this midwest metropolis, booked *Mystery* on second run and made it the backbone of his Friday-night program. He sold out the house every week but did not reckon on losing revenue due to the large percentage of children, whose tickets cost five cents as opposed to the dimes collected from adults. As Gilday was turning away adults every Friday night, he hit upon the idea of holding special late-afternoon matinees for children just out of school. For their nickels the youngsters got a full seven-reel program, which ended before the evening show commenced.

"In this way," Gilday explained to *Moving Picture World*, "I show to 300 or 400 children in the afternoon, and at the same time am not forced to turn down any ten-cent admissions at night. Besides, the children enjoy it more, because they go wild over *Million Dollar Mystery* and I allow them to yell and whoop all they want to, which I would not permit at the evening shows."

The 22nd and penultimate episode begins with remaining members of the Black Hundred (whose ranks by this time have been greatly depleted) redoubling their efforts to eliminate Norton and Jones, Florence Gray's protectors. But the latest scheme fails and the courageous reporter leads a police detail to the Hundred's recently discovered cave hideout, where the conspirators are routed after a pitched battle, with only Braine and Countess Olga escaping. They flee to the Hargreave mansion for one final assault on Florence.

Upon arriving at the millionaire's estate the two malefactors are shocked to learn that the long-missing Stanley Hargreave has at last identified himself to his daughter. In a surprising revelation he admits to having been near her all along. After shaving off his facial hair months earlier, Hargreave had noted his close resemblance to Jones. So he faked his own disappearance but hid nearby, exchanging places with the butler at crucial moments to lend assistance to Florence and Jimmy Norton.

(The improbability of master and servant so closely resembling each other as to be interchangeable without recognition likely was minimized by the use of double-exposure photography. *Mystery*'s scenario more than once refers to Flo La Badie's character as "Sid's daughter," indicating that actor Sidney Bracy was intended from the beginning to play a dual role in the serial's final stanza.)

In the last-ditch attack that follows, Braine is shot to death and Olga is apprehended. Surrounded by his daughter, faithful manservant, and future son-in-law (Jimmy and Florence having gotten engaged in Chapter Seven), Stanley Hargreave makes this portentous announcement: "Now I shall tell you the secret of 'The Million Dollar Mystery.' "

At this point the chapter ended, with the final episode promised for a later date.

Moviegoers caught up in the serial's central riddle took the $10,000 contest quite seriously. The company claimed to have received thousands of letters offering solutions to the mystery. Most participants believed the money had been secreted in the house or somewhere on the Hargreave property: inside a Bible, a fountain, a statue, a flower pot, an upholstered armchair, a loose brick in the fireplace; underneath a table top; tied to a chain in a well; under the water in a pit in the cellar; in the summer house beneath vines. But the correct deduction was made by Miss Ida Damon, a 24-year-old stenographer from St. Louis, Missouri.

The twenty-third and final episode was released on February 22, 1915, following conclusion of third-run engagements. Ida Damon's solution revealed that the million dollars had been hidden inside a large wooden picture frame, along with a picture of the girl's mother, behind the painting of Hargreave.

Within a few years serial fans would find themselves surfeited with criminal organizations whose masked members met in secret and financed elaborate schemes with seemingly limitless resources. Hidden fortunes also became ubiquitous in episodic thrillers, as did missing fathers who adopted disguises to aid plucky daughters and their champions. These and other soon-to-be-familiar plot devices, while not unique to the chapter play, earned widespread audience acceptance and approval as a result of their deployment in Thanhouser's serial sensation.

The Million Dollar Mystery reportedly was made for $93,000. An estimated 7,000 theaters booked the serial. Gross rentals totaled nearly $1,500,000; after factoring in costs related to prints, advertising, and distribution Thanhouser's chapter play returned a profit of 700 percent to Syndicate Film Corporation investors. By mid-November the per-share value of both preferred and common stock had approached $200. Unfortunately, Charles Hite did not live to see the serial successfully concluded. Thanhouser's president was killed on the night of August 21, 1914, while driving his brand-new, high-powered automobile. According to the accident report he skidded through a railing on the bank of a Harlem River viaduct and plunged to his death.

The Diamond from the Sky

(1915, American Film Company / Mutual Film Corp.)

THE MUTUAL FILM CORPORATION was home to most of the independent production entities that had not aligned themselves with Universal when the Motion Picture Distributing and Sales Company flew apart in 1912. Three years later, Mutual operated 56 exchanges in the United States and Canada; by then its reach extended beyond that of the General Film Company, which doled out pictures produced by member companies of the Edison-backed Motion Picture Patents Company. Thanhouser's *Million Dollar Mystery* and *Zudora* had benefitted from Mutual's efficiency. But the early months of 1915 were tumultuous ones for the powerful organization.

Among the many prominent filmmakers recruited by Harry Aitken were D. W. Griffith and Thomas H. Ince; the former lured from Biograph to produce and direct for Reliance and Majestic Pictures, the latter toiling in the same capacities for the New York Motion Picture Company owned by Kessel and Baumann. John R. Freuler and Samuel S. Hutchinson, who sat on Mutual's board and co-owned the American Film Manufacturing Company, came to resent the favoritism Aitken had shown toward Griffith and Ince. Their anger bubbled over upon hearing that Mutual's president had invested $40,000 of the company's money in Griffith's *Birth of a Nation*. Freuler and Hutchinson persuaded bankers Felix Kahn and Crawford Livingston, the firm's major financial backers, to support them in ousting Mutual's founder, who left in May, taking with him Griffith, Ince, and Mack Sennett, whose Keystone comedies had been distributed by Mutual. With these three top producers in his pocket, Aitken quickly established the Triangle Film Corporation and obtained the services of such major stars as Mary Pickford, Douglas Fairbanks, and William S. Hart. Freuler was installed as Mutual's new president at the annual stockholders meeting following the no-confidence vote in Aitken.

The American Film Manufacturing Company was formed in 1910 as a reaction to the Edison trust's crackdown on film exchanges that preferred independently made product to the General Film Company program of Patents Company licensees. One profitable exchange affected by this move was the Chicago-based H and H Film Service, owned jointly by Charles J. Hite and Samuel S. Hutchinson. The latter elected to produce his own films rather than submit to the monopolistic Patents Company. He staffed American by raiding the locally headquartered Essanay Film Manufacturing Company, founded in 1907 by exhibitor George K. Spoor and actor-writer-director Gilbert M. "Broncho Billy" Anderson.

By offering Essanay's employees more money Hutchinson was able to enlist many of them in his new venture. Among these were early fan favorite and resident leading man J. Warren Kerrigan, actor-director Tom Ricketts, and scenario writer Allan Dewan (later top director Allan Dwan). In the firm's salad days its general manager was Aubrey M. Kennedy, who would later make interesting contributions of his own to serial history.

American opened a plant and corporate headquarters in Chicago but shifted operations to California to evade Patents Company goons dispatched from New Jersey to harass independent filmmakers. The firm's production units hopscotched around the Golden State before settling in the beautiful coastal community of Santa Barbara, building a state-of-the-art facility that included a prop warehouse, carpentry shop, garage, dressing rooms, and film laboratory. Safe from Patents Company thugs and financially secure thanks to Hutchison's new distribution deal with Mutual, American quickly became a reliable provider of one- and two-reelers, its output heavily skewed toward Westerns. Talented actors and technicians gravitated to the Santa Barbara studio; actors Wallace Reid and Marshall Neilan found employment there, as did director William Desmond Taylor. The company trademark, a capital "A" with wings, gave American its brand name: "Flying A."

The successes of *Adventures of Kathlyn* and *Million Dollar Mystery* impressed Hutchinson, who had not yet caught the "feature fever" beginning to spread among program suppliers. Still committed to the mass production of short subjects, he reasoned that American was perfectly positioned to capitalize on the burgeoning popularity of episodic thrillers. Hutchinson forged an alliance with the *Chicago Tribune*, which in late 1914 launched a well-publicized "$10,000 Photoplay Contest" soliciting scenarios for a "continued novel" to be filmed by American.

The competition's entries were judged by Mutual's John Freuler, American's R. R. Nehls, and the Tribune's Mae Tinee, editor of the paper's "Right Off the Reel" department. The *Trib's* office was flooded with manuscripts during December and January; early reports estimated the amount between 9,000 and 11,000, but in *A Million and One Nights* Terry Ramsaye fixed the total at exactly 19,846 and claimed personally to have opened the prize-winning envelope, number 1616. (At that time Ramsaye was Mutual's publicity chief, based in Chicago.) It contained a professionally written and detailed scenario by erstwhile journalist, fictioneer, and dramatist Roy L. McCardell, whose moving-picture experience dated back to the early nickelodeon days, when he sold "spec" scripts for split-reel subjects to the American Mutoscope & Biograph company.

A New Rochelle native, McCardell spent two decades with the *New York Herald*, at various times working as beat reporter, rewrite man, city editor, and Sunday-supplement editor. He was best known to picture fans as the scenarist of a long-running series of Vitagraph comedies featuring the Jarr Family. Interviewed for a profile in the May 29, 1915 number of *Moving Picture World*, McCardell said of his work on *Diamond*'s original story: "I knew that competition would be keen. This simply proved an incentive to me. I worked harder on this competition than I have ever worked on any prize contest which I have entered."

Motography's February 13, 1915 issue carried a story announcing that the $10,000 Photoplay Contest winner had been chosen, although McCardell was not named; that revelation was made upon the serial's release. "The scenarios came from every state in the union," wrote an anonymous reporter. "Some of the best-known authors in filmdom, as well as thousands of unknown moving-picture fans entered the contest. Assistant judges were kept busy for weeks reviewing the scenarios submitted and classifying them for final inspection." S. S. Hutchinson was said to be in California, selecting cast members and arranging production details at American's Santa Barbara studios. Other trade papers reported similar accounts of progress.

Taking a page from Thanhouser's book, Freuler organized a separate entity to handle sales and merchandising of the proposed serial: The North American Film Corporation, with offices on Chicago's State Street and New York City's West 23rd Street. He also engaged the Nichols-Finn advertising agency, which had been instrumental in putting over *The Million Dollar Mystery*, to handle promotion and publicity. The chapter play would be marketed as a special feature, apart from the regular Flying A program. "Any theater may get this photoplay, no matter what its program affiliations may be," Freuler told *Moving Picture World* in late March. In a dig at Thanhouser and *Zudora* he added: "We realize that the manufacturer must stand back of his product. If what we give the exhibitor does not make good, it would be the height of folly to expect him to go along to an unsatisfactory finish." As principals in Mutual, American, and North American, Freuler and Hutchinson were poised to reap huge profits if the serial pleased audiences and hit big. Now all they had to do was make it.

According to several reports, Mary Pickford was offered the starring role for a staggering $4,000 per week but turned it down. Legend has it that, upon refusing, Mary suggested her equally experienced but less successful younger sister Lottie, who got the part. Industry cynics wasted no time circulating the story that Flying A was trading on Mary's popularity, and Hutchinson vigorously but not very convincingly disputed this claim in an interview for *Motography*: "In this choice the Pickford name, made famous through the successes of Lottie's sister Mary, had absolutely no weight. Lottie was chosen for herself alone. And she would have been chosen for the part if the name Pickford had never been heard in filmland before—because of all the actresses available she is so pre-eminently the one for the part."

Irving Cummings was cast as the hero and subsidiary parts were doled out to such capable Flying A regulars as William "Big Bill" Russell, Charlotte Burton, George Periolat, William Tedmarsh, and Orral Humphrey. Relative newcomer Jacques Jaccard, who joined American in late 1913 and both wrote and acted in numerous Flying A shorts before beginning his directorial career, was assigned to wield the megaphone. Of the 28-year-old Jaccard, American's chief had this to say: "He combines with in-born ability extreme accuracy and artistic confidence as a scene-builder. His experience has been of just such range as best fits him for his assignment. And great among his qualities is youth. Romance is illuminated only with the fire of youth."

Hutchinson chose George "Tripod" Hill, chief cinematographer for Hobart Bosworth Productions (and later a highly regarded director at M-G-M), to supervise the camerawork. Fred Priest, while given the title of technical director, actually served as more of a production designer, overseeing the construction of sets, selecting locations for exterior scenes, and supplying the appropriate props and costumes.

Trade-paper ads appearing in early April finally identified American's super-serial as *The Diamond from the Sky* and declared that production was already underway, with Chapter One scheduled for national release on Monday, May 3. As per custom, the first episode's prose counterpart would appear the previous day in the *Chicago Sunday Tribune* and, depending upon which report one believed, 300 to 500 other newspapers across the country, with Roy McCardell adapting his own screen story.

Principal photography had commenced in late March with a spectacular night sequence shot in Mission Canyon, not far from Santa Barbara. Intended as a prologue to the opening installment, it depicted the landing of a fiery meteor near an Indian village in Virginia. Jaccard hired some 40 Navajos as extras and transported them from a nearby reservation to the canyon, where they set up the teepees. Tipped off to the production activity, tourists sojourning in Santa Barbara and nearby Montecito gathered at the location and watched the proceedings from the sidelines. As a *Moving Picture World* correspondent reported, "The final scene taken showed a great meteor battling its way across the heavens and then striking the canyon wall with a tremendous shock, sending up a shower of fire that lighted the entire valley." Just how Jaccard achieved this effect is not known, but it must have greatly impressed the spectators in Mission Canyon that night.

A few weeks later, startled passengers on a Southern Pacific train bound for San Francisco witnessed a wild automobile chase on a road running parallel to the tracks. The first vehicle was a rakish roadster whose sole occupant, the driver, seemed to be bleeding from the head. In a large touring car not far behind, his pursuers repeatedly fired their pistols at the wounded man. A slight distance ahead the road wound to the left, intersecting the tracks. With a burst of speed the roadster's driver pulled ahead and swung directly into the train's path. His car barely cleared the crossing, its rear fender sheared off by the locomotive's cow catcher as he zoomed past. As the Pullman cars roared by, spectators noticed a camera crew grinding away and realized the chase had been staged for a motion picture.

This risky stunt, shot for *Diamond*'s third chapter, climaxed a sequence in which the character played by leading man Irving Cummings, having been falsely accused of murder, escaped police by diving through a window (hence the cuts to his head) and fleeing in the roadster. When a *Saturday Evening Post* article writer, after seeing the footage, penned an "exposé" accusing the serial's makers of resorting to camera tricks to achieve their ends, an indignant Hutchinson fired off a press release assuring readers that thrills in *Diamond* were authentic and that Cummings had performed the death-defying feat. *Moving Picture World* was among the publications in which the below excerpt appeared.

> I can explain it accurately in two words—it happened. There was no double printing nor any trickery, and the cameraman did not stand on his head nor did either the racing car or the locomotive pose on the track. . . .
> Officials of a certain Western railroad can testify to the fact that the scene was actually taken as it is shown on the screen, for the scare given one of its employees by the mad ride across the front of the speeding locomotive was such that it was necessary to relieve him from duty when the train pulled into the next station.
> Mr. Cummings first appeared on the train engineer's horizon about one-quarter of a mile from the crossing which is the climax of a mad race. The engineer whistled a warning. Mr. Cummings answered, giving the engineer the impression that he would drive his auto up over a nearby hill along a road branching off and away from the crossing.
> Naturally, the engineer—confident of this intention—put on more steam. And so did Mr. Cummings. Quick as a flash, the auto sped onto the track, crossed right under the headlight, careened off the track, swerved, righted itself, and down the road it went out of the scene.

Substantially accurate in his depiction of the event, Hutchinson deliberately misled *World* readers about the participation of Irving Cummings in this "mad race." The dangerous crossing was actually performed by stunt double Ted French, who spent a week rehearsing it. Every day at the same time he made the run, driving alongside the train to gauge the right amount of speed needed to pass it. Every day he waved at the engineer and applied his brakes before reaching the crossing. Naturally, the engineer was unprepared when French finally whizzed across the tracks in front of him, and the shock seriously unnerved him. He was indeed relieved of his duties at the next stop, just as Hutchinson claimed.

In late April a throng of exhibitors, exchange men, and trade-paper reviewers gathered in Mutual's Chicago screening room to preview the first three chapters of the eagerly anticipated *Diamond from the Sky*. Freuler and Hutchinson both addressed the crowd, as did Joseph Finn, who revealed the particulars of his massive advertising and promotional campaign.

The preview could not have gone better. *Motography*'s Neil G. Caward filed an enthusiastic report:

> Ere the showing was over, those who could find words in which to express their opinion of the picture were unanimous in declaring it one of the best that they had ever witnessed, from the standpoint of photography, the sustained interest of the romantic story, and in its sensational and thrilling developments that are bound to pull the public back to the theaters in which it is to be shown; while many others were so charmed by the picture that they found themselves utterly unable to put into words their appreciation.

Although one could easily be forgiven for dismissing Caward's account as rank hyperbole, available evidence indicates he accurately represented that advance screening. It generated dozens of bookings on the spot, as did a New York preview given shortly thereafter. "The production's beautiful photography, the rapid but well-sustained action as the compelling story is developed, and the superb acting of the principals won round after round of applause," noted a *Moving Picture World* correspondent. "Altogether, while the exhibitors who viewed the opening chapters had been led to expect much, they found that the reality vastly surpassed their expectations."

Following that second screening, Freuler's North American wasted no time placing double-page ads reproducing in facsimile a letter received from noted showman Marcus Loew: "I beg to state that I attended your private exhibition of the picturized romantic novel *The Diamond from the Sky* and was so much impressed with it that I have requested our Mr. Bernstein to close for it on our entire circuit, feeling satisfied that it will be a big drawing card for our theaters."

Theater patrons who attended Chapter One's first-run engagements on May 3 found *Diamond* uniquely absorbing, due in no small part to the prologue, set in 1685 Virginia. English soldier of fortune Sir Arthur Stanley has come to America make a new life. Captured by Indians, he is bound to a stake and threatened with death by fire that night. The savages' ceremonial dancing comes to a sudden halt when a blazing meteor streaks across the sky and thuds into the ground scant yards from the stake. The Indians regard this as a sign from the Great Spirit and release Stanley. A week later, he returns to examine the now-cooled meteor, in which is embedded a huge diamond. Sir Arthur gouges the stone out with his knife, and this diamond from the sky becomes a family talisman, handed down from generation to generation.

The story proper begins 200 years later. Virginia's Fairfax County is home to the aristocratic Stanleys, although a feud exists between Colonel Arthur Stanley and his first cousin, Judge Lamar Stanley. Both the diamond and the estate in England rightfully belong to the first-born male child of Sir Arthur's closest descendant, but if the Colonel does not produce a male heir the family holdings will transfer to the Judge's young son, Blair Stanley.

Arthur's wife dies giving birth to a daughter. Chagrined and desperate, the Colonel quickly devises a plan that will keep the Stanley fortune in his control. He surreptitiously visits the tent of a gypsy family camping on his property. Matt Harding (Jack Hoxie, billed as Hart Hoxie) and his wife Hagar (Eugenie Forde) have just become the proud parents of a boy. Paid with a bag of gold for his infant son, Matt tears the child from its mother's arms and gives it to Stanley, who spirits the newborn back to his home.

Doctor Lee (George Field), a long-time friend of the Colonel with an elastic conscience, agrees to swear that twins were born to the late Mrs. Stanley. In this way the son of a gypsy becomes heir to a huge estate and the fabulous jewel that goes with it.

Four years later Hagar Harding returns to Fairfax, hoping to recover her son. She steals into the Stanley home and confronts the Colonel, who drops dead at her feet from shock. Hagar steals the diamond but decides to leave the boy behind, knowing he will grow up with wealth and social prominence. A desire for vengeance still burns in the gypsy woman's heart, and she kidnaps Arthur's daughter Esther so that the girl will never have the advantages entitled her as a Stanley.

Doctor Lee, the only other living person who knows the truth, persuades Hagar to surrender little Esther, whom he raises as his ward. He also gets custody of the diamond by reminding the gypsy that it is part of her son's birthright, and vows to keep the secret of young Arthur's parentage.

Years pass and the two Stanley boys grow to manhood. The judge's son, Blair (William Russell), is jealous of his cousin Arthur (Irving Cummings), who not only inherited the family estate but also is his rival for the affection of Esther (Lottie Pickford), a friend to both. He believes that Arthur has the diamond, in actuality still held by Doctor Lee. The first chapter ends with Blair paying a visit to the Lee home and, peering through a window, seeing the Doctor with the glittering stone on a table before him.

In Chapter Two, Blair murders the aged medico and steals the fabled diamond from the sky. Arthur is framed for the murder and narrowly escapes the police. This sets into motion a complex series of events. Possession of the diamond changes hands many times as Blair and his new sweetheart, Vivian Marston (Charlotte Burton), conspire against Arthur and Esther. They are assisted by Luke Lovell (George Periolat), a member of Hagar's tribe, who covets Esther and believes he can only win her once Arthur is out of the way. Doctor Lee's ward has as her allies the hunchbacked gypsy Quabba (William Tedmarsh) and the eccentric lawyer Marmaduke Smythe (Orral Humphrey).

Diamond wowed nearly all who saw it, industry professionals and thrill-hungry moviegoers alike. The *World*'s James S. McQuade stated, "I am impressed that advantage has been taken of all preceding filmed serials by avoiding the mistakes made in various respects and by introducing improvements that will serve to heighten the value and interest of the story." One particularly welcome innovation was the addition to each chapter of introductory title cards presenting a brief synopsis of the story to date. Amazingly, this practice did not become routine for several more years.

Glowing notices from trade papers appeared with surprising rapidity. "One of the greatest serial conceptions that has yet been put forth," gushed *Billboard*. "Undoubtedly the best continued feature that has been put on the market," declared the *New York Telegraph*. "*The Diamond from the Sky* is in a class by itself," concluded *Reel Life*. Exhibitors were no less voluble with their praise, and the Nichols-Finn agency compiled dozens of showmen comments for double-page ads exhorting other theater owners to book the serial immediately and "make the summer months a joy season in the strong box."

Frank G. King, manager of the King Theatre in Estherville, Iowa, stated: "The first chapter was a terrific success, both financially and artistically. Played to the largest audience ever in my theater and received all kinds of congratulatory comments from my patrons as they passed out." He added that attendance at the second installment was even larger than the first, despite heavy rain all day and night. King attributed this to the "extraordinary interest" in *Diamond* displayed by his customers.

Charles P. Bailey, proprietor of Atlanta's Eighty-One Theatre, called the Flying A serial "a most wonderful success at my house," with 1,742 paid admissions on opening day—"far ahead of anything I have ever shown before."

C. W. Gates of Aberdeen, South Dakota's Bijou Amusement Company offered this admission: "I have given *Diamond from the Sky* the greatest advertising campaign that I have ever given any picture in my eight years' experience. Why? Because in those eight years I have never seen another picture that would warrant the expense."

Springfield, Ohio showman Phil Chakeres said the serial exceeded his expectations by a wide margin. "The first chapter we were a little in doubt about, as we thought it would be like all others, so I charged a five-cent admission, but after running same found it so much better that we have changed the admission price to 10 cents and can't take care of all the people."

James C. Bose, manager of Miami's Fotosho and Airdrome theater, tendered the following report: "We had one patron who was so delighted that he insisted we show it after hours even though he had to pay the [projector] operator for the extra time."

Freuler and Hutchinson had a tiger by the tail. But as weeks flew by, the serial's complexity and relentless pace of production eventually took its toll on director Jaccard, on whose shoulders rested responsibility for *Diamond*'s quality. He bowed out with fewer than half the episodes completed. American's owners assigned William Desmond Taylor to finish the chapter play. One of the most fascinating characters in silent-film history, Taylor sold antiques and prospected for gold before entering motion pictures in 1913 as an actor. He worked with Thomas Ince and Francis Ford, learning the business from every angle.

Taylor joined American in 1914 and cut his directorial eyeteeth on short subjects starring Ed Coxen, one of the firm's popular stars. Ambitious and capable, he hungered for better opportunities and cared little for serials, which he regarded (not entirely without justification) as crude melodramas with appeal only to puerile minds. Nonetheless, he met the shooting schedule's demands and distinguished himself with fine work. Tellingly, in press interviews granted after Taylor's assumption of *Diamond*'s direction, S. S. Hutchinson pointedly ignored Jaccard's contributions. "It takes a man like Taylor to make a stupendous thing like *The Diamond from the Sky* a big success," he told the *New York Telegraph* in late June.

Hazards abounded during the 35 weeks that *Diamond* was in production. William Russell was badly bruised while taking a fall down a flight of stairs. Later he was swept away in rapids while attempting to ford a river. George Periolat almost drowned while struggling with another actor in a flooded canal. Director Taylor accidentally stepped on a live electrical wire and was rendered unconscious by the shock. The shooting schedule underwent constant revision to reflect the unavailability of cast members suffering from illness or injury. Taylor's efforts to finish the chapter play on time were further complicated by the pregnancy of Lottie Pickford, who had married New York broker Alfred Rupp shortly before principal photography began. She conceived a child almost immediately but failed to inform anybody at American until her delicate condition became obvious. Changes in costuming and scene staging were required and Pickford's physical activity was necessarily limited.

The Diamond from the Sky unfolded in 30 two-reel installments, making it the longest serial ever produced. It kept audiences engrossed with a succession of plots and counterplots that found victory and defeat meted out to both factions with dizzying frequency. In the penultimate installment fortune seemed to favor Blair and Vivian, who had traveled to England and claimed ownership of the Stanley earldom by virtue of possessing the diamond. But the usurpers were exposed in Chapter Thirty, which ended with Arthur and Esther beginning a happy life together. The treacherous cousin and his wanton woman, however, remained at large and presumably available to engage in future mischief.

First-run engagements of *The Diamond from the Sky* ended in November of 1915. The final episode closed with subtitles reminding spectators to submit their ideas for a 10-chapter sequel: the *Chicago Tribune* was offering another $10,000, this time for a mere 100 words. On the 29th of that same month, the serial was made available to subscribers of Mutual's weekly program service at no extra charge. By then *Diamond* had already earned an estimated $800,000 in rentals.

In August 1916, a Mutual press release promised the company would imminently award $10,000 to a lucky writer who submitted the best scenario for the proposed sequel. That November, American proclaimed that the proposed 10-chapter follow-up would in fact be produced in four chapters and titled *The Sequel to The Diamond from the Sky*. The identity of the prize-winning scenarist "will be announced to the public on the screen only coincident with and in the fourth chapter of the sequel." Why so coy? Because said winner happened to be Mutual publicity director Terry Ramsaye. That his story was chosen from a reported 30,000 submissions would surely not have looked good, so better to keep it secret until the serial had been filmed and released.

Lottie Pickford, whose career had not significantly benefitted from her starring role in *Diamond*, was not available and her character written out. Cummings, too, was otherwise occupied. William Russell, Charlotte Burton, William Tedmarsh, and Orral Humphrey reprised their roles in the follow-up, which was filmed quickly, expeditiously and minus the usual trade-paper hoopla that accompanied the production of most early chapter plays. Esther and Arthur Stanley met off-screen deaths in a train wreck and their young son was removed from an orphanage and looked after by loyal Quabba, the hunchbacked gypsy. Eventually little Arthur was adopted by Louise Grafton (Rhea Mitchell), heroine of the piece. Blair and Vivian Stanley, unsuccessful in making one last attempt to steal little Arthur's inheritance, met a grisly end when they were struck by lightning while trying to escape with the diamond in a violent storm.

A July 28, 1917 news story in *Motography* conspicuously avoided mentioning the original serial at all. Titled "Two-Part Mutual Photodrama," this article gave the follow-up's title as *The Great Stanley Secret* and characterized it as "a highly dramatic production, eight reels of snappy action punctuated with thrills." The *Motography* story additionally claimed that *Secret* would play theaters in two parts of four reels each, but other trade-paper references called it a four-chapter serial in two-reel installments. Likely it was offered in both configurations. In any event, Mutual seemed eager to be rid of the sequel and gave it only minimal promotional support. *The Diamond from the Sky*, however, remained very much in the memories of pioneering exhibitors.

Francis Ford and Grace Cunard: The Original Serial Team

(Universal, 1914-1917)

IN EARLY 1914, desiring a permanent base of operations for his company, Universal Film Manufacturing Corporation president Carl Laemmle authorized West Coast studio manager Isadore Bernstein to purchase the Taylor Ranch, a 230-acre tract north of the Cahuenga Pass, for $165,000. The deal was closed with a down payment of $3,500 and Bernstein supervised the transfer of assets from Oak Crest to the new location, where construction of new structures began immediately. William Horsley, brother of Nestor president David, oversaw development of what would become Universal City. The lot's entrance and administration building fronted Lankershim Boulevard, at that time just a dirt road but later one of the main north-south thoroughfares in the San Fernando Valley.

At this time Universal, like principal competitors Mutual and General Film, marketed short pictures almost exclusively. Laemmle was the industry's leading proponent of what he called "the scientifically balanced program," presented in daily increments of four reels. Typically, the "feature" was a two-reel drama or Western, followed by a one-reel comedy and another drama of similar length, although in a different genre than the two-reeler. Occasionally the fourth part of the show was a "split reel" pairing, say, travelogues (then called "scenics") with animated cartoons or educational subjects. On Wednesdays it was the *Animated Weekly*, Universal's newsreel. In all, 1914 subscribers to the Universal Program received 28 reels per week under 14 different brand names: Bison, "101" Bison, Crystal, Eclair, Frontier, Gold Seal, IMP, Joker, Nestor, Powers, Rex, Universal, Universal Ike, and Victor. Some of the early brands, like Champion, had already been discontinued; others would soon be added. But at the dawn of the serial era the above-named were those in rotation, with Gold Seal productions generally considered the most meritorious. Product was distributed from 49 exchanges scattered across the United States and Canada. At this juncture exhibitors subscribing to the Universal program paid $105 per week, or $15 per day for four reels.

Universal was partial to male-female teams, and in 1914 many units featured them. There were Robert Z. Leonard and Ella Hall, George Larkin and Cleo Madison, Herbert Rawlinson and Anna Little, William Clifford and Marie Walcamp, Allan Holubar and Dorothy Phillips, and others. The lot was even home to married megaphone-wielders Phillips Smalley and Lois Weber, who collaborated so closely that their credit card read "Directed by the Smalleys." But when Carl Laemmle decided to compete in the chapter-play market, there was no question as to whom production of Universal's first episodic thriller would be entrusted: Francis Ford and Grace Cunard.

Born Frank Thomas Feeney on August 14, 1881 in Portland, Maine, the team's male half was a restless youth who dropped out of high school, impulsively married at 16, and just as impulsively abandoned his wife the following year. His father's political influence kept him out of the Spanish-American War after he attempted to enlist in the U.S. Cavalry. Frank Feeney toiled in a succession of odd jobs before joining a stock company as an actor and prop man. Later he claimed to have an unsuitable voice for stage work, using that as an excuse to try motion pictures.

In 1907 or 1908—sources differ on the date—Frank got his big break, such as it was, at the Centaur Film Company in Bayonne, New Jersey. Headquartered in a billiard parlor owned and operated by David Horsley, Centaur turned out comedies directed by Al Christie. Young Feeney won a part in one of them because, as he said later, "I looked funny." He also found acting work at the Edison Company (also in New Jersey) and Mèliés Star Films, the American branch of a pioneering French film concern. Around this time he adopted "Ford" as his stage name, inspired by a passing automobile and out of a desire to avoid embarrassing his family in Maine.

(Years later, Ford's famous younger brother John related the story differently. According to *his* version, Frank took the Ford surname from a drunken actor for whom he substituted during his brief stage career. John told interviewer Peter Bogdanovich that the older thespian subsequently showed up at Universal, looking for work from Ford and calling himself Frank Feeney. Readers of this book are urged to decide for themselves which account they care to believe.)

In December 1909 Ford and his wife, Elsie Van Name, accompanied the Mèliés troupe headed by Hector Dion and bound for San Antonio, where they spent more than a year grinding out one-reel Westerns and Civil War films. During this period Ford played a variety of roles, heroes and heavies alike, while also learning all aspects of motion-picture production. He even played Davy Crockett in *The Immortal Alamo* (1911), which despite its authenticity of location was panned by critics for a lack of realism.

Gaston Mèliés eventually tired of Westerns and decided to produce exotic films in the South Seas. Perhaps sensing that disaster lay ahead—and indeed it did, although that story is not relevant to this book—Ford joined the California-based unit of the New York Motion Picture Company owned by Adam Kessel, Charles Baumann, and Fred Balshofer. With a plant in Santa Monica, California, and elaborate exterior sets in nearby Santa Ynez Canyon, supervisor Thomas H. Ince was producing the best Western films then available. Ince had rented 460 acres and obtained the services of the Miller Brothers "101" Ranch and Wild West

Show, which relocated from Oklahoma to California to take advantage of the huge and still growing demand for Westerns. With large, sturdy sets, spectacular scenery, and real cowboys and Indians as performers, the "101" Bison brand stood for top quality.

Frank was tall and well proportioned, his most distinctive feature being the unruly mop of thick hair covering a large head. Handsome in a rugged way, he photographed poorly from the side; in profile his face appeared to have been flattened with a well-placed brick. But he projected strength, virility, and determination. Plus, he played heroes and heavies with equal facility.

In addition to acting, Ford routinely wrote and directed Bison two-reelers for Ince, a talented but self-aggrandizing filmmaker not above taking credit for exceptional work turned out by his employees. This rankled the easy-going Irishman, as did Ince's oppressive managerial style, which yielded uniformly good results but stifled creativity and inhibited experimentation. Frank found a sympathetic collaborator in actress Grace Cunard, with whom he first teamed in 1912, just as the New York Motion Picture Company joined Carl Laemmle in the Universal Film Manufacturing Company.

Cunard was born Harriet Mildred Jeffries on April 8, 1893, in Columbus, Ohio. Bitten by the acting bug at a young age, she was just 13 years old when her mother allowed her to join a stock company. (Mom accompanied Harriet when the troupe went on the road.) Over the next several years she gained valuable experience and learned a great deal about acting by working with accomplished professionals, including the great Eddie Foy. Legend has it she took her stage name from the Grace and Cunard steamship lines.

In 1910, while between theatrical engagements, Grace decided to take a flyer in motion pictures. Her first film appears to have been *The Duke's Plan*, a Biograph short directed by D. W. Griffith. She had parts in other one-reelers turned out by Lubin and Republic before making her way to the West Coast and joining the New York Motion Picture Company. Cunard worked in "Broncho" one-reelers and "101 Bison" two-reelers; the direction of most was attributed to Thomas Ince, but Ford acted in these and probably helmed some of them as well. He almost certainly directed *Custer's Last Fight* (1912), in which he also played the title role.

Kessel and Baumann had a change of heart and withdrew from Universal almost immediately, but in the protracted legal battle that followed they were forced to surrender their rights to the "101" Bison brand and pay $17,000 in penalties to boot. Eager to be rid of Ince, Frank and Grace negotiated their own deal with Laemmle and began producing shorts for the Universal program. Their films went out under the Broncho and Kay-Bee brands as well as Bison. By early 1914 most Ford-Cunard products—which occasionally ran to three reels—were among the prestigious Gold Seal offerings released every Tuesday.

A studio-written profile of Grace, published in the February 21, 1914 *Moving Picture World*, described her thusly:

> She is a beautiful woman with the natural talents and physique that redounds to the perfection of a woman on the stage. She leans towards strong roles, so far as her tastes and ability go, yet her lighter moods delightfully conform to the demands of ingenue in high-class comedy.
>
> Dark hair, with an agreeable suggestion of a wave in it, environs a face of classic contour, eyes that are sparkling and frank, and a nose that speaks of sauciness incidentally and dignity always. There is a charm about this young woman odd in the extreme. When she radiates roughness mostly there is an underlying seriousness that completely captivates with the "something yet to come unlooked for" which the mixture insinuates.

Upon relocating to the Universal lot Ford and Cunard initially continued making Westerns and Civil War pictures, but before long they had branched out to other genres, showing special affinity for crook stories and thrill-based melodrama. Grace did most of the scenario writing and Frank most of the directing, but their collaboration was such that each had a hand in the other's work.

Best of all, they labored autonomously, without the interference and credit-grabbing to which they had been subjected under Ince's regime in Santa Monica. The biggest problem they had in Universal's pre-serial era was scheduling shooting time at the small studio in Hollywood.

Frank and Grace shared an affection for the trappings of screen melodrama: trap doors, secret panels, hidden documents, and the like. Theirs was an unusually felicitous collaboration. Ford explained it in an unusually candid 1917 interview: "Miss Cunard and I are an ideal team. We even work out the story together. Sometimes one of us, sometimes the other, has the original idea, and then she usually puts it into scenario form. She can *dream* scenarios. We play into each other's hands. She is a very capable director herself, you know."

The Ford-Cunard team hit its stride during those early months of 1914. *In the Fall of '64*, a well-received Civil War drama, immediately preceded *The Bride of Mystery*, a three-reel melodrama that reworked George du Maurier's *Trilby*. Perhaps the most popular of their films in this period was *The Twin's Double*, in which Grace appeared as three separate but identical-looking characters, one of them a daring lady crook who traded on her resemblance to twin sisters to pull off a jewel robbery.

Ford played detective Phil Kelly, using the character name for which he had an unaccountable fondness. Kelly, occasionally nicknamed The Sphinx, became Frank's alter ego. In *The Twins' Double* he allows Grace's devil-may-care thief to escape after she risks her own safety to aid the drug-addled sister. (Cameraman Allen Siegler, a former cowboy, did such a remarkable job on the time-consuming double- and triple-exposure shots that Ford continued to use twins in his films for years afterward.) A sequel, *The Return of the Twins' Double*, was rushed into production immediately but held for several months before release that summer. Ford and Cunard had just finished their most elaborate film to date, a four-reel historical spectacular titled *Washington at Valley Forge*, when they commenced work on the project that would make them international stars.

Moving Picture World ran the following squib in its "Doings at Los Angeles" column for March 28: "*Lucile* [sic] *Love, the Mystery Woman* is the title of the two-reel Western that Francis Ford has started upon with Grace Cunard in the title role. Some of the scenes are supposed to be laid in Manila, P. I. The company is now at San Diego making some airship scenes."

Trade papers published in early April carried ad spreads heralding the coming of *Lucille Love, The Girl of Mystery*, now identified as a serial with a prose counterpart modestly described as "a 20th-century literary masterpiece" authored by "one of the best fiction writers in the world." Universal hired the A. P. Robyn Newspaper Syndicate of Chicago to place the novelization with leading newspapers and within a week some 40 sheets had booked the story. This prose adaptation, probably written by someone in the firm's publicity department, was credited to "The Master Pen."

A Universal statement published in various industry trades during the first week in April stated that *Lucille Love* would be released in 15 weekly installments of two reels each. "The first two reels of this story," it said, "a soul-thrilling one of love, devotion, danger, and intrigue, have already been produced."

Had the previously announced two-reeler actually been expanded to a serial? Possibly. It is certain that Ford and Cunard were asked to develop a chapter play in the wake of *Adventures of Kathlyn*'s success. Grace hastily wrote a one-page synopsis titled *Intrigue, or Lucille of the Secret Service*. The villain, to be played by Ford, was named Jacques but also known as "The Sphinx, who never smiles and seldom speaks." Lucille's last name was given as Browning and the précis indicated that Pete Gerald was to play her father, falsely accused of stealing "a valuable formulae" intended for the government. Cunard wrote that the plot could be extended by having the formula change hands repeatedly while Lucille and the Sphinx chased each other around the globe. "This is in the crude," she concluded, "but will work out nicely."

The following week's "Doings at Los Angeles" column reported that while in San Diego "doing some airship scenes for the *Lucille Love* series," Ford-Cunard stock-company member Ernest Shields nearly fractured his skull in a 25-foot fall on the rocky shore. Shortly after this incident Grace tumbled from the back of an elephant and sprained her ankle.

The firm took every opportunity to brag about the cost and effort that went into the serial. The trades, fed a steady diet of press releases charting *Lucille Love*'s progress, duly reported the company's location jaunts to San Diego, San Francisco, Mexico, and Manila. They published without question Universal's claims that hundreds of extras had been used. They ran photos of Ford and Cunard posing with Isadore Bernstein in front of a Chinese village built at a cost of $5,000 for use in a single chapter. One San Francisco trip involved shooting by the Golden Gate bridge, with Ford chartering an ocean liner for a single day. And yet, surviving candid shots taken during production in the small studio at Sunset and Gower reveal crude and perfunctory sets hastily erected for the taking of interior scenes. Moreover, principal players Keller, Schumm, and Shields all essayed multiple roles, an already-familiar cost-cutting practice.

By early April, Chapter One of *Lucille Love* was ready for shipping and previewed for trade reviewers, who watched in rapt attention as the story unfolded:

A prologue introduces West Point cadets Sumpter Love (E. M. Keller) and Hugo Loubeque (Francis Ford), who have both fallen for the same woman. After being caught stealing from other cadets, Loubeque is expelled when Love bears witness against him. And when Sumpter wins the hand of their mutual flame, the disgraced Hugo vows to spend the rest of his life seeking revenge.

Nearly 20 years pass and Love is next seen as a widowed U. S. Army general stationed in Manila. Sumpter's only child, Lucille (Grace Cunard), is engaged to marry his chief aide, Lieutenant Harry Gibson (Harry Schumm). Loubeque has become an international spy and installed his henchman Thompson (Ernest Shields) as a butler in Love's quarters. Hugo has long awaited the perfect opportunity to disgrace his former classmate and it arrives when a set of top-secret documents is entrusted to Love for safekeeping. Gibson locks the papers in the general's safe while surreptitiously observed by Thompson, who commits the combination to memory and removes the valuable documents after the aide has left.

When the theft is discovered, Love orders Gibson's arrest, fully aware of the effect it will have on Lucille. The heartbroken girl accidentally overhears Thompson's phone call to Loubeque, in which Hugo orders the butler to deliver the papers to him on board the steamship *Empress*. Determined to clear her fiancé's name, she begs a friendly aviator named Hadley (Eddie Boland) to fly her to the *Empress* in his hydroplane. As the aircraft swoops over the steamer Lucille prepares to leap out and the episode concludes.

Chapter Two introduces Lucille to Loubeque, who is stunned by the girl's resemblance to the woman he loved. The spy is injured when he blows up the ship's wireless set and, out of simple human decency, she nurses his wounds. When fire subsequently breaks out, Hugo removes the papers from their hiding place in his cabin and Lucille grabs them. She flees and boards a lifeboat reserved for women and children. It capsizes in the roiling sea, but Lucille saves herself by clinging to a floating timber that eventually carries her to a South Seas island. In the next chapter she is captured by natives who regard her as a white goddess. Loubeque, who also escaped the burning ship and made his way to the island, rescues her from the savages and regains possession of the documents.

Naturally, the white people are rescued by a passing ship, which dumps them off on the China coast, where the chase begins anew. Lucille and Loubeque play tug-of-war with the papers from San Francisco to Mexico and back again, with the spy gradually softening toward her and even rescuing the girl when danger threatens. His respect comes to mirror the love he had for her mother. In the serial's denouement Hugo surrenders the papers and disappears beneath a collapsing floor in his hideout. Lucille delivers the long-missing documents to the Secretary of War, clearing Harry Gibson and paving the way for their marriage. The final scene shows Loubeque writing the following words in his diary:

"My debt of hate toward Sumpter Love is cancelled, for no hate can outlive love in the man who has known Lucille."

Peter Milne reviewed *Lucille Love* for *Motion Picture News*, his notice appearing in the April 11, 1914 issue:

> This "de luxe" production of the Universal company is sure to be a success. From the very outset it scents of excitement and mystery. Two reels are to be produced every week for 15 weeks. As is always the case in pictures that are "to be continued," the last reel ends at an exciting moment, which is sure to cause the public to return for the next installment. . . .
>
> The photography is clear and the light effects are good throughout. . . . All the characters act their parts to perfection. The spy [Ford] is a fine, racy villain, and Lucille gives promise of developing into a most marvelous heroine.
>
> The excitement that abounds in these pictures from the opening scenes, and the feeling of suspense that the closing moments leave with the spectator, augur well for the stimulating power of the coming chapters of *Lucille Love, the Girl of Mystery*.

The serial's first episode, carrying the Gold Seal brand, went into release on Tuesday, April 14, as part of Universal's regular program. Non-subscribing exhibitors rented the chapter play on an *à la carte* basis and paid premium prices for the privilege. Within two months the A. P. Robyn syndicate tripled the number of papers carrying the *Lucille Love* stories, and not long thereafter Universal grandiosely claimed a total readership of 70 million for the serial's prose version.

Subscribers to the Universal program expressed considerable enthusiasm for *Lucille Love*. Fairmont, West Virginia's McCray Theatre—the area's only house charging ten cents for admission—reported doing Standing Room Only business for the duration of the serial. W. G. Conley, manager of Mercer, California's Colonial Theatre, filed a report after showing Chapter Nine, which he rated "by far" the best yet. "Our patrons were simply carried away," he wrote to *Universal Weekly*, "sitting on the edges of their chairs—on the arms of the chairs and craning away into the aisles. And many people told me on leaving that it was the best picture they had ever seen."

Tom Gaines, manager of the Best Theatre in Hillsboro, Texas, said he "boosted it as I have never boosted a film before, and jammed them in on a rainy day for [Chapter] Number One. When I checked up the box office, I was most agreeably surprised. When I checked up on Number Two, I could not believe so many could be gotten into a house of 500 seating capacity—a week's expenses [recovered] in one day's receipts, and some left."

"The town is simply Lucille Love crazy," declared Kansas City, Missouri exhibitor M. M. Sanford. "We have had to inaugurate a Wednesday matinee to accommodate extra business. There are Lucille Love parties in society circles and Lucille Love sundaes at the leading soda fountains."

John Paananen was the proprietor of the Star Theatre in South Range, Michigan, a mining town greatly affected by weak economic conditions. Yet he testified that *Lucille Love* drew more customers than any picture he had ever run:

> Every Thursday we have shown it we have had to open the doors at 6:15, and by 15 minutes to 7 the place had always been packed, even though the times here have been very poor for over a year, first on account of the strike, and now on account of the war and its effects on the copper market. The local mines are running only half the time. Still the people all manage to have money to see *Lucille Love*. One man, called Old Frank, whose age is 55 years, walked 15 miles to see last week's installment.

Exhausted by the sustained effort required to complete the serial, Ford and Cunard took well-deserved vacations after finishing the last chapter in early July; he returned to Maine to see his parents, she went to Ohio and then visited New York. Their fame and following increased exponentially as a result of *Lucille Love*'s success. Exhibitors who thus far had avoided paying $40 or $50 for five-reel features were delighted to have a special attraction guaranteed to pack their houses. Big-city critics predictably looked down their noses at Universal's first serial, mocking its lapses of logic and credulity-straining coincidences. But audiences marveled at the breathless action sequences and accepted without question the peculiar dynamic that existed between heavy and heroine. Historically, the Ford-Cunard chapter play is also noteworthy as the first whose episodes were released weekly rather than bi-weekly. That fact is often overlooked by serial historians.

Universal followed *Lucille Love* with another chapter play, *The Trey o' Hearts* (1914), starring Cleo Madison and George Larkin. Like its predecessor, *Trey* was offered to exhibitors as part of the regular weekly program. But Laemmle realized he was losing money by doing so, especially after reading accounts of Pathé's *The Perils of Pauline* and Mutual's *The Million Dollar Mystery* getting big money by selling those serials on an a la carte basis. Universal's third episodic thriller, *The Master Key* (1914), was the studio's first to be sold as a special attraction. The fourth, *The Black Box* (1915), also adhered to this strategy, which then became standard operating procedure.

In March 1915 Francis Ford and Grace Cunard accepted the responsibility of supplying Universal with another serial. They recycled characters and story elements from a brace of recent two-reelers, *The Mystery of the Throne Room* and *The Madcap Queen of Gredshoffen*, and fashioned a new story called *The Broken Coin*, to be released in 15 chapters. By this time Universal City was fully operational, so the team headquartered their unit on the new lot. Having so much space available to them, Ford and Cunard took full advantage of their new surroundings. For example, they ordered construction of a Balkan city street that stretched a full quarter mile, with some facades erected on a hill to provide a convincing backdrop for long shots. That would not have been possible at the old plant on Sunset and Gower. It would not even have been considered.

Ford and Cunard were riding high; they were Universal's most popular and profitable team, with a long string of successful releases trailing behind. But they could reach new heights with another serial smash, which would give them 15 weeks of exposure as well as sustained advertising and promotional support. *The Broken Coin* was produced on a considerably more lavish scale than *Lucille Love*.

Frank and Grace readied their unit for another lengthy endeavor. Trusted members of their little stock company such as Harry Schumm, Ernest Shields, Harry Mann, and Lew Short were assigned supporting roles, as were relative newcomer Jack Holt, Frank's younger brother Jack, and Grace's younger sister Mina. The unit's most prominent new player was one Eddie Polo, described at length below. Former cowboy Allen Siegler, by now the team's favorite cinematographer, served as first cameraman. He was spelled by R. E. Irish and Harry McGuire, with assistant Ralph Merollo turning the crank on a second camera to make a foreign negative.

Work began in late March. Carl Laemmle, having come to California for the March 15 ceremonial opening of the Universal City lot, was persuaded by Cunard to play a bit part in Chapter One. Afterward Universal's president, one of the film industry's giants, was issued a voucher for three dollars, the standard fee paid to day players. He collected the money from the studio cashier before returning to New York.

Production continued in April with a trip to San Francisco. Scenes were shot in that city's Chinatown and at the Panama-Pacific Exposition, a 635-acre fair celebrating completion of the Panama Canal. The following month Ford and Cunard took the unit to Oxnard, California, and in July to Tijuana, just across the Mexican border. They also spent a good deal more money on props and costumes. The biggest expense may have been incurred on a lengthy battlefield sequence employing hundreds of extras and capped by a large brush fire that got out of control and required the efforts of cast and crew to extinguish. One extra died from injuries sustained in the blast of an overloaded cannon.

As mentioned above, the man who would become Universal's biggest serial star got his big break in *The Broken Coin*. Circus star Eddie Polo was hired not for his acting ability but rather his athletic prowess. Frank and Grace willingly performed potentially dangerous stunts when the script required, but they were not physically equipped to supply the breathtaking thrills increasingly demanded by serial fans. The 40-year-old Polo, stocky and saturnine, doubled multiple cast members in perilous feats required by the script. Giving him one of the secondary parts was another way of justifying his salary and keeping his busy.

Polo's background has been fairly well documented, although his origin remains shrouded in confusion. Some sources give his true name as Edward W. Wyman and list his birthplace as Los Angeles or San Francisco. Others identify him as Edward W. Weimer and claim he was born in what was then called Austria-Hungary. (Eddie's guttural, heavily accented voice would seem to confirm the latter.) His year of birth is usually listed as 1875 but has also been reported as 1879. He entered show business at the age of four and apprenticed with the then-famous Worthley troupe of acrobats engaged by the Barnum and Bailey circus. After four years Eddie joined the Flying Hagelmans, trapeze and high-wire performers, and became a top aerialist. With brother Sam he created his own act and toured all over Europe with Barnum and Bailey, frequently playing to royalty.

In addition to acrobatics and aerial work, Polo excelled at horseback riding and often performed feats of strength calculated to draw appreciative gasps from audiences. He frequently provided thrills outside the big top to promote upcoming circus engagements in major cities. In Paris, for example, he once leaped from a plane circling above the Eiffel Tower, parachuting to the ground a thousand feet below. Eddie also wowed spectators with his prodigious strength and endurance; he once swam 325 feet below the surface without coming up for air. Stocky and saturnine, he cut an impressive figure and possessed a keen sense of showmanship. Also impressive was the size of his ego, although even his detractors agreed that Polo always delivered the goods.

In December 1914, with the circus in winter quarters, Eddie Polo went to Universal City—still in construction preparatory to its scheduled Grand Opening in mid-March—in hope of obtaining work as a stuntman and perhaps getting some acting experience. He immediately landed a small part in one of Henry "Pathé" Lehrman's knockabout comedy shorts released under the L-KO brand. Polo came to the attention of Ford and Cunard while they were producing *The Campbells Are Coming,* shot in late 1914 but not released until the following October. Eddie was hired to execute numerous falls from the top of an 80-foot-high fortress wall into a net hidden from camera view. He also made a 30-foot leap from a treetop and plunged from a severed rope bridge. Ford was thrilled with Polo's work and made him part of the Gold Seal stock company. Eddie appeared with Frank and Grace in the 1915 two-reelers *Nabbed* and *The Hidden City* before winning a supporting role in *Broken Coin.*

As the story opens, reporter Kitty Gray (Grace Cunard) visits a curio shop on her lunch hour and puzzles over an item for sale: one half of a large coin bearing an inscription in Latin. The word "Gretzhoffen" catches her eye and she buys the coin. Kitty has previously written an article about that impoverished Central European kingdom, making her curious about the partial inscription, which she translates at her home with the aid of a Latin dictionary. Although half the message is gone, the remainder hints at the location of hidden treasure. Returning to the newspaper office, Kitty persuades her editor (Carl Laemmle) to underwrite a three-month trip to Gretzhoffen. She bets a year of her salary against the expense money that she will land a scoop of worldwide importance.

Meanwhile, a mysterious foreigner (Eddie Polo) ransacks the girl's apartment looking for the coin, which he narrowly missed purchasing at the curio shop.

Later, on board the ocean liner that will carry her across the Atlantic, Kitty hides the broken coin. That night her stateroom is robbed by the same foreigner who had broken into her flat, but he fails to get the cryptically inscribed curio and makes no further attempts to find it.

Kitty arrives in Gretzhoffen and learns from the American consul that its monarch, King Michael II (Harry Schumm), is a puppet controlled by the unscrupulous Count Frederick (Francis Ford), secretly an international spy who covets the throne and undermines Michael at every opportunity. The tiny kingdom lacks strong financial underpinning, especially since the fortune in gold and jewels belonging to Michael's father disappeared when the old king died. The only clue to its whereabouts is the other half of the broken coin, owned by Michael and sought by Count Frederick. It develops that the sinister foreigner who tried to steal Kitty's half is Frederick's underling Roleaux. Upon learning that Roleaux has failed to acquire the other part of the coin, the Count beats his hapless henchman and decides on a new course of action. He learns where Kitty is staying and corners the American girl in her quarters as the first episode ends.

In subsequent installments the coin's two halves predictably change hands several times. Roleaux decides he has taken one beating too many from Frederick and becomes Kitty's defender. Additional intrigue is woven into the story with the introduction of villainous Count Sachio (Ernest Shields), Frederick's counterpart in the adjoining kingdom of Grahaffen. Eventually war is declared and Chapter Fourteen finds the two countries pitted against each other thanks to the machinations of a few malevolent schemers.

Presumably, *The Broken Coin* was to have ended with the resolution of that conflict and the recovery of King Michael's fortune. But the serial was extended from 15 to 22 episodes in response to letters and telegrams from exhibitors. The New York office cabled Universal City in late August and Isadore Bernstein okayed the additional funding needed to continue production. Novelist Emerson Hough, writing the serial's prose version for newspapers, hurried to California to consult with Ford and Cunard on expanding the story; the September 18 issue of *Motion Picture News* reported that the three went out to dinner together every night for a week to brainstorm the plot extension.

An item in the September 25 *Moving Picture World* broke the news that Cunard had been seriously injured on set and removed to a Los Angeles hospital for emergency surgery. Fortunately, Grace had already completed the scenarios for the final episodes, and Ford was able to shoot around her during the several weeks she needed to recover. By October 16 Cunard was back on the job. Eleven days later, almost exactly seven months after the first shot was taken, *The Broken Coin* wrapped. The added chapters took the story in a different direction; Kitty, Frederick, and Roleaux are shipwrecked and forced to share an island with savage natives. Upon being rescued, the Count is rather improbably revealed as the rightful heir to Gretzhoffen's throne. He unceremoniously deposes Michael and marries Kitty—whom he has come to love—making the plucky American reporter a princess.

The latest Ford-Cunard serial, rolled out in June, had elicited the most glowing reviews of any Universal chapter play to date. The *World*'s Lynde Denig, critiquing the first three episodes, predicted it was "certain of a cordial reception." He went on to say:

> These opening installments . . . are very well handled in that the story is fairly launched without undue delay; the essential characters are established and one realizes right from the start that the two parts of a broken coin are the pegs on which Mr. Hough's narrative [sic] is destined to be strung. . . . Mr. Ford, who plays the scheming count in addition to directing the picture, once more gives evidence of his ability to inject spirit into fight scenes, of which there is an abundance. . . . Well directed and acted, these opening episodes hold the attention.

Peter Milne's notice in *Motion Picture News* heaped praise upon Ford and Cunard:

> Those exhibitors who employ Universal service can readily realize the popularity of these two stars with the patrons of their houses. They are undoubtedly great favorites. Because of their daring and dashing manner this pair fascinates and astounds those whose ideas of the film

world are totally gleaned from the screen.

The Broken Coin is being written by Emerson Hough and scenarioized by Grace Cunard. Francis Ford is producing the picture and has already instilled in it some of his patented sensational, lightning action; enough in fact to give promise of a typical Francis Ford production.

The fights that appear in these first two installments are exceedingly strenuous. Most of them center around Eddie Polo, who plays Roleaux. He is truly a marvelous fighter, being fully capable of getting the upper hand against ten or twelve opponents.

The locale is confined to two imaginary European principalities. The atmosphere of these places is also imaginary. Men clad in modern clothes are stirred in with sliding panels and trap doors, automobiles, Arabs, camels, deserts, and robbers with a joyous incongruity that enshrouds the picture with a weird air of magnetism.

Moviegoers shared Milne's enthusiasm for Polo, whose daredevil stunts contributed mightily to *Coin*'s success. He began receiving copious amounts of fan mail, which swelled the circus star's head and made him difficult to work with. Having been an international sensation while under the big top Eddie expected no less when he moved into films, and by the time the serial was done Frank and Grace were heartily sick of him. But he had impressed Universal management and was destined for bigger things.

Following their triumph with *The Broken Coin*, Francis Ford and Grace Cunard returned to the production of two-reelers under the Bison and Gold Seal brands. *The Campbells Are Coming*, filmed in late 1914 and early 1915, saw release in October, and the "My Lady Raffles" series, pitting Grace's good-natured crook against Frank's dour detective Phil Kelly, was revived in March 1916. A squib in the April 1 number of *Moving Picture World* announced the team had just started a new serial, *Circus Sal*, to be released in 10 chapters. The next issue identified the chapter play as *Peg o' the Ring*, already in its third week of shooting. Ford was said to be directing "a large number of the stock actors and actresses of Universal City." But the following issue, dated April 15, claimed that Ford and Cunard were no longer employed by Universal and had been feted at a farewell dinner by 20 members of their unit.

Universal's house organ, temporarily renamed *Moving Picture Weekly* and now edited by Paul Gulick, carried in *its* April 15 number a full-page ad adding Eddie Polo and newly signed contract player Ruth Stonehouse to the cast of *Adventures of Peg o' the Ring*. A news story in the same issue promised "six or seven stars," not all of them to be seen in the first few episodes; others were slated to appear in Chapters Six and Seven, with still others to be introduced in Ten and Eleven. This same piece had Stonehouse playing Peg and Jacques Jaccard taking over as director. Ford and Cunard were demoted to supporting players in their own serial.

With Chapter One scheduled for distribution during the week of May 1, the *World* in its April 22 issue ran a brief review citing Frank and Grace but not mentioning Polo or Stonehouse—who were given top billing in a two-page ad for *Peg* the following week! Exhibitors by now were thoroughly confused. For the first time Universal serial publicity was not to be believed. Showmen must have been wondering, *what on earth is happening?*

Over the years film historians have surmised that Ford and Cunard bolted because they were tired of arguing with Eddie Polo, who had been cast in a supporting role he demanded Cunard beef up. More likely they clashed with studio manager H. O. Davis, exercising budgetary control over the first serial to begin production since he had taken over from Isadore Bernstein. The team was accustomed to operating with autonomy and undoubtedly resented the attempts of Davis to, in their view, hobble the chapter play's production with his bean-counting.

The exact timing is difficult to ascertain due to ascertain, but Ford and Cunard probably walked off the set during the second week of April, with three episodes in the can and the fourth about to go before the camera. Their publicists, engaging in damage control, insisted that Frank and Grace had been relieved of their duties. Meanwhile, the New York office wired the team to get back to work at once, but those telegrams were ignored. The aforementioned farewell dinner took place on April 11 at Delmonico's Cafe in Los Angeles. Ford and Cunard were not about to go gently into that good night, however, and immediately took a cross-country train to New York for a face-to-face showdown with Laemmle, already being deluged with complaints about his new West Coast studio manager.

Davis was now engaged in a game of chicken he could not afford to lose. With the national release date looming, he moved quickly to seize control of the serial. Columnist J. C. Jessen reported in *Motion Picture News* that the first four episodes had been remade with Stonehouse and Polo, with Jacques Jaccard directing from scenarios reworked by Olga Printzlau. But the Ford-Cunard Chapter One reviewed in the April 22 *Moving Picture World* was the chapter received by Universal's exchanges for shipping on May 1. The following week *News* columnist Jessen informed his readers that production had been suspended following receipt of a telegram from the New York office stating that Ford and Cunard would finish the serial. Laemmle had capitulated, overruling Davis and raising the team's salary in the bargain. Years later Cunard—who made $125 while shooting *Lucille Love*—recalled that Uncle Carl boosted her weekly wages to $450 and guaranteed a bonus of 25 cents per foot for usable scenes that exceeded 1,500 feet per week. In other words, Ford and Cunard were given a financial incentive to complete their films early.

The May 13 *Moving Picture World* ran a news story that quoted Frank extensively and put the controversy to rest. "Contrary to all previous announcements except the first one," Ford said, "Miss Cunard and I will appear in every episode of *Peg o' the Ring* as was announced in the first place. . . . It is all wrong about our leaving the serial." After assuring the interviewer that he and Cunard were still working on the chapter play's scenarios, he stated: "We are going back [to California] on perfectly satisfactory terms for everyone concerned, Mr. Laemmle and myself, the best proof of which is that Mr. Laemmle will accompany us as far as Chicago on our return tomorrow." Ford then added, "Oh, I might say also that neither Miss Ruth Stonehouse nor Eddie Polo will be in the serial." And they were not.

By early May, having railroaded cross-country twice on the Twentieth Century and safely ensconced at Universal City once more, Ford and Cunard began reshooting scenes Polo and Stonehouse had finished in their absence. It meant fast work, requiring the team to complete three chapters in two weeks. But the release schedule was not disrupted; exhibitors received their prints on time. Polo was suspended for several months before being assigned to the Marie Walcamp unit headed by Henry McRae. Stonehouse, severely injured in a trapeze fall, had required surgery and would be sidelined for weeks. Jaccard was reassigned to the Bison unit, for which he helmed two-reelers starring Harry Carey and another newcomer to Universal, G. Raymond Nye.

Additionally, Frank and Grace agreed to move their base of operations from Universal City back to the old lot on Sunset and Gower, which had been home to the L-KO unit making comedy shorts. This arrangement kept them away from Davis, who had been instructed not to interfere with the team.

Adventures of Peg o' the Ring sported a downright bizarre premise, one of many to emanate from Grace Cunard's fertile and occasionally off-kilter imagination. The serial begins by introducing La Belle Le Sieur (Grace Cunard), the star animal trainer in a successful circus. Having being attacked and seriously injured by a leopard, La Belle confides a secret to her faithful friend, Flip the Clown (Pete Gerald), who loves the trainer unconditionally. She is pregnant by a wealthy doctor named Lund (Marc Fenton), who eloped with her months before but refused to acknowledge the union after falling for another woman. La Belle later gives birth to a daughter whom she names Peg, but in her weakened condition the star performer realizes she is not long for this world. After writing a letter explaining the full story of Peg's parentage, she gives it to Flip and extracts his promise to raise the child as his own. Eager to keep something of his beloved La Belle, Flip readily agrees. The woman dies soon thereafter, comforted by the knowledge that Peg is in good hands.

Twenty years later, Peg (also played by Cunard) is a champion bareback rider with the same circus. Much beloved by her comrades of the tanbark, she suffers nightly from fits of temporary insanity during which she flies into a murderous rage. Her birth father, Dr. Lund, married a beautiful but avaricious woman (Jean Hathaway) after abandoning La Belle, thus acquiring a stepson named Frank (Francis Ford). In a wild coincidence Frank meets Peg at a party thrown for the circus members and is instantly attracted to her. Late that evening he introduces the girl to his mother, but at midnight Peg is overcome by one of her fits and attacks Mrs. Lund. Fleeing from the house, she passes out and is found by Flip, who guesses what has happened and spirits her away with Frank Lund in hot pursuit as Chapter One ends.

After that, the plot complications pile up with dizzying frequency. Dr. Lund, recognizing the resemblance between Peg and La Belle, learns about the incriminating letter and mounts a surreptitious campaign to get the document lest the circus queen use it in a future bid to claim the Lund inheritance. His greedy wife, employing the services of a Hindu rather improbably named Marcus (Irving Lippner), decides on the same course without her husband's knowledge.

As if all this were not sufficiently strange, Mrs. Lund in Chapter Five is revealed as the secret head of a counterfeiting ring, adding another layer of incredulity to a plot already bursting with it. Repeated attempts by both the Hindu and Dr. Lund's henchman (Frank's younger brother and future director John Ford, billed as Jack Ford) to steal La Belle's letter from Flip are constantly rebuffed, although the preparation of a forged letter wreaks considerable havoc in later chapters. Mrs. Lund poisons her unfaithful husband in Chapter Fourteen, and in the final episode Frank uses his own not-inconsiderable medical knowledge to cure Peg by "performing an operation with an X-ray apparatus," in the words of a studio-prepared synopsis. Mrs. Lund is apprehended and the circus queen's claim to Lund's fortune is established during the reading of the doctor's will when Flip produces the real letter establishing Peg's parentage.

The Polo-Stonehouse *Peg* would have deviated considerably from Cunard's storyline, as evidenced by a synopsis of the revised Chapter One accidentally printed in *Moving Picture World*'s May 13 issue. In this version Peg (Ruth Stonehouse) is an aerialist, not a bareback rider. Her lover is not Frank Lund but an athlete named Pierre Durand (Charles Munn). Dr. and Mrs. Lund are retained and the question of Peg's parentage remains paramount. The main villain is ringmaster Big Bill Barnen (G. Raymond Nye), whose chief henchman is a tumbler and strongman named Polo (guess who). During the evening performance Barnen deliberately engineers an accident in which Flip is fatally injured. As he lays dying, the clown begins explaining the story of La Belle Le Sieur. The installment ends with La Belle being injured by a big cat and taken into Flip's tent. Presumably, Grace would have been written out of the plot in Chapter Two after La Belle gave birth to Peg. Since he received billing on the ads with Cunard, Ford probably was slated to pop up in an early episode. But with Charles Munn established as Stonehouse's love interest, his appearance would certainly have been brief and perfunctory.

Despite its rocky beginning, *Peg o' the Ring* satisfied exhibitors and patrons eager for another Ford-Cunard serial, although its length was not extended as *The Broken Coin*'s had been. Joe Brandt attributed that decision to the necessity of rolling out *Liberty*, a "preparedness" serial pegged to current events in Mexico, on its scheduled release date of August 14.

Ford and Cunard followed *Peg o' the Ring* with several more two-reelers designed for inclusion in the Universal program. Several of their earlier shorts were retitled and re-released to keep exhibitors sated while they worked on their fourth and final serial, *The Purple Mask*, which went before the cameras in September 1916 as *The Adventures of My Lady Raffles*. The origins of this venture remain unclear, as it was early December before *Mask* was promoted as the chapter play following *Liberty*, scheduled to end its first-run engagements during Christmas Week.

Advertisements and press releases trumpeted the fact that the new Ford-Cunard opus was more series than serial, with each of its 16 episodes telling a complete story. This later turned out to be not quite the case, although a cynic might reasonably believe someone in Universal's front office decided it would be a good idea to string together "My Lady Raffles" series entries and rent them at serial prices rather than use them as program fodder. In any case, Frank and Grace provided enough connective-tissue footage to maintain the illusion that *Purple Mask* told a continuous story. (Actually, most of that work may have been accomplished in editing and titling.) Like *Peg o' the Ring*, the new production was mostly shot at the L-KO studio in Hollywood. The team would brook no interference from H. O. Davis.

In Chapter One we meet Patricia Montez (Grace Cunard), the niece of wealthy Eleanor Van Nuys (Jean Hathaway) and perhaps the most popular young American expatriate living in Paris. Ostensibly occupied with promoting endowments to her aunt's orphanage, the spirited Pat craves adventure. She is taken with American detective Phil Kelly, known throughout Europe as "The Sphinx," but when he snubs her at a social event Pat decides to make him look foolish in retaliation. She steals her aunt's valuable jewels, hides them in a dressing-table drawer, and engages Kelly to find them.

The plan backfires when the Van Nuys butler (Mario Bianchi) comes across the jewels and helps himself to them. When he begins acting suspiciously Pat follows him to the Café Chat Noir, a notorious dive frequented by Apaches. What she does not know is that Kelly and his assistants Pete Bartlett (Pete Gerald) and Bull Sanderson (Jerry Ash) are following *her*. Posing as an Apache's sweetheart, the daring American girl recovers the stolen gems. She leaves the Chat Noir and practically bumps into Kelly, dropping the jewels in her surprise. The disguised Pat makes good her escape but not without arousing the Sphinx's suspicion.

In Chapter Three Patricia, now fully committed to her cat-and-mouse game with Phil Kelly, is made "Queen of the Apaches" while wearing distinctive coronation togs consisting of black cape, black tights, and black velvet blouse. This outfit becomes her standard attire. Pat and her loyal henchmen make things tough for Phil and his assistants, always—but often narrowly—staying one jump ahead of the detective. Occasionally she leaves a purple half-mask at the scene of her crime, just to taunt Kelly. Later installments incorporate a subplot in which the Purple Mask and the Sphinx join forces to defeat a group of anarchists. In Chapter Sixteen, "A Prisoner of Love," Phil warns Pat that her criminous activities are sure to land her in prison and urges her to quit. She agrees to marry him, settling for a different type of confinement.

Ford and Cunard finished *The Purple Mask* in record time, lending credence to the theory that some chapters were independent entries of the "My Lady Raffles" series, recut and retitled for inclusion in the serial. The production was marred by an accident that reportedly devastated Grace and haunted her long afterward. One of the late episodes incorporated footage shot at the Vanderbilt Cup auto race held in Santa Monica on November 18. According to the script, Pat Montez was a passenger in one of the cars. While making the thirteenth lap at more than 100 miles an hour, driver Lewis Jackson lost control of his vehicle, which flew off the road and slammed into a refreshment stand. Jackson, two spectators, and a newsreel cameraman were killed. Mechanic John Ghianda, doubling Cunard, was hurled some 40 feet and badly injured.

Barring a few retakes shot some weeks later, *The Purple Mask* was done. So, essentially, was the Ford-Cunard partnership. They had been extraordinarily close, personally as well as professionally. In late 1915 Ford's wife, Elsie Van Name, had filed for divorce naming Grace as corespondent and citing alienation of affection as the reason. It never went through, possibly because husband and wife were Roman Catholics, but the following year Frank agreed to a legal separation and paid child support to Elsie, who lived in Brooklyn.

For unknown reasons the relationship ended abruptly. On January 17, 1917, Cunard surprised her family and friends by eloping with actor Joe Moore, whom she had met on the L-KO lot and known only a couple months. The following month Ford reconciled with his wife, who became a collaborator on his state-rights serials.

In the months after *Purple Mask* played off, the team was represented in Universal's program by another handful of reissued shorts. They did not appear on screen together in a new production until 1928, when both played members of a criminal gang in Joe Bonomo's Syndicate serial, *The Chinatown Mystery*. Yet both remained associated with episodic thrillers well into the sound era. Ford's last serial role was a bit part of Republic's *King of the Mounties* (1942); Grace played a German spy in two chapters of Universal's *Adventures of Smilin' Jack* (1943).

The Riddle Rider

(1924, Universal Pictures Corporation)

FOLLOWING EDDIE POLO'S abrupt departure from Universal in 1921, cowboy star Art Acord had become the Laemmle lot's top male serial star. He in turn was replaced by film favorite William Desmond, promoted by the firm as "the great feature star" and "hero of a million boys." Born in Dublin in 1878, Desmond grew up in New York and began his acting career in stock and vaudeville, debuting on Broadway in 1906. The burly Irishman's first motion picture was 1915's *Kilmany*, and the next year he attained screen stardom as leading man to Billie Burke in her first film, the smash hit *Peggy*.

While not an action-movie performer *per se*, Desmond acted in physically demanding Westerns and thrill-based melodramas early on. He supported William S. Hart in two 1916 films, *The Dawn Maker* and *The Captive God*, before moving to the Triangle Film Corporation and establishing himself with a series of popular starring vehicles, including a particularly successful Western titled *Deuce Duncan* (1918). After Triangle's collapse he freelanced for producers all over Hollywood, starring in another well-received horse opera, *Fightin' Mad* (1921), before signing with Universal in the spring of 1922. At 44, Desmond was older than most serial heroes (Ben Wilson had two years on him), but with his piercing eyes, square jaw, stocky physique, and thick wavy hair, he cut a dashing figure.

Universal rushed their new chapter-play star into a 15-episode thriller originally called *The Great Conspiracy* but soon retitled *Perils of the Yukon*. Loosely based on America's 1867 purchase of Alaska from Russia, *Perils* cast the Irish Desmond as Englishman Jack Merrill. Chapter One begins in the town of Sitka at a reception celebrating the transfer. Merrill is introduced to Olga Basanoff (Laura La Plante), daughter of a wealthy Russian trader with interests in Alaska. Their immediate and obvious attraction excites the jealousy of Ivan Petroff (Joseph W. Girard), an older and clearly outclassed suitor of Olga's. He challenges Merrill to a duel but is easily overpowered by the Englishman. In a break with serial tradition Jack and Olga become engaged before Chapter One ends. Needless to say, the marriage does not come off as planned. Trouble with Alaskan Indians and ruffians who invade the Yukon during the gold rush provide complications.

Desmond followed his successful debut with three more chapter plays, all released during 1923: *Around the World in Eighteen Days*, *The Phantom Fortune*, and *Beasts of Paradise*. After completing the latter he was scheduled to make a mystery serial titled *Hands in the Dark*. The November 10, 1923 *Universal Weekly* called it a 15-chapter release "crammed with mystery situations of exceptional suspense" and announced that Helen Holmes, not seen in Universal City since 1915, would be Bill's leading lady. But that was the last time *Hands in the Dark* was mentioned.

An item in the December 15 *Weekly* disclosed that Desmond's upcoming serial, a Western titled *The Riddle Rider*, would co-star Eileen Sedgwick and feature Holmes and *Beast of Paradise*'s William Gould as the two heavies. The same news story said, "A complete Western village was constructed for the preliminary scenes, and there will be a number of spectacular cliff and railroad scenes, incidental to thrillers, which experts are now laying off the ground for at the big studio." The village alluded to was a lengthy, downward-sloping, double-sided street that is instantly recognizable to fans of Universal's Twenties, Thirties, and Forties Western serials and feature films.

Why the change from mystery to Western? That has never been established. But Arthur Henry Gooden wrote the original story for William E. Wing and George W. Pyper to break down to scenario format. Production got underway shortly after Thanksgiving and reportedly proceeded at a rapid pace for the first couple weeks. On December 13, however, Sedgwick was seriously burned on the arms, hands, and shoulders while acting in a fire scene set in one of the cabins on the back lot. Sudden wind gusts sandwiched the actress between walls of flame, and only the foresight of production manager William Crinley prevented her injuries from being worse. As a precaution he had soaked several blankets in water prior to rolling the camera. Quick-thinking cowboy Artie Ortega grabbed one of them, dashed through the flames, wrapped it around the panicked actress, and hustled her off the set. Following the accident she spent several days recuperating while director William Craft shot around her.

Sedgwick played Nan Madden, a parentless young woman working as a Pony Express rider to pay off the mortgage on her small ranch outside Casper, Wyoming. The discovery of oil on other properties in the area has attracted a legion of crooks and sharpsters who prey on the townspeople and neighboring cattlemen. Chief among these is suave swindler Victor Sarles (Claude Payton), who either buys oil-rich land cheap or has his minions Jack Archer (William Gould) and Monte Blade (Albert J. Smith) terrorize the small ranchers until they abandon their spreads.

With the law represented—poorly—by a weak-willed sheriff (Yakima Canutt) fearful of antagonizing the town's Sarles-led faction, a mysterious cloaked figure suddenly appears to intervene in the gang's pillaging, righting wrongs while concealing his true identity. This "Riddle Rider" suspects dirty work when Sarles offers to buy Nan's property for the amount due on her mortgage. He warns the girl not to sell and helps her in numerous ways when she learns about the oil deposit beneath the ground on her property and begins drilling a well.

Nan's champion in town is mild-mannered newspaper editor Randolph Parker (William Desmond), who publishes the *Casper Star* with the help of his rotund "printer's devil" Willie (Hughie Mack) and bravely editorializes against Sarles and his partner in crime, Julia Dean (Helen Holmes), a false friend to Nan Madden.

The Riddle Rider foils every scheme Sarles mounts, even after he is discredited when Monte impersonates him and stages a robbery. Nan and the Rider survive fires, floods, stampedes, explosions, wagon crashes, falls from high places, and various assassination attempts. Finally, in a dramatic last-chapter confrontation with the villains, Randolph Parker tells the assembled townspeople that he is a U.S. government agent sent to expose the culprits responsible for Casper's troubles, and that he adopted the Riddle Rider persona to hold Sarles and company at bay while gathering evidence against them. The gang is vanquished and the survivors carted off to jail, whereupon Parker proposes to a delighted Nan.

Work on *The Riddle Rider* was completed in February but the serial's release was withheld until November. Fred J. McConnell, Universal's manager of short subjects and a specialist in film exploitation, devised numerous promotional tie-ins to boost what appeared to be a well-made but standard-issue Western chapter play. The early reviews, while favorable, gave no indication that Desmond's latest serial was anything to write home about. In fact, *Motion Picture News* critic Chester J. Smith, usually quite forgiving in his appraisals, went out of his way to point out Craft's shortcomings:

> The direction could stand a little improvement to make the thrills a trifle more realistic. When those bold, bad gangsters of the oil sharks chase Eileen Sedgwick into the narrow chasm just as the dam above breaks, they apparently have her in their collective cruel grasps. Seeing the onrushing waters, Eileen turns h dashing steed and charges back at her pursuers. The deluge apparently has her when

Desmond appears at the top of the chasm and lassoes her, dragging her up the cliffs to safety. There is no one left to lasso the desperadoes and one is left to believe that some miracle prevented their complete annihilation.

And when the same gang blow up the derrick over Miss Sedgwick's oil well as she is inspecting it, one shudders to think what has happened to the heroine, until she is dragged from a perfectly conceived protecting framework that not only restores her unscathed, but without a single hair a-ruffle or a spot of dirt to mar her beauty. And Desmond, so unconcerned over the whole episode and the harrowing experience through which he has just passed, jokingly holds up his fat office boy as he departs the scene of the disaster.

Of course, Smith went on to say "there is going to be a lot of excitement around where this Universal serial is shown," echoing the sentiments of his peers. But none of the industry's sage prognosticators foresaw the extent to which Desmond's latest would click with the serial-going public.

The *Exhibitors Herald*'s feedback column "What the Picture Did for Me" bulged with extravagant praise for *The Riddle Rider*. It had been years since any Universal chapter play generated such response, which doubtless inspired the owners of subsequent-run theaters to book the serial in record-breaking numbers. (On the strength of this surprisingly enthusiastic reception by second- and third-run houses Universal in early 1926 announced that a sequel—the first in Big U serial history—would be forthcoming.) Positive comments outnumbered negative by a ratio of nine to one, most of the complimentary remarks being unqualified raves. Those presented below are just a few representative samples from happy exhibitors:

Francis McGraw, Gem theater, Little Falls, New York: "I just want to say that *The Riddle Rider*, which I have just finished running, is absolutely the best chapter play I have ever run since I have been in business. This is no bunk!"

John Richardson, Jr., Princess theater, Olney, Texas: "One of the best serials I have played yet. It has the story, the star, the direction, and everything you could wish for. In fact, I believe Universal did their best on this one, and that is saying a lot for the picture."

Elmer Hughes, Opera House, Mesquite, Nevada: "This is my first serial and it looks mighty good to me. Will draw regardless of a weak feature [at the top of the bill]. . . . Already got more compliments on this than anything I ever ran."

Charles E. Lawrence, Star theater, Tuckerman, Arkansas: "The best serial I have ever had in my house. I am now on Episode Twelve and can say that I have enjoyed 12 packed houses since I started this serial. This is a business-builder."

J. H. Rubens, Strand theater, Newton Falls, Ohio: "Every exhibitor should buy this one. A great serial. Will make friends for your house. If Universal keeps up they will lead the world. Finest serial I ever saw. Don't let this one get away from you."

J. E. Draginis, Grand Theatre, Yoakum, Texas: "Boys, if you want a good serial book this one. It's a wow! Am now on the 14th episode and still going strong."

Horn & Morgan, Star theater, Hay Springs, Nebraska: "With country roads almost impassable, this serial is holding up better than any we have had in a long time."

The (anonymous) manager of the Family Theatre in West Frankfort, Illinois, estimated *Riddle Rider*'s box-office potency at "40 percent above average," adding, "A real Western serial that started out good and got better every week. Suited [patrons] 100 percent. Had many compliments and no knocks. If you have a Western crowd you can't beat this one. Absolutely the best I have run to date."

But praise for the serial, while overwhelming, was not unanimous. The consensus was challenged by highly opinionated Henry Reeve, proprietor of the Star Theatre in Menard, Texas. A regular contributor to "What the Picture Did for Me," the often bombastic Reeve fancied himself an influential exhibitor even though his was a 240-seat, second-run house in a town of just 1,200 people.

He booked *Riddle Rider* in November of 1925, well over a year after its release, and after running the fourth episode filed his first report in the *Herald*'s January 2, 1926 issue.

"A good serial," he wrote, "but we are too late on it, apparently. Very bad prints out of Dallas, which was a distinct disappointment after the excellent run we had with *The Great Circus Mystery* [a 1925 Universal serial discussed below]."

By the time Reeve next weighed in, at the end of January, he had changed his mind about the chapter play he initially described as "good." His second report: "Have gone through nine chapters and I'm still trying hard to see how come the almost unanimous reports I've read in the *Herald* say that this is the greatest serial ever. I've got a town that likes Westerns, but this serial is a total loss, or almost, for me. Got a dandy start on it at that. I think it's a mess myself, and the folks seem to agree with me for once. Oh, well, only six more thrrrrrilling chapters."

At this point Reeve—perhaps in a retaliatory frame of mind after getting tattered prints of *Riddle Rider* chapters from Universal's Dallas branch—took it upon himself to pan the serial on a weekly basis. He pulled no punches in subsequent comments. . . .

February 6: "The further we go the more I wonder how this thing got the rep it seems to have. Prints all shot, out of Dallas, haven't seen the end of a single episode since we started. Have to use a slide to let 'em know they have to 'come back next week' and lots of them don't."

February 13: "Only five more [episodes], thanks be. As I've said in previous reports, this is the only picture I've ever had to really totally disagree with *Herald* reports. The so-called thrilling climax to this chapter was a joke. Bright sunlight, not a breath of air stirring on land, and the heroine on a large boat with a hose throwing large waves—zabunk."

February 20: "Every week gets us nearer the finish is all I have to report on this stuff."

February 27: "Still meandering along. Very near the end, thank the gods. Can't hand this effort a thing. [I] see where the Riddle Rider is to do a return, but not here."

March 6: "Through with Chapter Fourteen and but one to go. That's good news for us."

March 13: "At last he rides no more; 'tis over, praise be, and the damsel knows that [Desmond's newspaper editor] is the Riddle Rider at last. Why it took her 15 weeks to find out is nobody's business, I guess. Never was so glad to see a serial end before. Been looking forward to it for the past three months."

Wisconsin showman William Tragsdorf, whose small-town patrons braved brutal weather to follow *The Riddle Rider* that same winter, took a shot at Reeve in his March 6 comment: "I actually read where one of the boys put in a squawk about this serial. That ought to make it 100 per cent.... Maybe all the rest of us are wrong. But I don't believe it. When [customers] come through 20 feet of snow and 40 below zero to see anything, it must be pretty good." So good, apparently that Carl Laemmle himself ordered Fred McConnell and William Lord Wright to cast Desmond in Western serials exclusively from that point on.

What explains *The Riddle Rider*'s remarkable popularity? With the serial itself lost to the ages, that is impossible to ascertain The situations depicted in its 15 chapters were hardly novel, nor was the idea of a heroic Mystery Man. Universal publicity compared Desmond's Rider to the Fra Diavolo of Alexandre Dumas novels and Daniel Auber's opera, but the character's likely inspiration was Johnston McCulley's masked avenger portrayed by Douglas Fairbanks in *The Mark of Zorro* just a few years before. Desmond, cloaked and disguised (though not very effectively, as stills from the film indicate), cut a dashing figure riding up and down the hills behind Universal's back lot—and after all, when have adventure-loving kids *not* loved a caped hero?

The Ace of Spades (1925) was William Desmond's first vehicle to result from Carl Laemmle's Westerns-only edict. Its creative team included Universal serial veterans William Lord Wright, who penned the original story; Isadore Bernstein, who minced the plot into chapter scenarios; and Henry McRae, directing his first episodic thriller since *The Dragon's Net*. Desmond was paired with Mary McAllister, the former Essanay child star who had grown into a beautiful young woman. Wright's yarn was set against the backdrop of the famous Oklahoma Land Rush of 1889, thrillingly recreated in the early chapters. Beyond that *Ace* held little appeal.

Desmond returned early the next year in *The Winking Idol*, based on a story by Charles E. Van Loan, author of many humorous baseball stories and the misadventures of early movie cowboy Buck Parvin, who delighted readers of *The Saturday Evening Post*. Eileen Sedgwick was back as leading lady, with Grace Cunard playing a villainess under the direction of Francis Ford. It marked the reuniting of Universal's first serial team. William Lord Wright supervised production and wrote story and scenarios with Isadore Bernstein. The title applied to a one-eyed figurine of an Aztec god, the key to hidden gold. But very few seem to have cared one way or the other.

Strings of Steel, worst of the 1925-26 lot, featured the last pairing of William Desmond and Eileen Sedgwick. Based on the one and only screen story written by Phillip Dutton Hern (with Oscar Lund), it was a half-hearted return to the Thrills from History concept and used Alexander Graham Bell's invention of the telephone as a jumping-off point. Desmond, a last-minute replacement for ailing Jack Daugherty, played a young engineer in the employ of Bell's chief rival, while Sedgwick was cast as a central operator for the Bell Company. The yarn seemed an odd choice for picturization in serial form and, lacking mystery and melodrama, pleased neither showmen nor patrons. Sedgwick left Universal after completing the film and Desmond returned to Western serials.

Universal's episodic thrillers had suffered declines in prestige and popularity. The latest campaign to elevate chapter plays was actually a throwback to the form's earliest days, when print tie-ins helped popularize the serial concept. A story in the April 17, 1926 *Universal Weekly* announcing the firm's five 1926-27 serials dubbed this quintet the "Famous Authors Five." In order of planned release, they were *The Great West That Was*, by Buffalo Bill Cody; *The Fire Fighters*, by John Moroso; *The Return of the Riddle Rider*, by Arthur B. Reeve and Fred J. McConnell; *Whispering Smith Rides*, by Frank Spearman; and *The Trail of the Tiger*, by

Courtney Ryley Cooper. While undeniably popular with readers, the scribes responsible for the original stories hardly qualified as distinguished men of letters, and their efforts could not by any stretch of the imagination be considered "the first great step to put serials on a literary plane with feature productions," as studio publicity averred. In fact, with just one exception the 1926-27 lineup of episodic thrillers continued a descent into mediocrity.

Universal's sole outstanding 1926-27 serial, *Return of the Riddle Rider* was produced at the request of exhibitors, not demanded by the sales department. Its inclusion in the "Famous Authors Five" lineup was dubious; Universal Short Subject Product Manager Fred J. McConnell actually devised the plot, although Arthur B. Reeve was said to have penned the scenarios. This is possible but unlikely: Reeve was no stranger to serials featuring Mystery Men, but he had never worked on a Western and by his own admission had no aptitude for the genre.

Once again the Wyoming town of Casper was depicted as a hotbed of crime and corruption. *Casper Star* editor Randolph Parker (William Desmond) still campaigned for law and order; apparently the town's population had completely turned over, because none of the citizens seemed aware of his previous activities as a cloaked avenger.

When crooked sheriff James Archer (Norbert Myles) and his henchman Buck White (Tom London) frame a reform candidate in the upcoming election for murder, disgusted Madge McCormack (Lola Todd) tells her father's friend James Thorley (Lewis Dayton) that were she a man, she would run for sheriff herself. Soon afterward "The Silencer," mysterious head of the county's lawless element, instructs Buck White to place her name in nomination for the office.

To the surprise of everyone, Madge is elected. The Silencer tries to exert control over her by threatening to ruin her father, Senator McCormick (Henry Barrows), suspected of mishandling the affairs of the Bonanza Oil Well, in which he is the leading stockholder. The Riddle Rider becomes Madge's defender and helps her defeat the gang.

Critics pronounced *Return* a worthy sequel and singled out director Bob Hill for praise. Perhaps in recognition of the first serial's amazing success, *Motion Picture News* reviewed the sequel in its feature-film section, an unusual deviation from protocol. Critic Paul Thompson's praise for the chapter play could easily be considered hyperbolic:

> Superlatives one uses sparingly. Consequently, when they are used they have a value that really means something. Only superlatives can do justice to the Universal thriller that marks the return to the screen of that character, the Riddle Rider, who possesses all the fascination of the unknown which intrigues us all. Granted that we are all children and love a detective story, whether it is written by "Old Sleuth," Gaboriau, Stevenson or Kipling. And from that premise you will deduce the hold that this serial is going to have on the fans who see it. You will emerge, as I did, from the first chapters admiring the kind of brain that can evolve so many complicated situations that you find yourself lost trying to figure out what will happen next and how the hero and heroine will be rescued from the scrapes into which the writer has plunged them.
>
> It is a sort of super-Western which not only includes hard riding and all the other things which you associate with that type of picture, but also intrigue, politics, a love story and every other ingredient that you can possibly ask for. For a matter of fact there are enough plots and complications to serve for several pictures. From the foregoing, I think, you will gather that I recommend absolutely *The Return of the Riddle Rider*.

Theater owners and their patrons were well pleased with *Return*, although the consensus held it did not match the original.

In January 1928 William Desmond fans got a double dose of their hero in *The Vanishing Rider*, which found him back in Riddle Rider mode, this time garbed entirely in black. William Lord Wright supplied the story but clearly did not spend much time cogitating over it. Saloon owner Butch Bradley (Bud Osborne) leads a band of outlaws determined to seize control of the Allen ranch after he finds gold on the property. Mary Allen (Ethlyne Clair) relies on her foreman Jim Davis (William Desmond) and sidekick Pop Smith (Nelson McDowell) to repel the Bradley gang's constant attacks, but she gets timely aid from the mysterious Vanishing Rider as well. The final chapter unmasked Davis and the Rider as twin brothers and Secret Service operatives. Ray Taylor directed from scenarios by Carl Krusada and George Plympton.

Sydney, Nova Scotia showman and unabashed serial enthusiast George Khattar expressed considerable fervor for *The Vanishing Rider* in his *Herald* report: "Boys, if you're looking for a box-office draw, get this latest Universal serial and if it doesn't smash all your past records of serials than nothing ever will. Each episode of *The Vanishing Rider* is not only equal to but better than the average feature. Any exhibitor who passes up this serial should make an apology to his patrons. Local exhibitors are kicking themselves for letting this serial pass without making a fight for it." (Apparently Khattar bid for exclusivity in the Sydney area.)

The Mystery Rider, released in December 1928, brought to an ignominious end Desmond's six-year run as a serial hero. He played the stalwart defender of leading lady Derelys Perdue, whose screen father developed a process for making rubber from the sap of the mesquite plant (!) before being murdered by an unseen assassin. The formula was pursued by a grotesque caped villain known as "The Claw" for his gnarled hand. To the surprise of absolutely no one, Tom London was unmasked as the miscreant; his presence in the cast had to have set off warning alarms to audiences everywhere. Desmond was gaining weight and slowing down, and his athletic feats were pared down dramatically. But it was the script's predictability that doomed *The Mystery Rider*. William Lord Wright, his own Universal tenure slowly drawing to an end, furloughed the star.

With talkies coming in, Desmond's stentorian tones made him easily adaptable to the new medium, although being typed as a serial star hindered his ability to secure speaking roles. Over the next two years he appeared in only two films—*No Defense* (1929) and *Murder on the Roof* (1930)—before returning to chapter plays, this time as a supporting player. He popped up in several Mascot serials and became a fixture in Universal's episodic thrillers beginning with *Battling with Buffalo Bill* (1931). Henry MacRae, who succeeded Wright as serial unit head following the sensational reception accorded *The Indians Are Coming* (1930), kept Desmond busy for years. Eventually, though, the venerable star was reduced to unbilled bit roles, which he was still seeking when he died in November 1949.

GALLERY 1 / 97

This photo with a printed-in signature was sent to fans of *The Perils of Pauline*.

Top: Crane Wilbur and Pearl White in *The Perils of Pauline* (Pathe, 1914). Bottom: Harry (Wilbur) and Pauline (White) thank their cowboy rescuers.

Top: Harry pulls Pauline from the wreckage of a car that's been sabotaged to kill her. Bottom: Harry seems to be giving Pearl some pitching tips while the treacherous Owen (Paul Panzer) none-too-subtly eavesdrops in this scene.

Top: Pauline at the mercy of gypsies in *Perils of Pauline*. Bottom: Sid Bracey (left), Flo La Badie and James Cruze, stars of *The Million Dollar Mystery* (1914).

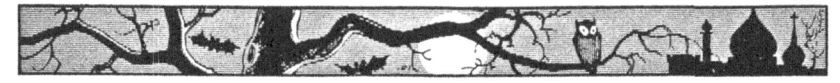

First Release June 22
Thanhouser's Million Dollar Motion Picture Production
The Million Dollar Mystery

Story by Harold MacGrath   Scenario by Lloyd Lonergan

Nine miles of film involving love, romance and adventure—forty-six reels of startling surprises, **new** thrills, stupendous staging—such is this gigantic, new serial production by the Thanhouser Film Corporation. The story itself by Harold MacGrath, the world famous author, will appear in nearly 200 leading newspapers, including the Chicago Tribune, Boston Globe, Cincinnati Enquirer, New York Globe and Buffalo Courier.

Two-reel installments will be released each week, starting June 22. $10,000 in cash will be paid for the best 100-word solution of the mystery. If you want a drawing card for the summer months—an attraction that will pack your house—get in touch with the Syndicate Film Corporation at once and arrange your bookings. The Million Dollar Mystery is an independent release and may be obtained regardless of the regular program being used.

SYNDICATE FILM CORPORATION
71 West 23rd Street   166 West Washington Street
NEW YORK   CHICAGO

or Syndicate Film Corporation representative at any Mutual Exchange in the United States and Canada

THE THANHOUSER THREE-A-WEEK

Tuesday, June 9. "Rivalry." A wonderful two reel production featuring Mignon Anderson, Harry Benham, Morgan Jones and James Cruze.

Sunday, June 14. "The Girl Across the Hall." A thrilling drama played by Harry Benham Madeline Fairbanks, Lila Chester, John Lehnburg and Harry Marx.

THANHOUSER FILM CORPORATION
NEW ROCHELLE, NEW YORK

Head European Offices: Thanhouser Films, Ltd., London, W. C., England

Thanhouser releases will continue to be features of the Mutual Program

---

Although *The Perils of Pauline* has always been remembered due to the legend of Pearl White and the accessibility of at least part of the serial, *The Million Dollar Mystery* was just as popular and just as influential. The Thanshouser organization had a well-deserved reputation for quality motion pictures featuring better-than-average actors and intelligent direction. By all accounts, director Howell Hansel gave serial fans the melodrama they craved but wrapped it up in an attractive package. This advertisement appeared in the major film-industry trade journals as an inducement to exhibitors still on the fence about the still-new chapter plays. It clearly worked, because the *Mystery* was a huge critical and commercial success.

Top: Frank Farrington (seated left) "takes it big" as Braine, leader of the villainous Black Hundred, in this scene from *The Million Dollar Mystery*. Bottom: *Mystery*'s breakout star was Marguerite Snow (with Sid Bracey), who played Countess Olga.

GALLERY 1 / 103

Another scene from *The Million Dollar Mystery*. Intrepid reporter Jimmie Norton (James Cruze) has just rescued heiress Florence Hargreave (Flo La Badie) from another trap laid by the Black Hundred. Cruze and La Badie were Thanhouser's top stars when *Mystery* was produced. Sadly, Flo died in 1917 at the age of 29.

Top: Frank Farrington (left) presides over a meeting of the sinister Black Hundred. Bottom: Lottie Pickford and her eccentric allies in *The Diamond from the Sky*.

Irving Cummings played Arthur Stanley, hero of *The Diamond from the Sky*.

Advertising Makes the Little Fellow BIG and the Big Fellow BIGGER

It doesn't make any difference how big or how little your theater is now, it will be bigger and better if you exhibit MUTUAL Movies, because we are spending thousands of dollars to make millions of people want to see

MUTUAL Movies

Get your share of the trade we create for you, and you will be that much better off.

We follow up our national and local newspaper advertising with a complete outfit for use in your own theater, so that people passing by will know that you can give them the advertised line of motion pictures.

If you want to get the money that MUTUAL Movies will get for someone in your town, get the nearest Mutual exchange to tell you all about it today.

MUTUAL FILM CORPORATION
Branches in 49 Cities   New York

In the film industry's early days, before feature films dominated the business, the Mutual Film Corporation was one of three major distributors, handling product not marketed by the Edison Trust's General Film Company or Carl Laemmle's Universal Film Manufacturing Company — including many notable early serials.

GALLERY 1 / 107

In this scene from Universal's first serial, *Lucille Love, the Girl of Mystery* (1914), General Love (E.M. Keller) bans Lt. Gibson (Harry Schumm) in front of Lucille.

Lucille Love (Grace Cunard) didn't hesitate to mix it up in Universal's first serial.

This incredibly rare 1914 photo, taken on the set of *Lucille Love* at the original Universal studio in Hollywood, show Francis Ford (seated) and Grace Cunard between takes of a restaurant scene. Note that the set was only partially built.

110 / Blood 'n' Thunder's Cliffhanger Classics 2

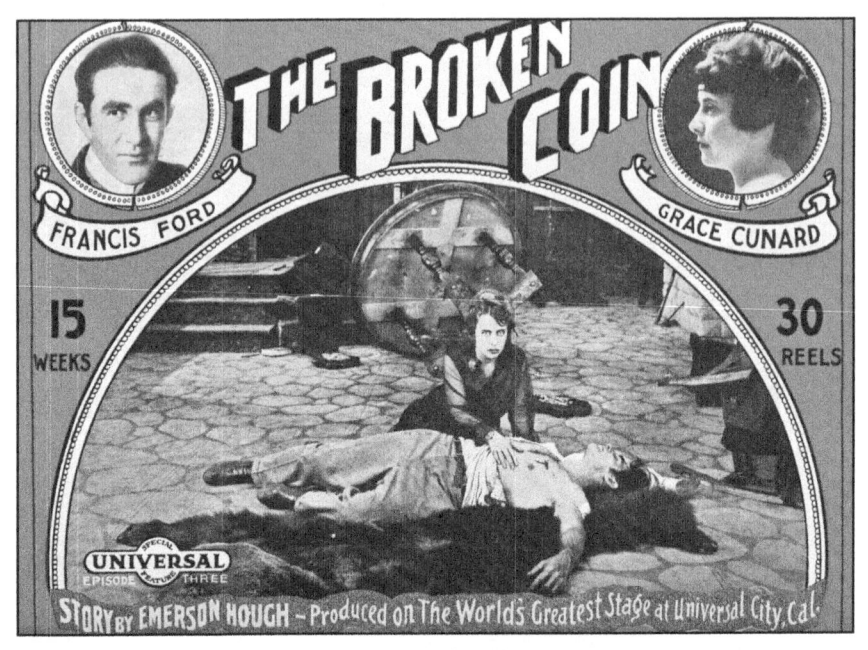

Top: early trade-paper ad for *The Broken Coin* before it was expanded in release. Bottom: Eddie Polo imprisoned in *Broken Coin*. Jack Holt sits on edge of table.

GALLERY 1 / 111

Top: Ford and Cunard direct Eddie Polo (on ground) on location. Note John Ford, standing with cap on. Bottom: scene from *Adventures of Peg o' the Ring* (1916).

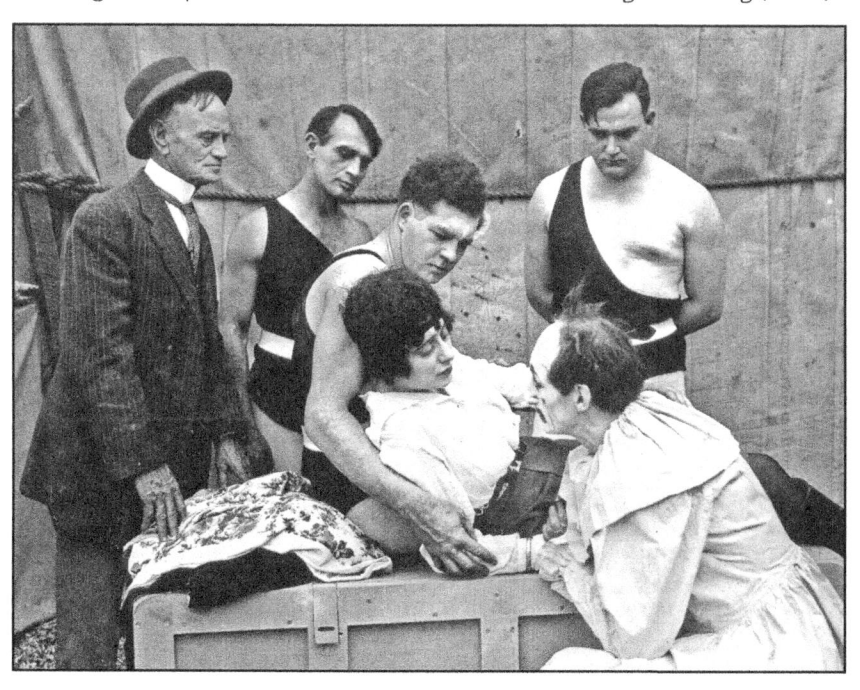

The last Francis Ford-Grace Cunard serial, *The Purple Mask* (1917), was intended to be standalone two-reelers in Grace's "My Lady Raffles" series, but Universal wanted another chapter play from the team. Unfortunately, this was to be their final episodic-thriller collaboration. Shortly after its release the pair split up and went their separate ways. Universal re-released some of their earlier short films with new titles to create the illusion that they were still together, but audiences soon saw through the ruse. Ford starred in several independently produced chapter plays through 1921; Cunard was leading lady to Elmo Lincoln and others.

GALLERY 1 / 113

Top: The Purple Mask mobilizes her gang of Apaches in the sewers below Paris.
Bottom: The Riddle Rider (left) recovers stolen money from the conspirators.

Eileen Sedgwick and William Desmond in *The Riddle Rider* (1924), one of the silent-movie era's most successful serials, reinvigorated the leading man's career.

Tarzan the Fearless

(1933, Principal Pictures Corporation)

ON JANUARY 14, 1929, director Jack Nelson and actor G. Walter Shumway contracted with Edgar Rice Burroughs to produce a serial to be titled *Tarzan the Fearless*. Burroughs insisted upon adding two stipulations: first, that the Ape Man was to be played by his son-in-law James Pierce (who essayed the role in 1927's *Tarzan and the Golden Lion*), and second, that he was to be paid $10,000 before principal photography commenced. Having dealt with Hollywood people of dubious character, Burroughs got the impression—correctly, as it turned out—that Nelson and Shumway might not be able to secure funding. If they did, he would get paid before a foot of film was exposed.

More than a year passed. As ERB had guessed, the option to the proposed serial went unexercised. When Metro-Goldwyn-Mayer came calling in the spring of 1931, Burroughs assumed that *Tarzan the Fearless* was a dead issue. His contract with Metro, signed on April 15, prevented him from licensing screen rights to any other producer for one year; doing so would entitle M-G-M to collect a sizable penalty.

What Burroughs didn't now was that there remained plenty of interest in *Tarzan the Fearless*. The character was very much in the public eye owing to the proliferation of popular-priced reprints of ERB's novels by Grosset & Dunlap, as well as the successes of two recent Universal serials (1928's *Tarzan the Mighty*, which Nelson had directed, and 1929's *Tarzan the Tiger*) and the syndicated Tarzan comic strip drawn by Hal Foster. Additionally, Burroughs was now licensing Tarzan's name and likeness for consumer products. Public awareness of the Ape Man had grown exponentially, which is one of the two main reasons M-G-M had been attracted to the property. (The other: developing a suitable follow-up to the studio's wildly successful jungle epic *Trader Horn*, from which a significant quantity of footage shot in Africa remained unused.)

Unable to obtain either production funding or a distribution deal on their own, Nelson and Shumway approached independent producer Benjamin F. Zeidman, who was making low-budget films for Sol Lesser's Principal Distributing Company. Zeidman offered to ask Lesser about financing and distributing the serial.

Born in 1890, Sol Lesser grew up in Spokane, Washington. As an ambitious young man he moved to San Francisco. In 1915, he learned that local authorities planned a cleanup of the Barbary Coast district, whose various dens of iniquity were notorious. With friend and cameraman Hal Mohr, Lesser made a cinematic record of the area for posterity. He self-distributed it as *The Last Night of the Barbary Coast* and reportedly made enough profit to buy a chain of theaters. For the next several years he was active in both exhibition and distribution, jumping back into production in 1922 after signing child star Jackie Coogan to an exclusive contract. After founding Principal Pictures Corporation he licensed film rights to the best-selling novels of Harold Bell Wright; these included *When a Man's a Man*, *The Mine with the Iron Door*, *The Calling of Dan Matthews*, and several others. His mid-Twenties adaptations of these stories, while not runaway hits, were sufficiently profitable to encourage future production ventures.

Lesser did business under several corporate umbrellas but found his opportunities limited as the Depression took hold, so he was receptive to Zeidman's overtures. A Tarzan film might be just the thing he needed to jump-start Principal. He was skeptical that the original contract remained in force, but Zeidman assured him it would be valid as soon as Burroughs was paid the agreed-upon $10,000. On October 10, 1931, Shumway accompanied Lesser's lawyer, Lewis Goldstone, to ERB's Tarzana home.

Burroughs, whose unsatisfactory experiences with movie people had persuaded him of the wisdom of making contemporaneous notes following each meeting with them, immediately wrote a memo describing the visit:

> I went to the door, and when I saw Shumway I told him that I knew what he had come here to talk about and that I would not talk to him about the matter. He said they had the money and were all ready to go. I remarked that it was a nice day. Goldstone said that he had come here to tender me $10,000. I told him that he would have to talk to [Max] Felix [ERB's lawyer]. He said he could not tender the money to Felix. He repeated, "I have come here to tender the money. I do tender the money." I said, "I have nothing to say." He did not show me any money nor any check. Mrs. Burroughs and Mr. Corwin were present and heard the entire conversation. . . .

Lesser's version of the meeting, recounted in detail for Theodore Fred Kuper in a 1970 oral history later published by Columbia University, differed in some details. According to the veteran producer, the amount in question was $20,000, not $10,000, although the historical record confirms the latter amount. Also, Lesser claimed that Goldstone handed Burroughs the cash, in thousand-dollar bills, which the author flung back in his face. The startled lawyer was then obliged to dive into ERB's front garden to chase the bills as they were scattered by brisk winds.

No stranger to contractual difficulties, the scrappy Lesser went ahead and publicized his intent to make *Tarzan the Fearless*. A squib in the October 30, 1931 issue of the trade paper *Film*

Daily stated: "Principal Pictures Corp. has associated itself with B. F. Zeidman in the production and distribution of the 'Tarzan' serial." This announcement put Burroughs squarely behind the eight ball, as he had assured Metro-Goldwyn-Mayer that no Tarzan film rights were outstanding. Lesser was prepared to file a lawsuit in declaratory relief, but ERB finally admitted he had overlooked the Nelson-Shumway contract when negotiating with M-G-M.

Not wanting any competition for their expensive Tarzan film starring Johnny Weissmuller, Metro dispatched lawyers to meet with Lesser's attorney and see if a compromise could be reached. A surprisingly conciliatory Lesser agreed to delay production until M-G-M's ape-man opus had been released. "Burroughs felt I was very fair and so he was willing to have another Tarzan picture made after Metro was through," the producer said in his memoir. "As a result of this cooperation, I established a real basic, friendly feeling all around, which ripened into a permanent friendship between Burroughs and me. . . ."

But Sol Lesser wasn't just playing Mr. Nice Guy. As an independent producer of limited means, he knew he couldn't compete with M-G-M's Tarzan picture, which reportedly incorporated African-shot footage left over from the studio's recent jungle epic, *Trader Horn* (1931). Clearly, his production would benefit from the release of a big-budget Tarzan feature film; if nothing else he would be able to piggyback on Metro's publicity, which was sure to be elaborate and extensive.

Tarzan the Ape Man was, of course, a huge success and Metro decided to make a sequel. But Burroughs was obligated to let Lesser produce and release *Tarzan the Fearless* first, and though he happily sold additional rights to M-G-M, the biggest studio in Hollywood was compelled to wait for the small independent producer to shoot his bolt.

(History has not been kind to the contract's original signatories. Nelson and Shumway were obviously bought out at some point, but nobody seems to know exactly when or for how much. Since they never invested cash in the project, however, it's reasonable to assume the amount of their settlement was minimal.)

Although Lesser was regularly distributing films through Principal—most of them wild-animal documentaries and English-made dramas—he had personally produced few movies since completing eight Buck Jones Westerns for Columbia release during the 1930-31 season. These six- and seven-reel Bs, made under the auspices of a shell company called Beverly Productions, were turned out for between $12,000 and $15,000 each. Lesser still retained the ability to raise *some* money, but he certainly wouldn't have the resources available to M-G-M, and doubtless Louis B. Mayer's minions didn't waste time worrying that Principal's Tarzan offering would steal much thunder from the Weissmuller film.

In late 1932 Lesser hired former Universal serial production chief William Lord Wright to devise a workable plot and supervise the writing of a screenplay. Wright had produced Universal's two Tarzan serials shortly before relinquishing his position to Henry MacRae in 1930, but since leaving Carl Laemmle's studio—his home for nearly a decade—he had done nothing in the picture business. Wright engaged veteran serial scripters Basil Dickey and George H. Plympton to flesh out his idea. Lesser had asked him to develop the story with economy in mind, and the plot Wright concocted was nothing if not thin.

The completed script was forwarded to Burroughs on January 10, 1933. Tarzan's creator objected to what he called "sex suggestiveness" in some scenes and asked Lesser to tone it down. (ERB was correct about the presence of this element, which remained in the script despite his protestations.) He also asked the producer not to use "Waziri" as the name of a cannibal tribe, since in Tarzan novels the Waziris were trusted allies of the Ape Man. Finally, he requested that a chimp's name be changed from "Balu" to "Galu." Lesser acceded to the author's wishes and moved forward on arranging to finance the project.

On March 22, 1933, *Film Daily*'s front page carried the news that Principal would be producing a Tarzan serial and 12 feature films for release during the 1933-34 season. Territorial sub-distributors entering into Lesser's co-operative plan to subsidize production would get first dibs on Principal's product.

The biggest obstacle to getting *Tarzan the Fearless* in front of a camera was the contractual obligation to use James Pierce in the title role. By early 1933 ERB's son-in-law had gone soft and flabby. His screen career had gone nowhere since *Tarzan and the Golden Lion*; he was playing bit parts without screen credit and had last been seen as a crooked football player in the 1932 Marx Brothers comedy, *Horse Feathers*. Despite his misgivings about Pierce as both an actor and a box-office draw, Lesser in early May screen-tested the actor. The results were unsatisfactory and the producer, as he had several times already, begged Burroughs to reconsider that stipulation of their contract. ERB adamantly refused, presumably to avoid hurting the feelings of his daughter and her husband, who had adopted a strenuous exercise regimen to get himself back in fighting trim.

At this point a frustrated Lesser warned Burroughs that he would make the serial a burlesque, depicting Tarzan as a "sissy" who needed a boost from wife Jane to scale a tree. ERB stood his ground but gave the producer an out by recommending Lesser negotiate directly with Pierce. If his son-in-law could be persuaded to stand down, Burroughs would do the same.

Lesser went to work on Pierce, citing the potential for scheduling difficulties (both the actor and his wife were appearing each weekday afternoon on the Tarzan radio show) that would wreak havoc with the serial's production. What cinched the deal, however, was Lesser's offer of $5,000, to be paid immediately should Pierce walk away. This proved a powerful inducement, since the actor was guaranteed only $500 a week for a maximum of four weeks' work. To the relief of everyone involved, ERB's son-in-law accepted the payoff. In writing.

The ink on this new agreement was barely dry when Lesser cast Larry "Buster" Crabbe as Tarzan. Like Johnny Weissmuller, Crabbe was an Olympic swimming champ; he had competed in both the 1928 and 1932 games, winning a gold medal in the latter for the 400-meter free-style race. Born in Oakland, California but raised in Hawaii, Clarence Linden Crabbe had spent a significant portion of his 26 years in the water, developing a magnificent physique that complemented his boyish good looks. Signed to a long-term contract by Paramount Pictures after his performance in the Olympics, Crabbe was immediately thrust into an imitation Tarzan movie, *King of the Jungle* (1933), based on a C. T. Stoneham novel titled *The Lion's Way*. In release only a couple months when Lesser screen-tested Jim Pierce, Paramount's jungle epic provided its newly minted contract player with an impressive first starring vehicle—and persuaded Lesser that Crabbe was an ideal choice to play Tarzan. Based upon the timing of events as we now know them, it's likely the producer was negotiating to borrow Crabbe from Paramount even as he was putting the skids under Pierce. The trade papers for May 19 announced that Buster Crabbe would become the screen's seventh Tarzan.

Lesser's deal with Paramount gave him Crabbe's services for exactly four weeks; any delay in commencing production could prove ruinous to the project, which was being filmed on a shoestring budget. The producer now moved quickly to hire cast and crew to make his scheduled start date of June 1. On May 24 Lesser hired chief heavy Philo McCullough and juvenile lead Edward Woods. The following day he formally engaged William Lord Wright to supervise the shoot. Screenwriter Walter Anthony, who had worked for Lesser several times, came on board to revise dialogue as needed and coach the players on line readings.

Casting the chief female role proved unexpectedly difficult, despite the fact that Poverty Row in those days had no shortage of young actresses experienced in the fast shooting of low-budget Westerns, serials, and melodramas. Frances Rich, Marceline Day, and Jeanette Loff were mentioned as possible ingénues, but the role ultimately went to 18-year-old Jacqueline Wells, at her tender age already a veteran of several chapter plays. Then under personal contract to Ben F. Schulberg, she was signed on May 29, just three days before the start of principal photography.

A proposed bit of "stunt casting" failed to work out: At the producer's request, the screenwriters had earmarked a supporting role for Helene Madison, like Crabbe a 1932 Olympic gold medalist in free-style swimming. But Lesser's ability to cast the 20-year-old athlete must already have been in doubt, because the script page describing her character's entrance carried this warning: "Note: This bit [is] so written that anyone will do if the Madison [is] not available." The part was ultimately taken by Carlotta Monti, whose lasting claim to fame is not her appearance in *Tarzan the Fearless* but, rather, her status as longtime live-in girlfriend of legendary screen comedian W. C. Fields.

The serial's exteriors were shot in easily recognizable Southern California locations. Jungle scenes were taken at Lake Sherwood and nearby Sherwood Forest in the Conejo Valley. (The area being so named for its use as the principal location used in the 1922 Douglas Fairbanks version of *Robin Hood*.) Iverson's Ranch, near Chatsworth, was employed for sequences requiring in a boulder-strewn area. Other chunks of the serial were filmed in North Hollywood, on the back lot at the old Mack Sennett studio, then being leased by Nat Levine's Mascot Pictures. The relatively few interior sequences were shot on rented sound stages at the RKO-Pathé lot in Culver City. The set used for Tarzan's cave had previously been used as the tomb of Christ in Cecil B. De Mille's 1927 biblical epic, *King of Kings*.

Director Robert F. Hill was an old serial hand, the 1921 *Adventures of Tarzan* being among the 16 chapter plays he had previously helmed. He was also accomplished in the turning out of motion pictures at a fast pace—a skill he would need to complete the 12 episodes of *Tarzan the Fearless* within four short weeks.

In later years Buster Crabbe was fond of denigrating the serial, calling it "the worst Tarzan movie ever made." He incorporated a few anecdotes about it into the hour-long speech he prepared for delivery at nostalgia-themed conventions and film festivals he frequently attended during the Seventies. Even in one-on-one conversations, including several I had with him, Crabbe would respond to questions about *Tarzan the Fearless* with those well-rehearsed digs. "None of us knew what was going on from one minute to the next [because] we shot it in six weeks," he would say. (Actually, it was 21 days spread over four weeks.) "For wild animals we had an old elephant, a nasty chimp, and a toothless lion. The rest was stock footage." (That was true.) "It was goddamned hot everywhere we went to shoot. I was the only one who didn't broil because I was the only one who wasn't wearing any clothes." (Unverifiable but probably true.)

Crabbe knew that *Tarzan the Fearless* was not held in high esteem either by serial buffs or fans of ERB's ape man. So the self-deprecating slaps were his way of begging the audience's pardon. Privately he believed that, given its meager budget and time constraints, the chapter play turned out about as well as could have been expected.

Jacqueline Wells, who developed a friendship with Edgar Rice Burroughs after posing for publicity photos with him, was far more forgiving of *Tarzan the Fearless* than Crabbe, whom she liked and respected. "Buster was wonderful, marvelous, an Olympic champion," she said in later years. "I thought him much better looking than [M-G-M's Tarzan] Johnny Weissmuller. There was no funny business with Buster—he was serious about becoming an actor—and with his looks and physique, how could he miss? He was excellent. Actually, I'd already known Buster [while] being under contract to Paramount [his home studio]. So we were already old friends when we worked on *Tarzan*."

While cutting the serial together, film editor Carl Himm interpolated heretofore unused wild-animal footage obtained by Lesser from Frederick B. Patterson, president of the National Cash Register Company in Dayton, Ohio. An authority on African hunting and a veteran of many safaris, the corporate executive shot this footage himself and only showed it privately until being contacted by Lesser. It's not known how the producer found Patterson, but the man's home movies gave *Tarzan the Fearless* much needed verisimilitude and production value.

It was apparently during the editing process that Lesser came up with the idea that *Film Daily* called "an innovation in the presentation of serials." As originally planned, *Tarzan the Fearless* was assembled in 12 chapters of two reels each. But Lesser had Carl Himm string the first four episodes—minus opening titles and recap footage—into an open-ended, seven-reel feature version of

5,634 feet in length, yielding a running time of just over 62 minutes. This feature could be offered to exhibitors as a special attraction to be followed by a coming-attractions trailer advertising that the subsequent eight chapters would be screened one per week according to normal serial custom. An early-August preview screening in Ventura drew the hoped-for response from audience members and demonstrated the viability of this novel approach. But the concept fell flat at the August 11 premiere in New York City's famous Roxy Theatre, whose projectionist neglected to follow the feature with the trailer. This confused Roxy patrons and prompted *Variety*'s reviewer (who attended that screening) to cast doubt on the idea's effectiveness.

Chapter One opens with Tarzan cavorting in the jungle, teasing his chimpanzee friend Galu and rescuing a fawn from a lion. The sound of far-off drums leads him to their source: the temple of Zar, home to a Caucasian tribe led by high priest Eltar (played by Mischa Auer). These strangely garbed people, who worship the God of the Emerald Fingers, have captured Doctor Brooks (E. Alyn Warren), a scientist interested in their history. The high priest believes this old man has come to loot their temple, which contains a statue of Zar with huge emeralds—each worth a fortune—embedded in its stone fingers. Eltar orders Brooks to be sacrificed. Tarzan arrives at the ceremonial chamber just in time to rescue the scientist and spirit him away. Eltar declares that the ape man has interfered with Zar's people for the last time.

Meanwhile, a safari guided by treacherous Jeff Herbert (Philo McCullough) and his dim-witted partner Nick Moran (Matthew Betz) have brought Mary Brooks (Jacqueline Wells) deep into the jungle—"Yugandi country"—to find her missing father. Mary is accompanied by her fiancé, Bob Hall (Edward Woods), who has become suspicious of their smooth-talking guides. And with good reason: Nick is using the safari as cover in furtherance of his own scheme, as yet unnamed.

Having been returned to the safety of his rough-hewn hut in the jungle, Brooks asks Tarzan to find Mary, whom the old scientist realizes must be searching for him. He gives the ape man a photo by which to recognize his daughter. Tarzan catches up to the safari and gets a tantalizing glimpse of the beautiful girl, who goes swimming in the river when the native bearers stop to rest. While admiring Mary from the top of a massive tree, he sees a crocodile gliding toward her. The ape man makes a daring dive into the river and knifes through the water, reaching the croc just before it can clamp the terrified girl between its jaws. In the vicious struggle that follows, man and reptile sink beneath the surface as Mary's scream is heard.

Chapter Two finds Tarzan victorious—naturally—and he befriends the Brooks girl before being frightened off by approaching white men. Jeff claims to have heard of Tarzan and describes the ape man as a jungle legend. But he knows better, being in possession of a letter from one of Tarzan's relatives back in England. If it can be proved that the ape man is dead, the family estate will go to the next of kin—who, not surprisingly, is willing to pay 10,000 pounds to anyone who disposes of Tarzan.

From this point the plot proceeds along dual tracks. The first involves the persecution of Doctor Brooks and his daughter by the natives of Zar, who remain determined to kill the white people lest they bring more interlopers to the sacred land. The second involves Jeff's efforts to kill Tarzan. The tracks intersect when the unscrupulous guide, upon finding Zar, steals one of the priceless emeralds adorning the God's statue. By repeatedly coming to the assistance of the Brooks party, Tarzan places himself in constant danger from both the Zars and Jeff Herbert.

The serial version of *Tarzan the Fearless* is lost, as is the seven-reel feature released by Lesser. What survives of the production is an 85-minute feature version edited by the film's British distributor and later shipped to America for domestic TV syndication. The British feature omits huge chunks of the narrative and scrambles the order of key sequences, resulting in continuity that is choppy to say the least. In 2005, Jerry Schneider's ERBville Press published a facsimile of the original shooting script, photocopied from Lesser's annotated copy, which was donated with the producer's other papers to the University of Southern California.

Close examination of this reprinted scenario—still available from Amazon—enables the serial fan to see just what is missing from the 85-minute feature version.

Much footage from the first four chapters is included, although some sequences do not appear in their proper order. A fascinating subplot from the middle four chapters, involving voodoo magic conjured up by the witch doctor of the savage Koso tribes, is missing altogether. In a sequence ending Chapter Six and going into Chapter Seven, the witch doctor turns himself into a tiger and is shot by Bob Hall. Chapter Eight ends with Mary wrapped in the tendrils of a giant man-killing plant. Chapters Nine and Ten revolve largely around the attempts of the alluring Madi, a priestess in the temple of Zar, to seduce Tarzan into surrendering the missing emerald, which he has recovered from Jeff.

As scripted, Chapter Eleven was a "recap" episode, built around flashbacks to earlier scenes. The repeated footage was, obviously, stripped from the feature version, although the startling chapter ending—leading into Tarzan's final confrontation with the crooked guide—was retained.

Interestingly, the British feature also omitted most scenes featuring the comic-relief character, a native bearer named Unga (played by Ivory Williams), who wore a monocle and affected an English accent. The script describes numerous instances of overly broad comedy that makes Unga the butt of jokes, and possibly U.K. audiences objected to humor involving racial caricatures.

Comparing script to film, one can see with relative ease why *Tarzan the Fearless* is not highly regarded: It couldn't have been a very good serial. A reading of the screenplay reveals that Wright, Dickey and Plympton were obviously instructed to devise a story devoid of expensive, time-consuming, or difficult-to-stage action sequences. Based on the page lengths of individual scenarios, the finished chapters could not have run more than 15 minutes each— several less than the average serial episode of that era. Shorter chapters meant less production time. Significantly, the most elaborate and memorable cliffhanger endings were those for the second and third installments, which of course were included in the seven-reel feature designed to induce exhibitors to book the rest of the serial.

The close of Chapter Two, which unfolds during a violent storm, finds Tarzan perched on a tree limb above the jungle hut in which Bob and Jeff are fighting over the Doctor's diary, in which has been drawn a map showing Zar's location. A bolt of lightning severs the limb and sends Tarzan plunging through the hut's thatched roof, collapsing it on the combatants.

Chapter Three ends with Tarzan rescuing Mary from Arab slave traders who have spirited her away from the safari. While racing down stream from the camp, the girl and the ape man are apparently trampled in a stampede of horses belonging to the Arabs. (The seven-reel feature ended, just before the cliffhanger of Chapter Four, with Tarzan bringing Mary to his hillside cave for safekeeping.) Most other chapter endings are banal; some, as scripted, could not have aroused much audience interest.

Bob Hill was a talented director, and one with many major successes to his credit. But the feature version of *Tarzan the Fearless* indicates that he was defeated by the unfortunate trifecta of a weak script, skimpy budget and short shooting schedule. And a decision made early on, reportedly by Lesser himself, hamstrung the director even more than the production's physical shortcomings. Crabbe explained it to me in a 1979 conversation: "Well, you see, this was just after Weissmuller's first picture. That 'Me Tarzan, you Jane' business went over very well. They only did it because Johnny couldn't act worth a damn, at least not at that point. But it got across. So Lesser decided that's how we'd play our Tarzan. Most of the time I just grunted like an idiot. On the one hand, I didn't have to worry about forgetting any lines. But, you know, this was a lead. Coming off the Lion Man thing [*King of the Jungle*] I was interested in showing what I could do, not only with the physical stuff, but as an actor."

Monosyllabic performance notwithstanding, Crabbe got better treatment from the critics than the serial itself did. *Photoplay* called *Tarzan the Fearless* "disjointed and inane" but admitted that "Buster *is* decorative." A *Motion Picture Herald* notice described him as "rather attractive and physically wholly accurate." And the *New York Times* opined that "Buster Crabbe is an impressive Tarzan . . ."

Variety's "Chic," who attended the feature version's New York premiere at the Roxy, cut to the heart of the matter. . . .

According to the sales plan the idea is to show the first chapter as a feature and then explain there will be eight more installments. Where the explanation is given in advance it probably will be regarded as an innovation but at the old Roxy, where nothing is said about the continuation, the film nosedives when the tailpiece shuts down on a lot of unfinished business. Probably many customers at this house are still wondering what happened to the rest of the story. In its feature length, plot is spread pretty thin. Action ends rather abruptly with Tarzan admiring the girl in his cave. For all the Roxy audience knows, they set up light housekeeping there.

Story is haltingly told in poor dialog and no one in the cast gets a chance with the material in hand. Picture should be sold as a serial in advance of the showing. And probably only in those houses which like serials.

Exhibitors commenting in the *Motion Picture Herald*'s "What the Picture Did for Me" column slammed *Tarzan the Fearless*. The appraisal shared by A. E. Christian, manager of Monticello, Kentucky's Wayne Theatre, represented the consensus: "This serial is proving a disappointment. It is cheap and prints are terrible. Too much visible faking. Poorest draw of any serial we have used."

Because the British feature version sports such ragged continuity and has only been available in substandard print quality, it's always been easy to make excuses for *Tarzan the Fearless*. But I doubt the complete serial, should it ever resurface, would make a better impression. Still, there's a good deal of fun to be found in Buster Crabbe's only outing as ERB's immortal ape man. Tarzan remains such a powerfully conceived character that almost every film version of his adventures has something to recommend it. The 85-minute feature, long in the public domain, has been marketed in every home-video format and is currently available on DVD from several companies specializing in uncopyrighted movies.

The friendship between Sol Lesser and Edgar Rice Burroughs continued to flourish. When M-G-M decided to reevaluate its commitment to the ape man following *Tarzan Escapes* (1936), Lesser jumped into the breach and produced an inexpensive "B"-grade feature, *Tarzan's Revenge* (1938), for distribution by 20th Century-Fox. It starred Olympic decathlon champion Glenn Morris—who, like Crabbe, played the role as Weissmuller had in his first picture. M-G-M quickly decided to continue its series, freezing Lesser out again. That studio finally gave up the ghost in 1942, Burroughs awarded Lesser exclusive rights to his most famous character, and the scrappy producer made Tarzan films for the next 15 years. Theatrically released by RKO, Lesser's series entries first starred Weissmuller, then Lex Barker, and finally Gordon Scott.

Chandu the Magician

A Brief History of the Character

ONE OF THE EARLIEST adventure serials broadcast on daytime radio, *Chandu the Magician* originated from the Los Angeles headquarters of Earnshaw-Young, Inc., an advertising agency specializing in the production and placement of sponsored radio dramas. Capitalizing on a nationwide fascination with Eastern and Oriental mysticism, the series was developed in 1931 by senior partner Harry A. Earnshaw with junior partner and creative director Raymond R. Morgan. My own belief, which I'll explain in depth later, is that they were heavily influenced by one of Talbot Mundy's high-adventure novels.

In any case, Earnshaw and Morgan made their protagonist an American named Frank Chandler, who spent the years after World War I in India and Tibet, learning the secrets of the East from a kindly, patient yogi. Having finally mastered the ancient arts of the "Three Times Three," the American was inducted into a small but powerful organization known as "the Inner Council." This secret society was charged with combating the forces of evil wherever they popped up to threaten the safety of mankind.

The initial episodes made clear that Chandler was known throughout the East as "Chandu the Magician." It was a catchy, exotic-sounding name but had been appropriated by one Will Lindhorst, a prestidigitator from St. Louis, nearly ten years earlier. The word "chandu" also referred to opium that had been prepared for smoking. Apparently, Earnshaw and Morgan didn't expect gripes about the name from listeners.

A decision was made to keep the extent of Chandu's supernatural abilities vague; in the very first episode he explained that the source of his powers resided in a small emerald casket given him by the yogi upon completion of his training. How he employed those powers depended upon the plot exigencies devised by scriptwriter Vera M. Oldham, a former Earnshaw-Young secretary.

Originally, *Chandu the Magician* was a local show, broadcast every weeknight at 8:15 in fifteen-minute installments on Los Angeles station KHJ. Gayne Whitman—one of broadcasting's busiest men, working on innumerable shows as actor, announcer, or both—assumed the title role. The series premiered on August 4, 1931 and immediately captured the fancy of listeners. The first installment took place at the Beverly Hills home of Dorothy Regent (played by Margaret MacDonald), widow of a famous scientist believed drowned when the steamship on which he was a passenger, *Light of Asia*, went down in the waning days of the Great War. Dorothy's children, 18-year-old Bob (Bob Bixby) and 16-year-old Betty Lou (Betty Webb), barely remember their father, but they are endlessly fascinated by legends surrounding their uncle, Dorothy's brother Frank. He is due back from the Orient any time, and the Regent siblings can hardly wait to see him.

Chandler's abrupt, mysterious arrival is heralded by the eerie, echoing sound of an "astral bell" (also referred to as a "psychic summons") that reverberates throughout the house. Bob and Betty pepper him with questions but Chandu has much more important things to discuss. During a crystal-ball viewing with the yogi, he has seen some unidentifiable menace lurking around the Regent home. This squares up with Dorothy's recent premonitions of danger.

Acting on a hunch, Chandu locates a secret room hidden beneath a wing of the house Robert Regent built for his office and laboratory. Valuable papers relating to the scientist's work are missing, and the only clue to their disappearance is a letter to Regent from a man named Max von Bodin. Another viewing of his crystal ball gives the magician reason to believe that his brother-in-law is still alive, but a prisoner.

At this point *Chandu the Magician* begins building a head of steam. In less time than it takes an announcer to read a commercial, Chandler, Dorothy, and the two children find themselves in Alexandria, apparently transported there by magic. Bob is convinced that his uncle has done some quick work with the emerald casket, but Chandu will neither confirm nor deny the use of hocus-pocus. Instead he trots out some cornball philosophy to confuse the issue: "Time . . . what is it, really? Why, I've known a year to go by like a cloud." (Oldham's scripts are liberally sprinkled with such juicy little bits of obfuscation.)

Chandu has important allies in this part of the world, none of them more capable—or alluring—than Nadji, last in a long line of Egyptian princesses and reportedly something of a sorceress. She is obviously attracted to Chandu but seems curiously unwilling to act on her feelings for him. Her memory seems to be all-encompassing and there are occasional hints that she has experienced reincarnation. Like Chandler, she is a member of the Inner Council. And she has learned that the American's suspicions are well warranted.

Nadji has wormed her way into the confidence of Roxor, a brilliant but thoroughly evil scientist who's also proficient in the black arts. He is bent on world domination and is racing to perfect a super-weapon of some kind to further his goals.

It develops that Roxor (sorcerers, we learn, adopt cognomens that are "palindromes"—names that read the same frontward and backward) is actually von Bodin, and that he sank the *Light of Asia* after having stolen papers and formulas belonging to Regent. But he ordered one of his henchmen to rescue the American upon discovering that the documents lacked information he desperately needs to complete the weapon or weapons—which, by the way, are never precisely described.

The search for Robert Regent takes Chandu and his party from Alexandria to Cairo, and from there to Algiers, and finally to Malta, where the imprisoned scientist is found in ancient catacombs where pagan rituals were conducted thousands of years ago. Roxor apparently meets his death when he falls into a bottomless pit while fleeing from Chandu.

The 14-week continuity, while hewing to a central plot, contains many subplots and superfluous characters. For example, much is made of Bob's decision to rescue from slavers a Russian dancing girl named Natasha, but she disappears after a few episodes. The same fate befalls young American tourist Judy Allen, presumably introduced to provide Bob with a romantic interest. She flits around during the Egyptian-set sequences and vanishes abruptly, although her name is invoked several times later on whenever Betty decides to tease her big brother.

A more significant romantic interest—one that's actually quite well handled by Oldham—is Abdullah, a young Bedouin prince who has fallen in with Roxor but betrays his master out of love for Betty Lou. He confesses his true feelings to Chandu and Dorothy Regent after they express justifiable skepticism about his apparent change of heart. They flatly forbid Abdullah to woo the impressionable girl, who has distrusted the Bedouin since he tried kidnapping her. The young prince reluctantly agrees to stay away from Betty but vows to aid the Americans to prove his sincerity. Subsequently, Abdullah sacrifices himself to save Chandler, and he dies without the girl ever knowing the depth of his feelings for her.

Although far too much air time is allotted the Regent siblings—too much for *my* taste, anyway—the first *Chandu the Magician* continuity teems with pulp-like adventure and melodrama, always tinged with mysticism. The brief diversions, while obviously padding, don't cause irreparable damage to the plot or significantly lessen the suspense. The ultimate fate of Robert Regent always hangs in the balance; every time Chandu and his allies seem close to rescuing the scientist, Roxor throws another obstacle in their path.

For a series so richly steeped in melodrama, *Chandu the Magician* in its early days is pleasantly restrained. There's none of the florid overacting often heard in later radio serials intended for youthful listeners. Whitman projects confidence and virility, and he sounds the properly plaintive note when appealing for guidance, as he does more than once: "Oh yogi . . . my teacher far across the sea . . . by the hidden secrets of the Three Times Three, I ask your help!"

I have been familiar with Chandu's adventures for many years, having heard the surviving episodes and seen the motion pictures adapted from them. For a long time I assumed the show's content and characters were solely the inventions of Harry Earnshaw, Raymond Morgan, and Vera Oldham. That changed when I read my first Talbot Mundy novel, *Jimgrim*.

Serialized in late 1930 and early 1931 issues of the pulp magazine *Adventure* as "King of the World" before being published in cloth by the Century Company, this bravura yarn was the last to feature James Schuyler Grim, a former American military officer introduced by Mundy in a 1921 short novel also published in *Adventure*. Mundy portrayed him as an operative for British Intelligence detailed to the Middle East in the years immediately following the Great War. "Jimgrim" was the name given the wise, stoic officer by his Arab friends.

The character's early exploits, some of them featuring historical figures of the post-WWI period, largely revolved around Grim's efforts to defuse tribal feuds and subvert nascent revolutions. Beginning with 1922's *The Nine Unknown*, however, Jimgrim's adventures increasingly incorporated mysticism—a development attributed to the author's growing fascination of Theosophy. At the conclusion of *The Devil's Guard* (1926), Grim accepted an invitation to study the ancient Eastern mysteries in Tibet.

Jimgrim begins several years later with the ex-military man newly returned from a Tibetan monastery. Grim and his pals—American adventurer Jeff Ramsden, British doctor Bob Crosby, and Indian *babu* Chullunder Ghose—stumble across a plot by a madman named Dorjé (pronounced Dor-ZHAY) to conquer the world using weapons and technology developed in Atlantis and found in long-forgotten ruins beneath the Gobi desert. One of Dorjé's spies, the beautiful Baltis, believes herself to be reincarnation from a long line of princesses. She loves Jimgrim and betrays the would-be King of the World on his behalf, even though the American spurns his amorous advances.

The similarities between *Jimgrim* and the first continuity of *Chandu the Magician* are too striking to be totally coincidental. Chandu is an American who spent years in the East after World War I learning the ancient secrets; so is Grim. Both men have telepathic skills, although the magician's are more highly developed. Nadji is the last in a line of princesses; so is Baltis. Nadji loves Chandu but restrains herself; Baltis loves Jimgrim but flaunts herself. Roxor is a brilliant scientist who hopes to conquer the world with devastating weapons as yet unknown to mankind; Dorjé is similarly brilliant and hopes to conquer the world with devastating weapons long forgotten by mankind.

Both stories play out in international settings. *Chandu the Magician* begins in California and moves to Alexandria, Cairo, Algiers, and finally Malta. *Jimgrim* opens in Marseilles and shifts first to Cairo, then to Delhi, and wraps up in Tibet.

There are, of course, important differences. But it is extremely difficult for me to believe that somebody in Harry Earnshaw's office, somebody connected to *Chandu the Magician*, didn't read Mundy's novel and, at the very least, draw inspiration from it. The borrowing stops short of plagiarism, but the similarities of tone and structure are too pronounced to be overlooked.

However original *Chandu* was or wasn't, it made quite an impression on KHJ listeners. The combined efforts of the cast, writer Oldham, and director Cyril Armbrister paid off in vastly increased sales of White King Soap, the show's sponsor.

Wisely, Oldham kept her characters on the move. The return of Robert Regent and his family to Beverly Hills was short lived, and a visit to the yogi found Chandler chagrined to learn that his work had not ended with the apparent death of Roxor. That deep-dyed villain, you see, had belonged a malignant secret society known as "The Brothers of Jeopardy." The brotherhood's members worked incessantly to undermine civilization's established order in all parts of the globe, and the Inner Council was committed to foiling their schemes at every turn.

It took a little stretching of Coincidence's long arm, but scriptwriter Oldham contrived to reunite Chandler with Dorothy, Bob, and Betty Lou in the mythical Balkan country of Montevania, where brotherhood members Count Metzos and Prince Dimitri plotted to assassinate young Prince Nicholas, rightful heir to the throne. This adventure soft-pedaled magic and mysticism somewhat, but it brought back one of the previous continuity's most interesting supporting characters, a malevolent dwarf known as Arigné the Spider. (Considerable confusion exists as to the proper spelling of the character's name. Some sources list it as "Arenia," and I've seen it in print as "Arenyé." Listening to the cast pronounce it doesn't help to clarify matters; some say Uh-RAIN-yuh, others Uh-REN-yay.) He is described by other characters as being thoroughly repulsive in appearance, and the sight of him scuttling across the room makes Dorothy and Betty Lou shudder. Arigné is nearly burned to death in a blaze from which Chandu escapes magically—as usual, without explaining exactly how he did it.

The closing chapters of the Montevania continuity delivers a blockbuster revelation: Roxor is still alive and working with Dimitri to usurp the throne. Chandler foils the malefactors, but they escape from him.

An island off the coast of Sumatra is the principal location for the next adventure, although there are side trips to Paris and Singapore. But it's in the steamy jungle, with his family at the mercy of cobra worshippers, that Chandu finds himself temporarily helpless. Previously, mention has been made of his one weakness: the susceptibility to fear. The magician has never feared for himself, but when Dorothy is captured by the cobra worshippers and sentenced to death for desecrating their holy temple, he becomes terrified and thus unable to rescue her when she needs him most.

Scripter Oldham, playing for suspense, drags out this sequence for days by having the high priest schedule Dorothy's "sacrifice" for a future date and imprisoning her in a hut while she waits. Rather improbably, Bob and Betty Lou are allowed to visit her frequently, resulting in lots of dialogue that doesn't advance the story. ("Oh, I do wish Frank could overcome his fear!" . . . "Don't worry, mother, we'll figure a way to get you out of here!") Finally, Chandu calls on the yogi and gets a much-needed pep talk that enables him to overcome his fear. With the sacrificial ceremony underway, he bursts into the temple and unleashes the full force of his magic powers on the natives.

Around the time this continuity was drawing to its action-packed conclusion, *Chandu the Magician* made news. The program's success had inspired Earnshaw-Young to syndicate it by recording the old episodes on transcription discs and offering them to other stations while continuing to broadcast new episodes live on KHJ. Another Los Angeles station, KNX, was the first to purchase syndication rights and in February of 1932 began running the series on disc from the beginning. In order to avoid competing with the ongoing live broadcasts, KNX ran *Chandu the Magician* at 5:45 p.m. while KHJ continued in the 8:15 time slot.

It was easy for prospective sponsors to advertise on *Chandu.* Each program opened with a 90-second version of the evocative theme composed by Felix Mills. That gave local announcers more than a minute to read ad copy—with a fully orchestrated musical background—before the recorded announcer cut in with a synopsis of the previous installment. The theme music ran for nearly as long at the episode's tail end, offering additional time for live voiceover commercials.

Syndication was still the exception rather than the rule at this time, making *Chandu the Magician* a pioneering series in more ways than one. The month of February saw six stations pick up the show. By May the number was 44. By year's end, the total had soared to 77. White King sponsored *Chandu* in most of the western part of the country; Beech-But Gum did the same for eastern stations carrying the program in such major markets as New York

City and Philadelphia. It was a sensation. In his history of early syndicated programs, *Points on the Dial: Golden Age Radio Beyond the Networks* (Durham: Duke University Press, 2010), Alexander Russo reports that one station carrying *Chandu* during this period claimed to have received, in a single week, more than one hundred thousand responses to a promotional tie-in.

Once *Chandu the Magician* went national, it was inevitable that Hollywood would come knocking on the doors of Earnshaw-Young, Inc. On March 29, 1932, Fox Film Corporation licensed screen rights to the series for a whopping $40,000—far more than many best-selling novels fetched—and announced that a film version would be released in the Fall. Early trade-paper advertisements listed Edmund Lowe and Marion Burns as the stars, and John Francis Dillon as director. The promotional copy was typically hyperbolic, but not that much: "Mightiest of radio names . . . Outstanding symbol of mystery and enchanting entertainment . . . Nightly, through the loudspeakers of the nation, he holds thrilling, throbbing millions in his spell."

Fox charged its top screenwriting team, Philip Klein and Barry Conners, with adapting *Chandu* to motion pictures. Klein and Conners had first paired the previous year to script *Charlie Chan Carries On*, first in the long-running Fox series to star Warner Oland. In the last 12 months they had also written scenarios for two additional Chans (*The Black Camel* and *Charlie Chan's Chance*), two Zane Grey Westerns starring George O'Brien (*Riders of the Purple Sage* and *The Rainbow Trail*), and, perhaps most importantly, Fox's adaptation of a much-talked-about Broadway thriller by Fulton Oursler and Lowell Brentano, *The Spider*.

A murder mystery that unfolded largely in real time in a packed theater, *The Spider* starred Edmund Lowe (1890-1971), one of Fox's top male stars. The scion of a distinguished Southern California family, Lowe contemplated entering the priesthood before attending college. He pursued a short career in education, teaching English and elocution before being bitten by the acting bug. He went on the stage shortly before World War I and made his Broadway debut in 1917, securing his first film role not long thereafter.

Lowe became a Fox contract player in 1924, earning his first rave reviews in the studio's 1925 adaptation of *East Lynne* and winning stardom the following year opposite Victor McLaglen in the first screen version of *What Price Glory*, Maxwell Anderson's acclaimed play featuring boisterous soldiers Quirt and Flagg. (McLaglen and Lowe would go on to play the same characters— or some like them—in a half-dozen films.) *The Spider* cast him as headlining stage magician Chatrand, who employs hypnotism, thought transference and elaborately contrived illusions to ferret out a killer among the members of his audience in a darkened theater. The Klein-Conners continuity was not a particularly effective adaptation of the source material, but it gave former art director William Cameron Menzies, co-directing the movie with Kenneth MacKenna, ample opportunities to experiment with visual effects while staging Chatrand's eye-popping magic tricks.

Given Hollywood's penchant for making unnecessary alterations to licensed properties that had already achieved success in other media, Philip Klein and Barry Conners generally remained faithful to Vera Oldham's scripts for *Chandu*'s first continuity, "The Search for Robert Regent." What changes the screenwriters *did* make were beneficial to the narrative: They removed extraneous characters (Judy Allen, Gordon Douglas, Arigné the Spider, and Natasha the dancing girl, among others) and stripped the narrative of time-wasting diversions that had only been padding in the first place (such as a sequence in which Bob and Betty Lou got lost in secret passages beneath an Egyptian pyramid).

There *were* some significant changes. The secret invention on which Regent was working at the time of his kidnapping by Roxor, never described with specificity in the radio show, was revealed to be a death ray capable of leveling entire cities. The film's Abdullah never reformed, as did radio's Bedouin prince, and his interest in Betty Lou was motivated by lust rather than love. No reference was made to Roxor's former life as Max von Bodin. Also omitted were any references to the Inner Council, the Three Times Three, and the Brotherhood of the Lotus—all mentioned frequently in those early episodes of the radio show.

The one dubious addition to *Chandu*'s cast of characters was Albert Miggles, included for comedy relief. Identified as a former soldier under Chandler's command during the Great War, he is a whiny, unrepentant rum-hound. The magician hypnotizes Miggles into believing that a hectoring miniature version of himself materializes whenever he starts drinking.

Hypnosis, in the Klein-Conners script, becomes the primary source of Chandu's power; there is no emerald casket, no mystic incantations other than those used by the magician for dramatic effect. At one point Roxor urges his henchmen to blindfold the American as soon as they capture him. "Samson's strength was in his hair," he says. "Chandu's is in his *eyes*."

Last-minute script revisions were made by Harry Segall, Bradley King and, surprisingly, musical-comedy playwright Guy Bolton. Marion Burns, originally slated to play the princess Nadji, was replaced by 21-year-old beauty queen and former Earl Carroll showgirl Irene Ware, who arrived in Los Angeles on May 9 to begin her tenure as a Fox contractee.

That same day, the studio formally exercised its option on Menzies' contract. He was summarily assigned to co-direct the Chandu picture with a recent import from France, Marcel Varnel. The former would handle straight dramatic scenes while the latter would helm sequences involving visual effects, of which there would be many. By early June the first-draft screenplay had been finished and Menzies began conferring with innovative cinematographer James Wong Howe on the most feasible way of effectively realizing the pictorial effects specified by Klein and Conners.

Varnel, for his part, oversaw the casting of supporting players. Veteran actor Henry B. Walthall, who achieved fame as the leading man in D. W. Griffith's *Birth of a Nation*, was hired to play Robert Regent after Ralph Morgan, the producer's first choice, dropped out. Virginia Hammond was picked for Dorothy, with Nestor Aber and June Vlasek taking the roles of Bob and Betty Lou. *Chandu the Magician* provided 15-year-old Vlasek with her first screen credit; several years later she changed her name to June Lang and achieved some notoriety as the wife of Chicago mobster

Johnny Rosselli. British character actor Herbert Mundin won the part of Miggles, and darkly handsome Weldon Heyburn—once touted as "the poor man's Clark Gable"—signed on as Abdullah.

The real casting coup, however, was the signing of Bela Lugosi as Roxor. After several months at liberty following completion of *Murders in the Rue Morgue* for Universal, the *Dracula* star was desperate for work and accepted a flat fee of $2,500 (with a two-week guarantee) to play *Chandu*'s master villain. At this point of his career Lugosi made notoriously poor choices, grabbing any part offered him by major studios and Poverty Row outfits alike. After finishing *Chandu* he accepted a meager $800 from the Halperin brothers to assume the leading role in *White Zombie*, which remains one of his best-remembered starring vehicles.

Bit by bit, combining photographic tricks with mechanical devices, Menzies and Howe devised the illusions that, from the film's very first sequence, established Chandu as a formidable prestidigitator. To portray the famous "Indian rope trick," in which a young man climbs a robe seemingly anchored to nothing, they had riggers build a harness by which the stunt player could be hoisted into the air and pulled up beyond the rope's length. Chandu's nonchalant stroll across hot coals was achieved by sprinkling the sides of his path with broken glass lit from beneath, while steam was pumped through concealed pipes and lycopodium flames blazed merrily. Optical-effects technician Fred Sersen designed a death ray that involved filming a beam of light against black velvet and superimposing it over footage of miniature city spaces representing Paris, London, and New York. Electrical devices needed for Roxor's lab was supplied by Kenneth Strickfaden, who during a long career rented his equipment to every studio that ever made a "mad scientist" movie. At the time he was best known for his contributions to Universal's *Frankenstein* (1931). Additionally, Menzies supervised the design of elaborate miniatures through which Howe's camera would glide fluidly.

Once producer approval of the planned special effects had been secured, Klein and Conners incorporated description of the visuals into a revised final script draft dated July 7, 1932.

Principal photography commenced on July 11 and continued for six weeks. During filming some of the effects sequences had to be modified on set, limiting the staging of actors. As director of those sequences, Menzies was forced to make compromises he feared would negatively impact the final product, but he soldiered on. By late August post-production special effects were already being added and the editing process rushed to enable Fox to meet the film's pre-arranged national release date of September 18. *Chandu*'s "negative cost"—which included all expenditures up to preparation of the printing negative for release prints—was $349,456, about average for a medium-budget program picture that, with a running time of 71 minutes, could play either half of a double bill.

Chandu the Magician was clearly intended for young moviegoers, the same demographic that comprised the radio show's audience. Fox miscalculated badly by marketing it as a prestige picture, a strategy that was pursued based on the marquee value of the Lowe and Lugosi names. Therefore, in the major markets it played the lavish downtown movie palaces owned by Fox and patronized by relatively sophisticated urbanites, who gave it the horse laugh.

In New York City the film opened in Manhattan's premier showplace, the opulently outfitted Roxy Theater. It was a glaringly inappropriate venue for a picture of *Chandu*'s type and the notices were poor. "If *Chandu the Magician* were bad enough to be funny, it would have its virtues," said the *Herald Tribune*'s critics, "but it has the misfortune to fall dismally between the burlesque and the dramatic, with the result that it offers scant entertainment."

"Char," a reviewer for the show-business bible *Variety*, lambasted the film:

> *Chandu* carries the fantastic, the inconsistent and the ludicrous to the greatest lengths yet achieved by the screen. Were it to be taken seriously, there'd be no enjoyment for anyone. If it's accepted strictly as hoke growing out of the horror cycle, it's not so bad, but it's still hoke.

While a variation of the horror cycle through the magical angle, picture often reaches the point in its continuity where it reminds of serials. In that respect it will probably prove oke to those radio followers of Chandu's adventures.

Fox, from accounts, may do the next thing to a serial in the usual manner by making another or several features around Chandu and Roxor, the menace. . . . Audience on finish of picture does not know whether Roxor perishes or not, this probably being a Fox angle in order to still have the character for a possible sequel.

But there wouldn't be any sequel. Domestic film rentals of *Chandu the Magician* amounted to $488,496. Factoring in distribution fees and the cost of prints and advertising, the picture lost approximately fifty thousand dollars. It was a black eye for the whole Fox organization and proved to be the last film Lowe made for the studio on his original contract. *Chandu* was supposed to be Irene Ware's big break, but its failure dashed her hopes of attaining stardom. She played supporting roles for the duration of her two-year contract and left Fox in 1934 to freelance.

Although considered a major disappointment when released in 1932, *Chandu the Magician* is highly regarded today by devotees of fantastic cinema. The rehabilitation of its reputation began with early 1970s screenings in such prestigious venues as the Museum of Modern Art and the New York Cultural Center. Long considered a lost film, it survived in the form of a single 35mm nitrate print discovered by archivist Alex Gordon. He had a 16mm printing negative copied from the original and included *Chandu* in a package of obscure Fox early talkies syndicated to television stations in the mid and late Seventies.

Personally, I find *Chandu the Magician* delightful, and a better than fair representation of the radio program. Visually it's a stunner, thanks to special effects carefully planned by Menzies and future Oscar-winning cinematographer James Wong Howe. The use of oblique angles, diffusion lighting, double exposures, elaborate shadow patterns, deep-focus camerawork, and intricately constructed miniatures gives the film a unique look that conveys a dreamlike quality.

The dialogue—especially in romantic interludes featuring Chandu and Nadji—borders on fruity, and Varnel elicits dangerously ripe performances from his players. Lowe seems for the most part to have ignored the director and is his usual breezy self, but Lugosi, prone to overacting anyway, chews the scenery hungrily. He really goes over the top during a sequence in Roxor envisions the destruction of the world's greatest cities by the death ray he hopes to perfect, describing the annihilation of London, Rome, Paris and New York while his apocalyptic fever dreams appear on screen, superimposed over close-ups of his face.

Yes, it's impossible to take *Chandu the Magician* seriously. Yes, it's serial-like in structure, offering climaxes in every reel. Yes, the acting is charitably described as overripe. But if you approach the film with your sense of wonder engaged, and if you happen to be a fan of the radio show, you won't be disappointed. 20th Century Fox Home Entertainment made it available on DVD several years ago as part of a "Fox Horror Classics" box set, and the digitally remastered transfer of that lone surviving 35mm print is a joy to behold. It is now also available as a Blu-ray.

The box-office failure of *Chandu the Magician* didn't have any appreciable effect on the radio series, which chugged right along and picked up new stations on a regular basis. Gayne Whitman made a cameo appearance as Chandu in a 1933 *Hollywood on Parade* short subject that showed Mae Questal, the voice of Betty Boop, being menaced by Bela Lugosi as Dracula ("You have booped your last boop," he intones solemnly).

The original KHJ run ended late that year, having presented approximately 480 episodes. Whitman had added lucrative motion-picture voiceover work to his busy schedule, and there's some evidence that Oldham was all written out, so to speak. To her credit, *Chandu* remained reliably exciting, with each new adventure taking place in an exotic locale. Magic, mystery and melodrama were never far from the forefront, and she continued to devise intriguing situations and colorful characters.

The series continued in syndication for several more years. As late as 1936 some markets were airing transcriptions of installments presented live in 1933. Earnshaw licensed the property to other broadcast entities and several versions of *Chandu the Magician* were produced with new casts. A Chicago edition of the series has been documented, as has a Canadian counterpart. At least one surviving transcription disc with a 1935 air date features Jason Robards Sr. as Frank Chandler.

Chandu's second foray into motion pictures took place in 1934, after independent producer Sol Lesser, whose Principal Pictures Corporation released product on a scattershot basis, acquired the larger company's unexercised option to film a sequel to *Chandu the Magician*. A scrappy businessman with two decades of experience in production, distribution *and* exhibition, he enjoyed "favored nation" status with Fox—a relationship thus far unexplained. Shortly after receiving the Chandu rights he also inherited the contract of long-time Fox star George O'Brien, whose above-average Westerns cost more than the cash-strapped studio could afford. Producing O'Brien's films independently, Lesser cut their budgets by a third. Fox contributed to distribute them, an arrangement that continued even after the company merged with Darryl F. Zanuck's 20th Century Pictures the following year.

In 1933 Lesser entered the chapter-play market with *Tarzan the Fearless*, which had been made available as both a 12-episode serial and an hour-long feature film to be followed by eight weekly chapters. (The feature simply combined the first four chapters, ending at a logical point in the narrative but leaving numerous plot threads unraveled.) He proposed to do something similar with his Chandu picture.

The assignment of Fox's sequel rights to Lesser took place on December 30, 1933. The producer wasted little time preparing his film, and in typical fashion made grandiose announcements to the trade press. A brief news story in the February 8, 1934 issue of *The Hollywood Reporter* claimed Lesser had hired Vera Oldham to adapt Chandu to the screen, and that prolific serial scribe Basil Dickey would perform the shooting-script carpentry. Oldham received screen credit with Earnshaw and Morgan for the radio series but none for adaptation or original story, so the extent of her involvement in the serial is unknown. The same can be said of Dickey, whose name does not appear on the title cards.

Lesser assembled a crew accustomed to the fast pace and short budgets common to chapter-play production. Director Ray Taylor was recruited from the Universal serial unit, as was cinematographer John Hickson. Production manager Theodore Joos had been an assistant director on several Mascot serials as well as Lesser's *Tarzan the Fearless*. But the canny producer also retained several key staffers from his documentary and feature-film crews, including production supervisor Frank Melford and editor Carl Himm.

Freelance scenario writer Barry Barringer penned an adaptation of a later continuity from the radio series. It revolved around efforts of the Ubasti, worshippers of the Egyptian cat-goddess, to kidnap Chandu's sweetheart Nadji. The Ubasti believe that the lost island of Lemuria—"the birthplace of black magic"—will be restored to its ancient glory if they sacrifice the last surviving Egyptian princess. Chandler, returning from the East, foils the first attempt on Nadji at a party Dorothy has staged in her Beverly Hills home. Ubasti's high priest, Vindhyan, directs the cult's efforts to spirit Nadji away.

Eventually the action shifts to a secret temple where Chandu interrupts the sacrificial ceremony and kills Vindhyan in hand-to-hand combat. He brings Nadji and the Regents back to Beverly Hills, but they have only a brief respite before Vitras, another high priest, launches a new campaign against the princess from the Ubasti's island stronghold. He uses black magic to have her transported to Lemuria. It is believed that when Nadji is sacrificed, her soul will be transferred into the body of Ossana, which the Ubasti have preserved for centuries.

Chandu and his family sail to the island but are shipwrecked and captured. In an underground maze beneath the temple, Chandler meets Tyba, a white magician imprisoned by the Ubasti long ago. He encourages Chandu to use the fabled High Incantation, the only spell powerful enough to stop the ceremony and destroy the temple. In the resulting confusion, Chandler escapes with Nadji and the Regents.

Barringer's screenplay streamlines the Lemuria continuity but makes several alterations. Like Klein and Conners did with their script for the 1932 feature, he eliminates some minor characters while expanding the role of others. Certain sequences are telescoped for translation to the screen, those taking place in Lemuria and on the yacht of Chandler's friend Prince Andra. On radio Vindhyan and Vitras have more to do, and last longer, than in the film adaptation.

Fox's Chandu was primarily a hypnotist, but Barringer makes him a full-fledged master of the occult sciences. There's no equivocation; the magician calls upon his yogi several times and casts several spells to counter moves made by the Ubasti. The radio show's "astral bell" (aka "psychic summons") rings far more in the serial than it did during the feature film.

Unfortunately, Lesser had access neither to Fox's financial resources nor a director as talented as William Cameron Menzies. Reportedly, the serial was budgeted at $90,000. Barringer's script was complete and the financing in place by late June, with shooting scheduled to begin on July 9. But the title role had yet to be cast and time was running out.

At this time Bela Lugosi, the malevolent Roxor of Fox's *Chandu* feature, languishing on Poverty Row and making bad career choices, had wearied of playing villains and vampires. Eager to capitalize on the Hungarian actor's connection to the property and still-potent box-office allure, Lesser offered him the role of Chandu. For his part, Bela leaped at the opportunity to play a hero and accepted a weekly salary of $750 with a four-week guarantee. He was, of course, fundamentally miscast as an American of Anglo-Saxon heritage named Frank Chandler. Barringer gamely attempted to explain Lugosi's thick accent by having Chandu's nephew Bob tell a reporter in Chapter One that his famous uncle "has spent most of his life in the Orient." Presumably, young audience members wouldn't be able to tell Burma from Budapest.

Lugosi's casting was announced in a June 25 *Hollywood Reporter* piece, which identified *The Return of Chandu* as a feature film to be followed by "a series of eight two-reelers which will be a continuation of the feature story." Doubtless some exhibitors looked askew at this report: Lesser had employed the same strategy with *Tarzan the Fearless* only to meet withering criticism when showmen booked the feature alone and learned to their dismay that it ended with several unresolved plot points. But the producer was not about to repeat his mistake.

Commencement of principal photography was rescheduled for July 11, giving Lesser another few days to fill out the cast. Spanish actress Maria Alba, desperately trying to secure a foothold in Hollywood, signed with Lesser to play Princess Nadji. A striking beautiful woman, Alba naturally looked more Castilian than Egyptian. But her voice almost perfectly matched that of radio's Nadji.

Silent-era star Clara Kimball Young made a convincing Dorothy Regent, although it's doubtful that a single moviegoer accepted her as Lugosi's younger sister. Young Universal contract players Dean Benton and Phyllis Ludwig were borrowed to essay the roles of the Regent children. Sinister-looking Lucien Prival was cast as Vindhyan, Jack Clark played Vitras, and Murdock McQuarrie appeared as the Voice of Ubasti. Cyril Armbrister, director of the Chandu radio program, was not only engaged as Ubasti cultist Sutra but also as the serial's dialogue director. Josef Swickard, well schooled in the portrayal of attenuated and avuncular father figures, perfectly embodied Tyba, the elderly white magician.

Without a back lot or sound stages of his own, Lesser and his production supervisor shot *Return of Chandu* on rented sets and locations. Scenes taking place aboard Andra's yacht were filmed in San Pedro's harbor. A chase sequence was shot on Lookout Mountain, and several homes in the San Fernando Valley were used as backdrops. Lesser also rented the "Egyptian Quarter" on Universal's back lot and, most impressively, the massive wooden gates built on the RKO Pathé lot for *King Kong*.

Director Ray Taylor, a long-time helmer of serials who was accustomed to working on short budgets and schedules, finished work in exactly four weeks. That's two weeks less than was required for Fox's *Chandu the Magician*, which had a running time of less than half the serial's length. At that point editors Carl Himm and Lou Sackin took over.

Still stung by exhibitor annoyance over the *Tarzan the Fearless* feature assembled from that serial's first four episodes, Lesser had obviously instructed Barringer to construct his adaptation of the radio show's Lemuria sequence in two clearly definable segments. Chapters One through Four pit Chandu against Vindhyan, who is dispatched in an exciting last-minute rescue of Nadji and Dorothy. With minor trims and the elimination of chapter-opening recaps, the quartet of installments made a compact seven-reel feature, also titled *The Return of Chandu*, running just under 65 minutes. Any showman who booked the feature without the following eight two-reel episodes would not have to worry about frustrating his patrons. Both chapter play and feature went into national release simultaneously on the first of October. The serial was rented for the customary five dollars (in some cases less) per chapter; the seven-reeler was leased for a flat fee of ten to twenty-five dollars based on the size and location of theaters booking it. And, of course, the film was made available in 12 two-reel chapters with running times between 16 and 20 minutes.

Chapter Five begins with Nadji and the Regent family safe, but only temporarily. The Voice of Ubasti orders Vitras to complete Vindhyan's mission by kidnapping the princess and bringing her to Lemuria for proper sacrifice alongside the perfectly preserved corpse of Ossana. Chandu and his family, sailing to the island, fall victim to the Ubasti and spend the second half of the chapter play trying to rescue Nadji and escape.

This plot segment, unlike the first, is padded to an almost ridiculous degree. An average of nearly four minutes per chapter is devoted to main titles, printed synopses of previous episodes, and recap footage leading up to the chapter endings. Individual shots and complete sequences are repeated numerous times. Chapter Ten repeats nearly the entire reel of the previous installment, the first new scene appearing eight minutes in. Then, adding insult to injury, there's almost five minutes of recaps from Chapters One through Four.

Lesser's second feature version of the serial, titled *Chandu on the Magic Island*, bears a 1934 copyright notice (although no record of its registration appears in Library of Congress copyright files) and was submitted to the Production Code Administration for approval that same year. Apparently condensing Chapters Five through Twelve into seven reels, this second feature is every bit as compact as the first. The padding is stripped out and the narrative flows smoothly.

It's my belief that Barringer, at Lesser's urging, scripted *Return of Chandu* as two standalone features and the editors stretched the available footage to fill 12 chapters. There's no other way to account credibly for so much repetition in the eight-episode plot segment unfolding on Lemuria. The features-first approach would also explain why several chapters have situational rather than "cliffhanger" endings. (Speaking of which, close viewing of both serial and features puts the lie to an oft-repeated but totally erroneous contention: that chapter endings were reshot for added suspense. This is simply not the case.) It was much easier for Barringer to structure the adaptation without resorting to the artifice required for building to sensational stunt-filled climaxes.

Setting aside concerns over padding, I still enjoy *Return of Chandu* immensely and remain willing to go toe-to-toe with its detractors. It has historical significance as one of only two chapter plays (the other being 1916's *The Mysteries of Myra*) built around occult phenomena and the eternal struggle between white and black magic. I can readily understand why it might not appeal to fans conditioned to judge serials based on the number of fistfights, car chases, and gun battles they contain. Those who take a more expansive view of the form, however, should be able to appreciate *Return*'s qualities. It's steeped in mystery and melodrama and additionally flavored with Eastern exoticism; in that respect it's quite faithful to the radio series. Moreover, it's not predictable. Chapters don't end with exploding warehouses, set-demolishing donnybrooks, or cars sailing over the sides of cliffs.

Indeed, devotees of radio's Chandu will find much to like in the serial. Lesser was able to procure the show's music cues and sound-effects recordings; the psychic summons and the Ubasti drums heard in *Return* are those used in KHJ's early-Thirties broadcasts, as are the unforgettable Felix Mills compositions backing the main titles and chapter forwards. On radio an announcer read synopses of previous events, punctuating them with a deeply intoned "Chaaaandu . . . the Magician!", which was followed by the sound of a gong. The movie serial presents its chapter synopses via title cards superimposed over a large gong, which is struck by a silhouetted figure. A circular wipe, recalling to mind the silent-era irising-in of a camera lens, blots out the text and picks up the action.

With the obvious exception of Lugosi, the screen actors are surprisingly well matched to their airwaves counterparts. But Bela overcomes the infelicity of his casting with the sincerity of his portrayal. Universal's failure to provide him with sympathetic roles, much less heroic ones, drove him from that studio. *Return of Chandu* gave him an opportunity to play the good guy, the romantic lead, and he clearly relished it. Yet the otherworldliness he summoned up as Dracula also informed his characterization of Chandu, and when mesmerizing an Ubasti cultist there was about him a decidedly menacing aspect. It gave his Frank Chandler an edge than Edmund Lowe's lacked.

The Return of Chandu is a product of its time; that is to say, there's no disguising its provenance as a low-budget film emanating from Poverty Row. (For all his major-studio connections at the time, Sol Lesser made his Principal releases on the cheap and distributed them via the state-rights method until he partnered with George O'Brien.) Its most easily recognized characteristics— the rented sets, the supporting cast studded with silent-era actors, the familiar stock music leased from Abe Meyer's library—indelibly stamp the serial as an early Thirties production of modest means. To some, the picture seems crude and dated. To others— myself among them—it has inexplicable charms unique to films of its grade and period. When Chandu in the closing minutes of

Chapter Twelve unleashes the power of the High Incantation, producing from his fingers an animated fireball that explodes and brings down the Ubasti temple's rock ceiling, his action is every bit as satisfying as the room-leveling fistfight between hero and villain that ends a Forties Republic serial. Maybe more so, now that I think of it.

Lesser seems not to have offered trade screenings of the serial, as most critics reviewed the first feature. *Film Daily* offered its appraisal in the October 9, 1934 issue:

> This is the good old hoke, but is done with class and intelligence, and with strong story interest building logically to a tense climax. Bela Lugosi is the man who has studied Oriental magic, and is acquainted with all the occult science of the Yogi, and knows also the dark secrets of those who practice the Black Art. . . . It is all done with a polish and class that lifts it out of the thrill-hoke division, and makes it an hour of thrills for an intelligent audience to enjoy.

Variety's anonymous critic, catching the feature as the bottom half of a double bill in New York's Criterion theater, was quite a bit tougher:

> Some action in this, but it is neither fish nor fowl. This might be expected when a serial of some 12 episodes is trimmed and pasted together for feature length. The trimming is good at times, but some of the padded stuff remains. And there are several yawning gaps in the continuity that spoil whatever effect was intended. . . .
>
> It is thin stuff and rather obvious. The build-up to each in a series of climaxes are readily spotted, each one generally denoting where episode of original serial closed.
>
> Bela Lugosi is wasted. Even at that he stands head and shoulders above rest. Maria Alba is satisfactory while conscious, but is doped by yogis [sic] and stays in a coma

nearly half of footage. Others are stooges for Chandu's manipulations. Aside from Clara Kimball Young and Wilfred Lucas, they act like serial performers.

Juveniles might fall for Chandu's popularity and radio build-up may help. Otherwise, [picture] is weak even for duals.

Film-rental totals or box-office grosses for Lesser's *Chandu* films are not available, but it's likely the feature-serial combo was not particularly profitable. Sol Lesser stopped producing serials after *Return of Chandu*, which would lead one to believe that his novel exercise in chapter-play marketing failed to yield the expected results.

By 1936 most stations carrying *Chandu the Magician* had exhausted the backlog of transcription discs, and with no new episodes being produced the series went into limbo. Like many other successful shows from the Thirties, it was revived by the Mutual-Don Lee Network. In 1948 Raymond R. Morgan persuaded the original sponsor, the Los Angeles Soap Company, to bankroll the series again, and updated commercials for White King Soap were included in newly recorded transcription discs. Morgan hired Armbrister and Oldham, commissioning the latter to do light rewrites of the original scripts to reflect changing time and a post-World War II world.

Tom Collins, as prolific a radio performer in the Forties as Gayne Whitman had been in the Thirties, was engaged to play Chandu. In addition to serving as the announcer on *Cavalcade of America*, he regularly acted on episodes of *The Whistler*, *Lux Radio Theater*, and *The Adventures of Ellery Queen*. Collins was joined by Irene Tedrow (as Dorothy Regent), Lee Millar (Bob) and Joy Terry (Betty Lou). Veola Vonn took the role of Nadji.

The Mutual revival, a cheaper production all around, used organ music rather than the full orchestra that accompanied the original Los Angeles run. The Felix Mills theme lent itself to Korla Pandit's organ playing, as it sounded like something a snake charmer might play.

In most respects the Mutual program—which began on June 28, 1948—was more than adequate, but one suspects Armbrister coached his people to overact. Whitman projected confidence, Collins projected intensity. Where Margaret MacDonald's Dorothy seemed concerned, Irene Tedrow's Dorothy seemed panicked. Millar and Terry played the Regent siblings as several years younger than the script identified them.

The Mutual five-a-week run repeated the first three continuities in full: the search for Robert Regent, the adventure in Montebania, and the struggle with the cobra worshippers. Other major story arcs, including the Lemuria plotline, were overlooked. The early episodes were reshaped to satisfy Mutual's 1949 demand for a half-hour series. Newly written episodes downplaying mysticism failed to thrill listeners, and by the following year the once-mighty Chandu was off the air for good.

The Lost City

(1935, Super Serial Productions Inc.)

AMONG ALL FORMS of cinematic storytelling, the cliffhanger serial was perhaps the least controversial. Since most chapter plays were aimed at children (or, at best, unsophisticated adult viewers from small towns and rural areas), their producers generally eschewed such plot elements or questionable scenes that might arouse the ire of local censors. This was especially true after 1922, when the Motion Picture Producers and Distributors of America (MPPDA, forerunner of the much later MPAA) hired former U.S. Postmaster General Will H. Hays to administer the self-policing Production Code governing the inclusion of potentially offensive material into movies. The Hays Office worked overtime to keep the nation's screens clean, but it was not possible to regulate tastelessness.

That's where *The Lost City* comes in.

In 1934 the movie serial was enjoying renewed popularity after several years in the doldrums. By that time the problems regarding sound recording had been ironed out and it was possible for producers of low-budget films to absorb the extra costs without spending a small fortune. The chapter-play market, while not exactly wide open, nevertheless allowed for independently produced offerings that could be rented cheap to cash-strapped exhibitors who used serials to boost regular attendance during those Depression days. Universal was the only large production and distribution company still in the game. Nat Levine's Mascot Pictures, formed in 1927, had outlived its competitors from the late silent era and was Universal's main competitor. Independent producer Sol Lesser had supplied a couple chapter plays, but most Poverty Row entities avoided the market.

Ambitious but perpetually undercapitalized New York-based entrepreneur Sherman S. Krellberg entered the motion-picture industry in the Teens, when he was in his mid-twenties. He had participated in all phases of the film business: production, distribution, and exhibition. He formed tiny corporations to accommodate fly-by-night investors interested in completing one or two projects. If any one corporate entity showed a loss or got bogged down in dent, he folded it and moved on to another. Krellberg's first serial, a 1919 Helen Holmes starrer titled *The Fatal Fortune*, was produced under the auspices of the SLK Serial Corporation, which was dissolved shortly after Fortune flopped. Since then he had avoided the chapter-play market. But sometime in the late summer of 1934 he decided to take another chance and formed Super Serial Productions, which listed its corporate headquarters at 729 Seventh Avenue in Manhattan.

After Labor Day the movie-industry trade papers began running news squibs about Super Serial Corp's inaugural production, which was to be called *The Lost City*. A 1920 chapter play with the same title, set in darkest Africa, had been a sensation that actually launched an entire cycle of jungle serials. Krellberg's offering was also a jungle-set thriller, but the producer remained uncharacteristically mum as to whether it would be a remake of the earlier episodic epic.

The Lost City was hastily written by as odd a conglomeration of picture people that ever shared screen credit. The original story was credited to part-time actress Zelma Carroll and silent-serial veterans George M. Merrick and Robert Dillon. Merrick had supervised production of several late Twenties serials released by the Weiss Brothers. Dillon was an older hand at the game, having scripted many of Universal's biggest serial hits during the first half of the Twenties, then writing and producing chapter plays for Rayart release. Neither man had been involved in serial production for years; how or why Krellberg chose them to work on *The Lost City* is anybody's guess.

The shooting script was produced by another team of unlikely collaborators. Perley Poore Sheehan had been a top-notch pulp fictioneer since before World War I. He was fascinated by the motion-picture business even then. One of Universal's earliest feature-film hits, *The Bugler of Algiers* (1916), was based on one of his pulp yarns. And he landed the well-paying job of writing the scenario for Lon Chaney's *Hunchback of Notre Dame* (1923). Sheehan earned kudos for his work on Paramount's 1927 smash starring Emil Jannings, *The Way of All Flesh*. But he had not worked in motion pictures since, and recent years had seen him once again grinding out penny-a-word fiction for pulp magazines, both under his own name and the *nom de plume* of Paul Regard. How he fell into Krellberg's clutches is another of the enduring mysteries connected to *The Lost City*. Sheehan's fellow scripters were assistant director Eddy Granemann (with only one previous screenwriting assignment to his credit) and Leon d'Usseau (with just four to his). Although this trio was charged with writing scenarios based on the original story, not one of them had ever been involved with a serial before. It was all very strange.

Ever the shoestring producer, Krellberg pushed the writers to strip out of their script anything that might be expensive. Although nominally a jungle serial, *The Lost City* sported only one sequence involving a live animal—and that sequence, by a wild coincidence, employed stock footage from the 1920 *Lost City*. The titular metropolis itself was never seen: Krellberg refused to pay for miniatures, mock-ups, or painted backdrops of it. All that was seen of the city, inside or out, were a couple laboratories, a few small chambers, and some short hallways supported by silvery girders.

Imposing electrical devices in the mad scientist's lab were rented from electrical engineer Kenneth Strickfaden, who built them for lavish features, including classic Universal's horror films of the early Thirties. Native villages and a trading post, with their bamboo doors and thatched roofs, were standing sets rented cheaply.

On October 26, 1934, trade papers carried the news that former major-studio contract players William "Stage" Boyd and Claudia Dell were cast. Both were falling into obscurity. Boyd, a notorious drunk and carouser, had destroyed a promising career and was doing the same to his liver. Shortly thereafter the hero role went to Kane Richmond, a promising young leading-man type and recent Fox Film Corp contract player, blackballed by major studios after falling in love with the girl friend of a prominent producer while on location outside the country. Krellberg filled in the cast with character actors frequently seen in low-budget serials and independently made "B" pictures: George (later "Gabby") Hayes, Eddie Fetherstone, Josef Swickard, Milt Morante, and the like.

Shooting began on December 1 at the old Mack Sennett plant in the San Fernando Valley. The Sennett lot, then being leased by Mascot's Nat Levine, had its own "jungle," but an unseasonably cold fall had denuded the trees. Instead of lush foliage, Krellberg's cast and crew filmed in and around thorny tangles of brush and bare tree limbs.

The serial was originally scheduled for a 35-day shoot that was pared down to 21 days. Three units shot simultaneously. Director Harry Revier (whose maimed right hand was behind the acquisition of his nickname, "Three-Finger Harry") handled the main unit and worked with the principal players. Bennett S. Cohen, better known as a screenwriter, took command of the second unit. Robert Dillon headed a third unit, which shot only silent action footage over which sound effects would later be dubbed. The final day of shooting fell on Christmas Eve, and despite protests from cast and crew Revier insisted that the serial be finished on schedule. Krellberg had decided to release *The Lost City* in both serial and feature lengths, and film editing was rushed to accommodate him.

On January 24, 1935, Sherman K. Krellberg returned to New York with prints in hand. The serial extended to 12 two-reel episodes; the feature collected the first three chapters and Reel One of the fourth, breaking the continuity at a logical point. As Sol Lesser had done with his *Tarzan the Fearless* and *The Return of Chandu*, Krellberg intended to offer exhibitors the feature version followed by the remaining installments.

The serial's plot is as follows:

When the world is ravaged by a series of historically violent storms and earthquakes, electrical engineer Bruce Gordon (Kane Richmond) determines that the upheavals are being caused by a destructive power, possibly electrical in nature, emanating from Africa. With his assistant Jerry Delaney (Eddie Fetherstone) and fellow scientists Reynolds (Ralph Lewis) and Colton (William Millman) in tow, Bruce travels to the Dark Continent and locates the source of the destructive rays: the fabled lost city of the Ligurians, whose last surviving member, an evil scientist named Zolok (William "Stage" Boyd), hopes to bow the civilized world to his wishes and restore Liguria's lost glory.

Zolok has captured and imprisoned a brilliant inventor named Manyus (Josef Swickard), who reluctantly aids the evil genius to protect his beautiful daughter Natcha (Claudia Dell) from harm. The mad Ligurian also controls a strongman named Appolyn (Jerry Frank) and a dwarf named Gorzo (Billy Bletcher). Together they rule an army of giant, mindless black natives whose bodies have been expanded by one of Manyus' inventions. The most fearsome of these poor creatures, Hugo (Sam Baker), often accompanies Appolyn and Gorzo when brute strength is required.

Bruce and Jerry quickly figure out what's what and who's who. Reynolds and Colton attempt to spirit Manyus away and bend him to their will. Butterfield (George Hayes), an unscrupulous trading-post owner who controls a native tribe, at first opposes Bruce but eventually aligns with him against Zolok. Additional complications are provided by exotic Queen Rama (Margot D'Use) and the Wanga tribe. There also exists a race of spider men who dwell in caves and trap victims for sacrifice to giant arachnids.

Eventually Rama, Colton, and Reynolds meet unfortunate ends and Zolok mounts one last desperate effort to conquer the others. Finally he goes mad and blows up the entire mountain in which the lost city resides, killing himself and obliterating every last trace of the Ligurians. Bruce and the others, having escaped the city, return to civilization.

The Lost City has been labeled a racist work on the basis of scenes depicting howling natives being subjected to the Manyus enlarging process—which, judging from the shrieks, must have been painful. Then, too, the process seems to render each native incapable of independent thought and unable to communicate with anything but a grunt. Characters utter such lines as, "That sounds like a white woman's scream!"

However offensive these things might seem today, they were not included maliciously or deliberately. The serial's depiction of African natives is no different than that one would see in, to take one example, M-G-M's early Tarzan movies.

No, what makes *The Lost City* so objectionable is its breathtaking tastelessness and total lack of restraint. Harry Revier, an old-school silent director whose previous serials included the quite good *Son of Tarzan* (1920), obviously demanded his cast overact floridly, and the writhing, shrieking natives were intended to frighten young children based not on racial stereotyping but on the severity of the torture they were forced by Zolok to undergo. Revier's directorial style was already outdated in 1934, but it doesn't seem to be motivated by racial animus.

Still, the entire production seems to have been regarded as unwholesome. Even Kane Richmond, in a 1962 face-to-face interview with *Screen Thrills Illustrated* co-editor Sam Sherman, winced at the very mention of the title. "Of every movie I've ever done," said Richmond, "that's the one I'd like to forget." He went on to explain that the punishing schedule and unceasing demands of three directors made for a spectacularly unpleasant shoot. According to Richmond, it was especially rough on 68-year-old Josef Swickard, who was rather feeble to begin with and suffered the indignity of being carried around under Sam Baker's massive arm like a sack of potatoes, then dropped to the hard ground with no consideration for his safety or fragile physical condition.

Moreover, continued Richmond, Harry Revier seemed to delight in tormenting Swickard, punctuating his directorial orders by jabbing the old man's chest with his deformed hand. Finally, disgusted with these antics, Richmond grabbed the director and pulled him off to the side. "If you don't quit riding that poor old guy," he said, "I'll walk off this picture and tell everyone in Hollywood what you've been doing." Revier hated being challenged this way but couldn't risk losing his leading man, not even for an afternoon. So his abuse of Swickard stopped then and there.

William "Stage" Boyd, whose scenes were grouped together and shot in just a few days, couldn't hold himself together even for such a limited time. He imbibed constantly and finished his final scene in a drunken stupor. Boyd's last-chapter meltdown shows him with tousled hair and rumpled costume; he slurs his lines and staggers across the laboratory set. Since Zolok is supposed to have gone completely insane at that point, Boyd got away with his unprofessional behavior. It appears to be in character, and Revier probably figured the little kiddies in the audience wouldn't suspect the truth anyway. (Boyd, by the way, died on Wednesday, March 20, 1935—less than three months after finishing the serial—from cirrhosis of the liver.)

Remarkably, both serial and feature version received laudatory reviews from members of the notoriously merciless New York press. Both trade and consumer publications treated *The Lost City* with kid gloves, lending credence to the rumor that Krellberg bought them off. Take this appraisal from *Film Daily*: "This new serial produced by Sherman S. Krellberg possesses thrills, novelty, suspense, and continued interest. Moreover, it is well produced and well performed in its principal roles." A review of the 74-minute feature pronounced it good for the first seven reels but slumping in the last one.

The *New York Daily News* gave the feature three-and-a-half stars, calling it "easily one of the best pictures of its kind since *Frankenstein*. . . . Sure to be a Broadway success."

The *New York American* declared: "Whee! Here's a wild one! A regular baby-scarer! It calls for exclamation points between each word!"

The *New York Evening Journal* dubbed it "an extravagantly fantastic adventure yarn."

Variety, the most independent trade paper, was not so easily impressed and apparently immune to Krellberg's method of persuasion, whatever it has. The paper's critic "Chic" filed the closest thing to an objective review, with a generous helping of *Variety*'s patented "slanguage":

> Possibly a little more production coin and considerably more thought would have brought this in as big-time stuff, but with poor photography, sometimes faltering direction and story inconsistencies, the yarn falls into the second division, though it's good fodder for the ballyhoo grinds.
>
> Story is misshapen in that it comes to its peak too soon, with about 12 minutes of falling action, which permits whatever effect has been gained to fade out. There is too much running around and tag-playing to hold the suspense and several times what is intended to be another shocker merely brings a laugh. . . . Tod Browning could have made a whizzer out of this in his heyday, but it's out of Revier's usual style and he is handicapped by a faulty script.

The glowing notices obviously helped, but I still find it amazing that *The Lost City* was held over for three weeks at New York City's Globe theater. And that it was booked into two prestigious Warners houses: Newark's Capitol and Paterson's Rivoli. And that it also secured dates at some RKO houses in the metropolitan area, and was distributed in Latin American countries by United Artists—hardly a schlock outfit.

Perhaps Depression-era serial audiences were more forgiving. In the early Fifties, however, New York parents deluged WOR-TV with complaints when *The Lost City* was televised on the weekday kiddie show *Buster's Buddies*, hosted by Buster Crabbe. Some viewers objected to what they saw as disgusting racism, others to horrific scenes of shrieking natives being subjected to the tortures of Manyus' inventions. The serial was quickly withdrawn; in later years Crabbe admitted being embarrassed by the debacle.

Krellberg squeezed every last drop of profit out of *The Lost City*. Contemporaneous with release of the serial and the eight-reel feature version, he prepared other feature that was 11 reels long. A third feature, edited with different emphasis, was released in 1941 as *City of Lost Men*. And as late as the mid Seventies, he prepared a fourth feature version; where, how, or even if this final cut was exhibited in not known definitively, but as Krellberg at that time still owned theaters in New York—including on the famously decrepit 42nd Street—it might well have been.

Today one can see *The Lost City* in all its tastelessness on DVD. One can call it many things—racist, tasteless, bizarre, misogynistic, disturbing, and more. But boring it's not.

Radio Patrol

(1937, Universal Pictures Corporation)

THE WORD "CLASSIC" is tossed around rather loosely in discussions of noteworthy motion pictures, and this author will cop to employing it promiscuously in the pages of *Blood 'n' Thunder*. In truth, very few cliffhanger serials deserve that appellation, especially if they are being appraised objectively.

But some serials defy such appraisal and are recognized as "classics" because they possess virtues that are amorphous and indescribable. A few, especially those that became ubiquitous as a result of constant exposure on television in the late Forties and early Fifties, have retained their popularity in recent years despite clear-headed analysis that has exposed flaws and limitations willingly overlooked by earlier viewers. Universal's *Radio Patrol* is one of these.

Radio Patrol began life in 1933 as a localized daily strip running in the *Boston Record* and incorporating real-life locations and landmarks in Beantown and the New England countryside. At that time it was called *Pinkerton, Jr.* after the protagonist, a boy detective named Pinky, whose sidekick was an Irish setter not very originally named Irish. *Boston American* crime reporter Eddie Sullivan and bullpen artist Charles Schmidt handled the feature in a workmanlike manner, avoiding the improbable situations and grotesque villains already beginning to pop up in *Dick Tracy,* the nation's most popular cop strip.

The Hearst-owned King Features Syndicate acquired *Pinkerton, Jr.* little more than a year after its debut, changed its title to *Radio Patrol,* and added it to the prestigious lineup in *Puck, the Comic Weekly,* the 16-page color section that came with Sunday editions of the Hearst papers and other sheets that exclusively used King Features' syndicated material. Although Pinky and Irish still figured prominently in most of the continuities, the strip's hero was Sergeant Pat O'Hara. A uniformed cop who toured in his radio-equipped patrol car, ruggedly handsome Pat was aided by his pudgy partner, "Stuttering Sam" Maloney and plainclothes policewoman Molly Day. They didn't solve locked-room murders or chase death-ray-wielding mad scientists; the crimes they investigated were fairly typical ones: fraud, petty theft, bank robberies, insurance swindles, and the like.

Of course, by 1934 police radio cars were no longer a novelty, but that didn't impede the strip's popularity. Will Gould's violent *Red Barry*—another King Features crime strip launched that year—competed more directly with *Dick Tracy,* but the less showy *Radio Patrol* steadily built its own fan base. Sullivan's stories may not have been innovative, but they were smoothly developed and carried by personable characters who spoke easy-on-the-ear dialogue. Charles Schmidt's drawings employed the semi-illustrative style favored by King Features art directors, falling somewhere between the "bigfoot" style of *Wash Tubbs* artist Roy Crane and the impressionistic, cinematically influenced work of *Terry and the Pirates'* Milton Caniff and *Scorchy Smith's* Noel Sickles.

The same year that King Features gave *Radio Patrol* a national rollout, Universal released its first serial adapted from a comic strip. *Tailspin Tommy,* a primitive aviation-adventure feature distributed by the Bell Syndicate, written by Glenn Chaffin, and illustrated (poorly) by Hal Forrest, reached the screen with Maurice

Murphy essaying the title role and Noah Beery Jr. playing Tommy's pal Skeeter. Although the 12-chapter adaptation was loosely plotted and its villains nondescript, it proved enormously successful. The youthful theatergoers who dutifully attended Saturday matinees at their local picture palaces were also the most loyal readers of comic strips, and they were thrilled to see one of their favorites brought to life on the screen.

Producer Henry MacRae, who had been involved with Universal chapter plays since 1914 and headed the company's serial unit, now realized the box-office potential in popular figures from the funny pages. That view was shared by members of the sales department charged with feeding the maw of exhibition. At their urging Universal licensed motion-picture rights to a slew of King Features strips: *Flash Gordon, Ace Drummond, Jungle Jim, Secret Agent X-9, Tim Tyler's Luck, Red Barry* . . . and *Radio Patrol.*

MacRae's production of *Flash Gordon* (1936) was a box-office phenomenon that became Universal's second most profitable release of the year, its earnings surpassed only by singing star Deanna Durbin's debut film, *Three Smart Girls*. It was also the final serial released by Universal under the regime of founder and president Carl Laemmle, shortly to be forced out of the company he had led since 1912. Financiers behind the ouster named former Paramount executive Charles R. Rogers as studio head and gave him a mandate: reduce production costs whenever and wherever possible. MacRae had been the fair-haired boy of "Uncle Carl" from Universal's earliest days and was an unabashed Laemmle loyalist. His serial successes, most recently including *Flash Gordon*, made him valuable to the company's new owners and kept him safe from the purge that forced most of Uncle Carl's friends and (many) relatives out of their cozy positions at Universal.

But MacRae's influence was somewhat diminished and his production methods now subject to second-guessing by newly installed executives looking to burnish their reputations. The average Universal serial at that time was produced for between $150,000 and $175,000. *Flash Gordon* reportedly cost twice that much, although it played in first-run theaters normally indifferent to chapter plays and therefore earned significantly more than its less-expensive brethren. Universal's new management insisted that serial expenditures could be cut without several impacting the quality or competitiveness of the company's episodic thrillers. MacRae was forced to share his department with associate producers Ben Koenig, younger brother of Universal's newly minted executive general manager, and Barney Sarecky, who had written and supervised production of serials for Nat Levine's Mascot Pictures and briefly, Republic Pictures.

Together, and once in collaboration with MacRae, Koenig and Sarecky turned out several chapter plays adapted from King Features Properties: 1936's *Ace Drummond*, the duo's first production, was followed by *Jungle Jim* and *Secret Agent X-9* the following year. During the Thirties Universal typically opened its annual "season" with a Western serial, and 1937-38 got underway with a Johnny Mack Brown starrer, *Wild West Days*, which MacRae and Koenig jointly produced. Koenig was back with Sarecky for that season's autumnal offering, which was *Radio Patrol*.

MacRae had relied on the same basic group of writers and directors for years. He entrusted the direction of most Universal serials to Ray Taylor and the scripting to Basil Dickey, George H. Plympton, and former secretary Ella O'Neill, with occasional contributions by Het Manheim and George Morgan. Under MacRae these collaborators had enjoyed virtual autonomy, protected from front-office interference by their avuncular chief, who had Laemmle's complete confidence. Universal's chapter plays were predictably profitable and supplied the company with critical cash flow during the Depression years.

Koenig and Sarecky assembled their own creative team, which labored under constant pressure to devise episodic thrillers that could be filmed more economically. A per-serial savings of ten or twenty thousand bucks made the unit's bottom line look a lot better to the company's green-eyeshade boys. Sarecky's key hire was Ford Beebe, who joined Universal in the early Twenties as a public-relations man and occasional scenario writer. He left the studio to partner with second-tier cowboy star Leo Maloney, for whom he wrote, directed and occasionally produced two-reel shorts and feature films. Maloney's surprising, untimely death in 1929, shortly after completing his first sound Western, sent Beebe scrambling for work, and he briefly returned to Universal's serial unit, titling *Tarzan the Tiger* (1929) and scripting *The Lightning Express* and *The Indians Are Coming* (both 1930). In the early talkie years he wrote and co-directed Mascot serials on which Sarecky too had worked. Accustomed to the parsimonious procedures endorsed by Mascot's Nat Levine, Beebe knew all the shortcuts needed to bring chapter plays to completion on short money and shorter shooting schedules. He signed a seven-year contract in 1936 and teamed with Cliff Smith (aka Clifford S. Elfelt) to direct *Ace Drummond*, first of the Koenig-Sarecky serials.

From the first Beebe was cognizant of underlying tension, which he correctly attributed to resentment held by long-time members of the serial unit for these johnny-come-latelys. "MacRae had a lot of pull in the front office [even after Laemmle's departure]," Beebe told film historian George Geltzer in a 1965 interview. "He'd been with the company for years, and had been its manager three times. And he *did* make good serials. His friends wanted to see the Koenig-Sarecky combination come a cropper, and since this feeling spread through many of the departments, Sarecky was on very much of a hot seat. He needed a non-partisan director who would both do a good job and not sell him out to the opposition. That's when he called me. [Cliff Smith and I] came through with what Koenig had promised—a good serial for less money than had been expected. From then on, MacRae would produce a serial while Sarecky was scripting and planning his next one, and then the positions would reverse. It worked out very well, but the political struggle never really ended."

Screenwriters Wyndham Gittens, Norman S. Hall, and Ray Trampe—Mascot veterans all—were given syndicate tear sheets of early *Radio Patrol* continuities and from them developed a plot in the spring in 1937. They retained most of the strip's principal characters but altered a few surnames and relationships. The basic situation was an old serial standby: the pursuit of a "weenie," in this case a valuable formula. Koenig and Sarecky were fond of stories that, instead of having just one villain, pitted rival factions against each other. One of the factions might be revealed in later chapters as having benign motives for impeding the hero's progress, but initially the dueling interests made for unpredictable plot complications.

Grant Withers, a MacRae favorite who took the title in *Jungle Jim* and owed Universal one more serial per his two-picture deal, was cast as Pat O'Hara. Adrian Morris (brother of Chester), who co-starred with Withers in one of Mascot's episodic epics, *The Fighting Marines* (1935), contracted to play Sam. No doubt their re-teaming was the idea of Sarecky, who had co-written and co-produced *Marines* for Nat Levine. Newly signed contract player Catherine Hughes, who had appeared in Republic serials and Westerns as Kay Hughes, was assigned the role of Molly and experienced child actor Mickey Rentschler hired to play Pinky. The dog Irish was impersonated by a well-trained German Shepherd named Silver Wolf.

Radio Patrol was shot over a four-week period during June and July. Directors Beebe and Smith, who had worked in tandem on Universal's four previous chapter plays, relied on predictable cost-cutting measures and were aided by the scripters, who wrote much of the back lot into their scenarios. The studio's dump site was pressed into service as a junkyard. One of the antebellum mansions built for the company's 1927 production of *Uncle Tom's Cabin*, already overgrown with weeds, had its windows boarded and thus became a haunted house. Familiar city-street sets were visible on numerous occasions, as well as the "Egyptian Quarter" facades constructed in the silent era.

When Beebe and Smith ventured outside the lot, it was always to locations employed in at least a handful of sequences. Auto chases taking place within city limits were filmed in North Hollywood and the adjoining Studio City neighborhood; cars careened around the same Ventura Boulevard corner no less than a half-dozen times. When pursued and pursuers were seen outside urban areas they invariably wended their way around Mulholland and

Coldwater Canyon Drives in the Hollywood Hills. A nearby steel mill was the site of several extended chase-and-fight sequences, including the Chapter One climax in which Pat O'Hara fell from a catwalk and nearly met a fiery death.

Another time- and money-saving device pressed into service ranks as one of the most annoying things in the serial. Withers, backgrounded by a simple flat with the shadow of a stepladder to his left, was lensed in close-up, throwing and taking punches. This one shot, always used fragmentarily, appears in practically every fistic encounter regardless of background—even those taking place outdoors. It enabled the directors to substitute stunt double Eddie Parker for Withers as soon as someone took a swing at him. Parker, a big lummox who stunted (sloppily) for all the leading men in Koenig-Sarecky serials, would whale away at his opponents for minutes at a time, and it was expected brief snippets of Withers from that close-up could be spliced into the fights at intervals, supposedly convincing kiddie audiences he was the one pummeling the heavies. It's difficult for this author to believe that even a moderately observant ten-year-old would have been fooled by this clumsy trick, but suspension of disbelief—a must at any age for enjoying serials—can be a beautiful thing.

Kay Hughes had been making serials and Westerns at Republic when her agent, who also represented Universal's top star, Deanna Durbin, promised to secure a berth for her at the bigger studio. Seduced by the promise of better career opportunities, Hughes broke her Republic contact and reported to Universal City after visiting an ailing relative back east. To her surprise and disappointment, she was offered parts similar to those she had essayed at Herbert Yates' studio. *Radio Patrol*, in fact, was her first assignment on the old Laemmle lot. But when I met Kay in 1992 she didn't seem unhappy about the serial; indeed, she believed it to have turned out rather well.

"I was used to working long days on the serials," she told me, "so the schedule we had on *Radio Patrol* didn't surprise me. It always amazed me how the directors could keep things straight, you know, because one minute we could be shooting a scene from

Chapter Two and then the next set-up would be for something in Chapter Ten. Ford Beebe was a dear to me. I don't really remember the other fellow, but we got along together."

Hughes also got along with Grant Withers but recalled that the star's drinking forced modifications to the schedule. "He was okay in the mornings," she said, "but he'd start drinking at lunch time and would sneak nips all afternoon between takes. By three or four o'clock he'd be slurring his words. The directors started juggling script pages so that our dialogue scenes could be shot before lunch. That way they could do the physical scenes, you know, the fights or chases, in the afternoon. Grant's double [Eddie Parker] would be the one doing most of the work in those."

Kay's one significant annoyance was fellow supporting player Mickey Rentschler, who frequently jostled her in trying to cop a feel. She thought him surprisingly self-confidant and sexually aggressive for an adolescent boy. "He got to be a nuisance," she confessed. "He was all hands, that boy. And not at all bashful about his intentions. He made passes at me practically every day! At least, that's how it seemed to me. But he knew his lines, I'll say that for him."

Principal photography wrapped in mid-July and by mid-August the first several episodes had been edited and submitted to the Library of Congress for copyright and to Production Code administrators for their Seal of Approval. Chapter One's national release date was October 4, 1937. In first-run markets *Radio Patrol* competed with Republic's *S.O.S. Coast Guard* and Columbia's first serial offering, *Jungle Menace*.

The initial stanza got things off to a flying start. Impoverished inventor John Adams (Harry Davenport), experimenting at a steel mill owned by kindly industrialist George Wellington (Montague Shaw), has perfected his formula for flexible steel and is murdered by an unseen assassin after making a successful demonstration. A furtive figure later identified as ex-con Harry Selkirk (Max Hoffman Jr.) sneaks into Adams' workshop and steals the formula, which the inventor had committed to paper mere moments before being shot down mysteriously.

Called to investigate the murder, radio cop Pat O'Hara (Grant Withers) finds himself confronted with various suspects having diverse motives. The most obvious person of interest is Selkirk, who apparently wants to use the formula as a bargaining chip in another game. Wellington's unscrupulous rival, the steel magnate W. H. Harrison (Gordon Hart), plans on acquiring the murdered man's formula, revolutionizing his industry, and reaping a fortune. Then there's an Iranian envoy named Tahata (Frank Lackteen), engaged in negotiations with Adams for the secret of flexible steel; he stood to save a million dollars by acquiring the formula via other methods. Tahata's chief henchman, a man named Franklin (Leonard Lord), appears to be under a hypnotic spell and naps in a mummy case when not engaged in deviltry.

"Pinky" Adams (Mickey Rentschler), son of the late inventor and now rightful owner of the missing formula, is taken under Pat's wing and becomes privy to whatever information the police uncover. Molly Selkirk (Catherine Hughes), sister of the prime suspect, eventually reveals that Harry was framed by Harrison, for whom she works under an assumed name in a bid to locate evidence that will clear her brother's name.

Pat and his partner Sam (Adrian Morris) have their work cut out for them, tangling with two sets of tough heavies—Tahata's and Harrison's—while trying to flush out the murderer. The much-coveted formula changes hands several times over the course of 12 chapters. The murder of Adams is finally shown to have been effectuated by a cleverly constructed pistol triggered when the inventor unknowingly crossed an electric-eye beam.

Scripters Gittens, Hall, and Trampe play fast and loose with logic, a quality sorely lacking in most serials but in particularly short supply in Universals of this period. Narrative cohesiveness is sacrificed to keep the action moving at a cyclonic pace, and much emphasis is placed on the supposedly short memories of viewers attempting to follow the plot and correctly deduce the killer's identity. Final-chapter revelations, theoretically explaining everything that has gone before, leave the spectator with more questions than answers.

Trying to be objective about this serial runs the risk of conveying disapproval not actually felt. On the contrary, *Radio Patrol* is extremely enjoyable and one of the best Koenig-Sarecky efforts. The chapter play sustains itself by virtue of constant forward motion. The action is plentiful and almost non-stop, with fight leading to chase and chase to another fight in practically every installment. Innumerable fistic brawls, loosely choreographed (if at all), find Withers' double Parker swinging wildly and often missing altogether, while fellow stunt performers Tom Steele, Carey Loftin, and George Magrill (among others) do their best to make him look good. Parker must have worked cheap, because he continued to double serial leading men at both Universal and Columbia through the mid-Forties.

Released on October 4th with the hoopla typical to serials based on popular comic strips, *Radio Patrol* did brisk business. Notices were generally favorable, especially those filed in the movie-industry trade papers. *Box-Office Magazine* reviewed the latest Koenig-Sarecky opus in its September 18 issue. "Based on a newspaper cartoon series of the same name," observed the anonymous reviewer, "this serial employs the sure-fire ingredients that make youngsters ask for more.... Although at times incredulous, each chapter moves along at a fast pace and ends with a sufficient amount of suspense."

Variety's critic "Wear" elaborated, using his paper's famously terse prose style and idiosyncratic jargon:

> Filled with customary implausibilities, new chapter play by Universal holds high potentialities for exhibs. Fact that the King Features *Radio Patrol* strip has been well popularized in newspapers throughout country inspires groundwork for attracting juvenile attention....
>
> Makers of *Radio Patrol* have departed more from the old serial formula than a few years ago would have been thought feasible. Producers are wise to the fact that the present-day youngsters like their thrills served with some degree of conviction. Presence of a modicum of improbable

events in this serial, some first-rate acting, a minimum of trite or melodramatic lines and careful building of plot helps this one vastly. There's the ever-present chopped climax to sustain or hold over interest until next week's chapter, but it is not quite as blatant as customary.

Plot implausibilities and budgetary vagaries aside, *Radio Patrol* possesses the indefinable qualities that make the best Thirties chapter plays so enjoyable. While hard to put one's finger on, they're best summed up in this case by a single live-action shot that prefaces each chapter synopsis (done in comic-strip style, another Koenig-Sarecky innovation). Following the main titles, the camera fades in on a long shot of a young boy in his bedroom. He's totally engrossed in something he'd reading. The camera quickly dollies in to reveal that the lad is absorbed in a *Radio Patrol* comic book. His eyes bulge and he clutches the magazine tighter as the scene dissolves to the comic-strip panels recapping the events of the previous episode. No other single image so effectively conveys the joyous appeal of Depression-era motion-picture serials. The awestruck boy reading that comic book was just one of millions who, week after week, suspended their disbelief to be entranced by the live-action adventures of their four-color favorites.

Red Barry

(1938, Universal Pictures Corporation)

IN LATE 1933 Joseph V. Connolly, president of King Features Syndicate (a division of the William Randolph Hearst media empire), was desperate for a detective-action comic strip that would compete with the wildly successful *Dick Tracy*, drawn and written by Chester Gould for the rival Chicago Tribune-New York Daily News Syndicate. To this end Connolly secured the services of Dashiell Hammett, creator of *The Maltese Falcon*'s Sam Spade and the nation's foremost writer of hard-boiled crime fiction. Together they developed the concept for *Secret Agent X-9*, which revolved around an unnamed federal operative.

Hammett's byline guaranteed instant marketability for the new strip, freeing Connolly to employ an unknown cartoonist for the art chores. Numerous men were considered but two finalists quickly emerged: Alex Raymond and Will Gould (no relation to Chester). Of the two Raymond, then ghosting King Features' *Tim Tyler's Luck* for Lyman Young, had the more polished style and was awarded the prestigious assignment. Fate had something else in store for the runner-up.

Born in 1911, Bronx native Will Gould was a high-school dropout who toiled as an ad-agency clerk, department-store stocker, and Western Union messenger boy in addition to boxing and playing semi-pro baseball. He dabbled in song writing and paid close attention to Broadway's night life. Finally exploiting the only talent with which he felt secure—drawing—Gould began cartooning for the Bronx *Home News*, creating a humorous strip called *Felix O'Fan*. Soon thereafter he moved to the New York Graphic, where he wrote and drew *Asparagus Tipps*, whose pint-sized protagonist dispensed tips on each day's horse races.

Eventually Gould found a berth at King Features, doing sports cartoons. He ran afoul of Connolly with his lackadaisical attitude about deadlines and was *persona non grata* at the syndicate for many months. During that time he relocated to Los Angeles, quickly becoming enamored of Southern California's climate and impressive array of golf courses. Fortunately, he had a loyal friend and sturdy ally in Brandon Walsh, writer of the *Little Annie Rooney* strip and confidant of Joe Connolly.

Walsh believed Gould capable of adapting his "big foot" style to an adventure strip. He persuaded the easygoing cartoonist to knuckle down and spend more time on *X-9* samples than Gould typically spent on his sports work, which had a slapdash quality. Although Raymond (who was developing *Flash Gordon* and *Jungle Jim* at the same time) got the job working with Hammett, Joe Connolly encouraged the runner-up to submit his own detective strip for consideration.

Egged on by Walsh, Gould eventually came up with Red Barry, a college football star who joined the police force after graduating and became the department's top undercover man, infiltrating criminal gangs and breaking them up from the inside. Crude but vigorous, the proposed strip seemed to be strong competition for *Dick Tracy* and Connolly okayed it. *Red Barry* debuted on Monday, March 19, 1934, and within a few short weeks generated its first controversy when Gould presented a sequence—inspired by true events—in which young children were cut down by bullets during a shootout between gangsters. The cartoonist heard from

William Randolph Hearst himself, but it was not a message that he relished getting. Hearst's terse note read: "I will not tolerate such disgusting violence in my comics pages!"

Gould submitted to a mild dressing-down by Connolly and went back to work. The strip's supporting cast filled out rapidly. Barry answered only to his immediate superior, gruff and walrus-mustached Inspector Scott. Even Police Commissioner Trent, a stuffed-shirted blowhard, didn't know Red was the department's ace undercover man. He constantly hectored Scotty to make use of his pet, gentleman sleuth Valentine Vane, a monocle-wearing fop who affected a British accent and always seemed otherwise occupied when dangerous assignments presented themselves.

Barry's circle was small. He got tips, and occasional aid, from an ex-crook nicknamed Benny the Boom-Boom. In the first continuity he befriended a youngster who had the unwieldy name of Archibald Galahad Lancelot Lee but answered to "Ouchy Mugouchy," a much catchier handle. Ouchy's sister, Loretta Lee, was intended to be Red's love interest but never quite caught on with the strip's readers. They clearly preferred a feisty sob sister named Mississippi, who played a more prominent role in the narrative.

Red Barry attained national prominence in early 1935 with an extended continuity that found the undercover man trying to prevent the execution of a young man framed for murder by exposing the real killer, a mobster named Black Milano. Gould maintained suspense throughout the story (which lasted several months) by periodically devoting an entire strip to the innocent man on Death Row, invariably pictured counting down the days, and later the hours, before his scheduled march to the electric chair. Gould sustained the feature's popularity with lurid, violent melodrama; several of Red's subsequent adventures took place in Chinatown, involved mysterious murders, and added to the cast such regular characters as Hong Kong Cholly and a slinky *femme fatale* known only as The Flame. Rather less appealingly, *Red Barry* began sharing the spotlight with Ouchy Mugouchy and his two pals, Elmer and Butch (a tomboy born to one of New York's socially prominent families), who called themselves "the Terrific Three."

Although *Red Barry* never came close to unseating *Dick Tracy* as the country's most popular detective-adventure strip, it built a strong following and predictably attracted Hollywood's attention. 20th Century-Fox contacted Gould about licensing *Red Barry* not for the title character but for the Terrific Three: the studio was giving child actor Jane Withers a build-up to leverage her against Shirley Temple if the latter's salary demands got too onerous. Withers was to have played Butch; no other casting decisions were made.

More attractive to Gould was a deal offered him by Bryan Foy, executive producer in charge of Warner Brothers' "B"-picture unit. A loyal follower of *Red Barry*, Foy thought the character perfect for up-and-coming contract player Wayne Morris, who had made a strong impression on moviegoers as *Kid Galahad* (1937). Like Red, Morris was a brawny former college football star. Moreover, his dark blonde hair photographed as red in the black-and-white cinematography of the day. Foy envisioned a series of six "B" pictures to be produced and released during the 1938-39 season. Knowing that Gould wrote the strip's dialogue and continuities, the producer offered to pair him with an experienced scriptwriter and pay him a starting salary of $500 per week to pen the screenplays. Should the first two films prove successful, his wages would be bumped to $750 weekly, and eventually to $1,000.

"I couldn't believe my ears!" the cartoonist recalled in a 1970 interview for *Graphic Story Magazine*. "That kind of dough for such a breeze! Hell, if it took me more than three weeks to turn out one of those scripts, I'd be loafing."

An ecstatic Gould wired King Features, from whom Warner Brothers would have to obtain screen rights to the strip. The next morning he received from the syndicate a telegram with soul-crushing news: *Red Barry* had been licensed to Universal only a month before. The property was intended for a serial. As owners of the strip, King Features were entitled to sole screen credit. Not only would Gould be denied a percentage of the licensing fee, he wouldn't even be acknowledged as Red's creator. The cartoonist was outraged but, contractually, he didn't have a leg to stand on.

He had signed away his rights to the character. Furthermore, he had alienated Joe Connolly by consistently running late with his strips, forcing the syndicate to spend extra money on engravers who worked overtime to finish the printing plates. King Features, having already established a congenial working relationship with Universal (with such popular strips as *Flash Gordon*, *Jungle Jim*, *Ace Drummond*, *Radio Patrol*, *Secret Agent X-9*, and *Tim Tyler's Luck* already adapted by the studio into chapter-play form), clearly felt Will Gould entitled to no consideration whatsoever.

On May 10, 1938, Universal announced its slate of product for the upcoming 1938-39 season. As had been the case for the previous two seasons, responsibility for the year's quota of serials was divided between Henry MacRae (assigned to produce *Flaming Frontiers* and *Scouts to the Rescue*) and Barney Sarecky (who got *Red Barry* and *Buck Rogers*). Interestingly, when the trade papers published Universal's 1938-39 titles in mid-May, Buster Crabbe had already been chosen to play Red Barry.

Serial-unit chief director Ford Beebe was scheduled to share the megaphone with Alan James (aka Alvin J. Neitz), who joined Ray Taylor on Universal's season opener, *Flaming Frontiers*, after being lured away from Republic, where he had co-directed *Dick Tracy*, *The Painted Stallion*, and *SOS Coast Guard* in 1937. Like Beebe, he was a solid, unpretentious journeyman who turned out salable product in a workmanlike fashion. As a grizzled veteran of Poverty Row Westerns and melodramas, James knew every one of the directorial shortcuts needed to compensate for low budgets and short schedules.

Norman S. Hall and Ray Trampe crafted the 13-chapter screenplay using a melange of events, locations, and characters pulled from the comic strip. Fortunately, they omitted any mention of the Terrific Three. They also significantly changed the motivations of two of the strip's principals. Primarily, they adhered to Sarecky's mandate: write something that can be produced cheaply and expeditiously. This meant reusing key sets numerous times and shooting most of the serial on sound stages and within the back lot's confines.

Additionally, Hall and Trampe returned to the formula that had distinguished recent Universal chapter plays. Instead of pitting the hero against one villain, they placed him between rival factions competing for the same "weenie"—in this case, stolen bonds worth $2,000,000. Three distinct groups vied for possession of the bonds, and whenever Red got his hands on the papers it was only temporary.

Sarecky cast Universal contract players Edna Sedgwick and Frances Robinson in the two chief female roles; curiously, the less experienced (and less talented) Sedgwick was billed ahead of Robinson, who had very capably essayed the female lead in *Tim Tyler's Luck* the previous year. He cast 51-year-old English actor Cyril Delevanti as an attenuated Asiatic—a favor to director Beebe, married to Delevanti's daughter Kitty. Legendary serial veteran Frank Lackteen was signed to play a sinister Chinese villain, and extremely prolific character actor Wade Boteler hired on in the role of Inspector Scott. *Red Barry* gave Boteler his first serial role in 15 years; during 1923 he'd worked on the Universal lot in a brace of chapter plays, *The Social Buccaneer* and *Around the World in Eighteen Days*. The Pina Troupe, a family of circus acrobats, were hired to do their specialty act for a vaudeville-theater scene in Chapter One.

Production got underway during the first week of June. Sarecky felt that the Hall-Trampe script, written with standing sets in mind, could be shot in a month or less. Beebe and James resigned themselves to another back-breaking schedule. Typically, one filmed with cast and crew while the other prepared for the next day's shooting, pre-selecting camera setups and mentally blocking scenes and sequences. On occasion, both directors worked simultaneously, Beebe with the principal players and James with a second unit covering fights or car chases performed by stunt doubles. The nearby Hollywood Hills were almost exclusively used for chases in Universal serials; residents living along Laurel Canyon Boulevard and Mulholland Drive had long since become accustomed to cars and camera trucks scudding across their dust-covered roads. The area was just minutes from Universal City and therefore the most convenient place to shoot chases, and the picturesque Hills offered scenic advantages as well.

Much of the action unfolded in a vaudeville theater. Scenes taking place in the cavernous auditorium were shot on Universal's famous Stage 28, built as a replica of the Paris Opera House for 1925's *The Phantom of the Opera* and altered for use in countless later films with theatrical settings. Scenes taking place back stage and in dressing rooms were filmed on standing sets employed recently in such Universal musicals as *You're a Sweetheart* (1937).

Exteriors utilized numerous structures on the back lot. The European village, with its cobblestone streets, was redressed with Oriental props and banners to simulate the forgotten byways of New York's Chinatown. Valentine Vane's luxurious home was actually the "Shelby Mansion" erected in 1927 for Universal's multi-million-dollar production of *Uncle Tom's Cabin*. Built at a cost of $62,000, the Mansion was not a facade but instead a "practical" set—a real house with nine rooms and staircases, outfitted with generators and built-in light banks to facilitate interior shooting. Such other sets as *Red Barry* required were modest in size and construction, with carefully chosen props and furnishings making them seem more impressive.

Principal photography zoomed along at the breathless pace that members of the Sarecky unit had learned to live with. Problems that cropped up during filming were solved rapidly on set or left for fixing in post-production.

Asked about *Red Barry* nearly 40 years after making it, Buster Crabbe shrugged dismissively and replied, "It was just another serial, as far as I was concerned. Didn't have near the production the Flash Gordons had. Not much of a script, either; we did plenty of running all over the back lot, back and forth. It was a tug-of-war sort of thing. First I had the bonds, then the heavies had the bonds, then I got 'em back. That was pretty much the whole story." Did he blame directors Ford Beebe and Alan James? "Oh, no. Hell, no. They were working their tails off trying to get the damn thing finished on schedule. You know, we worked very fast on serials. Not at all like feature pictures. We had to shoot enough footage for three features on half the time and money Universal spent on one Deanna Durbin picture. Maybe *less* than half. The directors did the best they could under those conditions."

Crabbe also had praise for his fellow cast members. He characterized Frances Robinson as "a cute kid," adding: "Damn good little actress, too. She read her lines with a Southern-girl accent, you know, that 'sho-nuff' kind of thing. I remember one afternoon doing speeches with her in the back of a taxicab. One setup, a two-shot. No close ups. No retakes. We ran 'em off in one take. One after the other—boom, boom, boom. Enough dialogue for them to splice into three or four chapters. She didn't miss a line." Like Frankie Thomas, Robinson's co-star in *Tim Tyler's Luck*, Crabbe seemed puzzled that "Francie" didn't go further than she did. "I have no idea why she didn't get better parts. I only worked with her the one time. But she struck me as having a lot on the ball. I guess she just didn't get the breaks."

Buster also liked Cyril Delevanti, referring to him as "a great little guy . . . a real trouper, you know, like Charlie Middleton. He spent a lot of time in makeup every morning; they had to paste all those whiskers on him. He never complained, though. And when he got out of that chair, boy, he was Chinese through and through. Another guy who rarely blew a line. You had a lot of those oldtimers on the serials because they were real pros; they did their speeches in one take. We didn't get lots of takes, so you had to get the lines right the first time. Every now and then there was a camera problem, or the sound wasn't picking up right. In those cases we did the second take. But most of the time, you walked through the scene once with the director and then you did the business in one take. It was pretty much the same thing when I did the Billy Carson Westerns for [Sam] Newfield. One rehearsal, one take. In and out. Move on to the next setup."

Although I have been unable to pin down the date on which *Red Barry* wrapped production, the serial was ready for its national release on October 19, 1938. Advance reviews in the trade papers were favorable if not glowing. Said the *Film Daily* critic after screening the first two chapters: "Serial fans, to whom super-heroes are balm to the heart, will doubtless journey to picture houses regularly to see whether Buster Crabbe can emerge victor from his grapplings with wily foes, domestic and Asiatic. Since plausibility is an unwanted ingredient in the modern serial recipe, its total absence will be an anticipated factor. . . . So actionful is the yarn that considerable credit must be given at even this premature stage to Ford Beebe and Alan James." The anonymous reviewer singled out Frances Robinson, describing her Mississippi as "a comely newspaper gal whose Deep-South accent is a relief after the dialogue in the American language purporting to be the accents of Far Eastern folk."

Variety's "Barn" had this to say: "*Red Barry* is a followup on the successful serial ventures concocted thus far by Universal using characters popularized with the kids in newspapers. It has full quota of stolen bonds, lurking shadows, trapdoors, fistfights, and gunplay, done in waterfront setting coupled with Oriental intrigue. . . . Weekend traffic, in houses asking for kid traffic, will be helped by the *Barry* serial. The Ford Beebe-Alan James directorial combo savvies the juve want and delivers in usual style. Norman Hall-Ray Trampe screenplay moves fast."

Indeed, *Red Barry* is nothing if not briskly paced. Chapter One opens in an unnamed Asian country that clearly is China, at war with an unnamed invader that clearly is Japan. Beleaguered General Fang (Guy Usher) presents two million dollars in negotiable bonds—a gift from the Russian government—to Wing Fu (Cyril Delevanti), a Chinese patriot and antiques importer with a curio shop based in New York's Chinatown. Wing is to use the bonds in America to purchase fighter planes for Fang, but the mission must be kept top secret because it violates the Neutrality Act passed by our Congress. One of Fang's top men, Captain Moy (Charles Stevens), accompanies Wing Fu to safeguard the bonds and facilitate the deal.

Just before the steamship carrying Wing docks in New York Harbor, the securities are stolen from the purser's safe and thrown overboard. The theft has been engineered by underworld chieftain Quong Lee (Frank Lackteen), who doubles as proprietor of the

Eurasian Cafe on Pell Street. He dispatches henchman Weaver (Wheeler Oakman) and several thugs to Pier Ten, where one of them dons diving gear to recover the bonds.

Police detective Red Barry (Buster Crabbe), detailed by Inspector Scott (Wade Boteler) to investigate a series of Chinatown murders, is getting nowhere fast when one of his pals, a spunky newspaper girl named Mississippi (Frances Robinson), dashes into headquarters with a coded message from a Chinese Secret Service agent working undercover. Red is tipped off that something big is breaking at the Lyceum, a downtown vaudeville house not far from Pell Street. But shortly after he, Scott, and Mississippi reach the theater, the agent is mysteriously slain while performing with a troupe of Oriental acrobats. Manager C. E. Mannix (William Ruhl) promises to cooperate with the police, and Red learns that the theft of the bonds is linked to someone in the theater.

Patrolling the waterfront in a police cruiser, the inspector spots a diver working from Pier Ten. Red slips overboard, swims to the dock, and surprises the thieves. In the struggle that follows, the dazed Barry falls into the water in front of a coal chute. Weaver opens the chute and tons of coal slide down, presumably burying the police detective as Chapter One concludes with a coming-next-week title card superimposed over a shot of the mechanical fire-breathing dragon that adorned episode endings of *Ace Drummond* (1936).

Chapter Two formally introduces Natacha (Edna Sedgwick), a Russian ballet dancer performing at the Lyceum. She wants the bonds for herself and relies on the aid of two countrymen, Petrov (Stanley Price) and Igor (Earl Douglas, better known as Ernie Yaconelli), to help her get them. Also taking a hand in the game is Red's old pal Hong Kong Cholly (Philip Ahn), who plays dumb and speaks pidgin English when he's around police but, in fact, is an educated and articulate Chinese working with Wing Fu to recover the bonds. Meanwhile, blustery Commissioner Trent (William Gould) orders Scott to take Barry off the Pell Street Murders and instead use society detective Valentine Vane (Hugh Huntley), a pompous fop.

Although it takes him a few chapters to get the lay of the land, Red ultimately deduces he's vying for possession of the bonds with three factions: Wing Fu's own men, headed by Captain Moy; Quong Lee and his man Weaver; and finally Natacha and her two Cossack buddies. But *Red Barry*'s plot complications don't stop there, and a major twist presented in Chapter Eight effectively changes the story's trajectory: At that point the viewer learns that Quong Lee, long-time owner of the venerable Eurasian Cafe, is actually Mannix in disguise. (How he had time to run two legitimate business enterprises, rule Chinatown's underworld *and* scheme to steal two million in bonds is a mystery the serial not surprisingly refuses to tackle.) The surprises keep coming, with the unexpected killing of one major character and the surprising treachery of another. These events camouflage the fact that *Red Barry*'s plot, centering around possession of the bonds, never evolves. Different factions simply take turns obtaining the securities, only to lose them after a chapter or two. Other things are thrown into the mix simply to keep viewers from getting bored. And, it should be noted, the strategy works.

There's plenty to criticize about *Red Barry*, including its deliberate misdirection and lapses in continuity. To begin with, the Russian dancer Natacha—a major figure in the story—is never actually introduced. But the Chapter Two recap presented in comic-strip form refers to the girl as if she had. References to the Pell Street Murders and a femme fatale called the Flame (a nod to one of the strip's best-remembered sequences) aren't fully explained, and while Quong Lee appears to be behind the slayings, there's no motive given for them. More than one character is shown being shot in one episode only to pop up uninjured in the next. A trap supposedly laid for Red by Wing Fu is sprung by Quong Lee, which makes no sense whatsoever.

Yet the serial entertains. It's particularly appealing to fans of Universal movies from the Thirties, which offer special delights relating to the constant reuse of familiar music cues, interior and exterior sets, and even extras and supporting players (many of them veterans of Laemmle's studio going back to silent films).

Like most Sarecky-produced serials, *Red Barry* features not a single piece of music written just for the serial. But the score is both effective and evocative, beginning with the main-title and chapter-forward cues, lifted from a 1936 "B" starring Bela Lugosi, *Postal Inspector*. Pieces written for *Parole, Sutter's Gold, Crash Donovan, Goodbye Broadway, East of Java, East Is West, Remember Last Night*, and other mid-Thirties Universals were put to good use by editors Alvin Todd, Lou Sackin and Saul Goodkind, although one plodding Oriental motif was repeated far too often.

And Buster Crabbe is a major asset. His performance for the most part is relaxed and breezy, with the actor tossing off lines as though they were improvised rather than scripted, but he's properly determined in dramatic scenes and extremely affecting in a Chapter Ten sequence that finds him swearing over the body of a slain friend to bring the man's killer to justice. A fine, understated bit of acting that wouldn't be out of place in a major "A" picture, it reminds the viewer that Crabbe was not just a charismatic athlete but a talented actor as well. He considered *Red Barry* "just another serial," but thanks in part to his excellent work it's considerably more than that.

As for Will Gould . . . well, he lost interest in his brainchild after the serial came out. He'd grown weary of deadlines anyway and was more interested in playing golf, chasing women, and hobnobbing with Hollywood big shots who promised him writing deals that never quite materialized. Ultimately he walked away from the strip that had made him famous. By the time Universal's *Red Barry* finished making the theatrical rounds in late 1939, its pen-and-ink counterpart had vanished from the Hearst papers. The final story continuity depicted the breakup of the Terrific Three, but King Features never printed the last Sunday page, in which an ironic Gould had Ouchy Magouchy asking, "Gee, I wonder when Red Barry's comin' back?"

Top: (L to R) Philo McCullough, Buster Crabbe, Edward Woods, E. Alyn Warren.
Bottom: Buster Crabbe appraising Jacqueline Wells in this shot from Chapter Two.

Top: Tarzan captures high priestess Madi (Carlotta Monti, mistress of W.C. Fields).
Bottom: After rescuing Mary Trevor, Tarzan brings her to his cave for safekeeping.

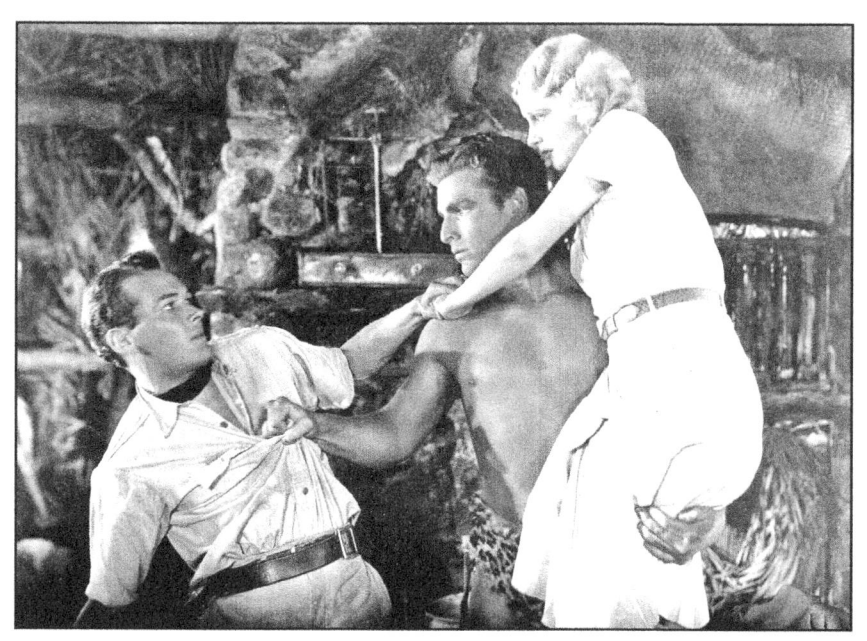

Top: Tarzan mistakenly thinks Bob (Edward Woods) is trying to take Mary away by force, when he's actually trying to protect her himself. Bottom: After wounding at the hands of Eltar's warriors, Tarzan is saved from the lion pit by faithful Tantor.

Original one-sheet poster for the serial's 1934 theatrical release. Separate artwork was created for both feature versions, which played to enthusiastic Chandu fans.

GALLERY 2 / 191

Top: An incredibly rare photo of the original Los Angeles radio cast of *Chandu the Magician*, taken in 1933. That's series star Gayne Whitman in center. Bottom: Chandu (Bela Lugosi) watched by Bob (Dean Benton) and Betty (Phyllis Ludwig).

Top: Beauty queen Irene Ware played Princess Nadji and Edmund Lowe took the title role in Fox's *Chandu the Magician* (1932). Bottom: Bela Lugosi played the malevolent Roxor in Fox's feature, which was generally faithful to the radio show.

GALLERY 2 / 193

Top: Chandu leads a rescue party of sailors on the island of Suva. Bottom: Chandu hypnotizes an Ubasti cultist in an effort to learn where Nadji is being held.

Top: Chandu welcomes Nadji (Maria Alba) to the home of his sister Dorothy (Clara Kimball Young) and her children Bob and Betty Lou. Bottom: Chandu disrupts the Ubasti's attempted sacrifice of Nadji by invoking the sacred High Incantation.

This striking poster was one of several designed for the feature-length versions of *The Return of Chandu*, the first released in 1934 and *Magic Island* a year later.

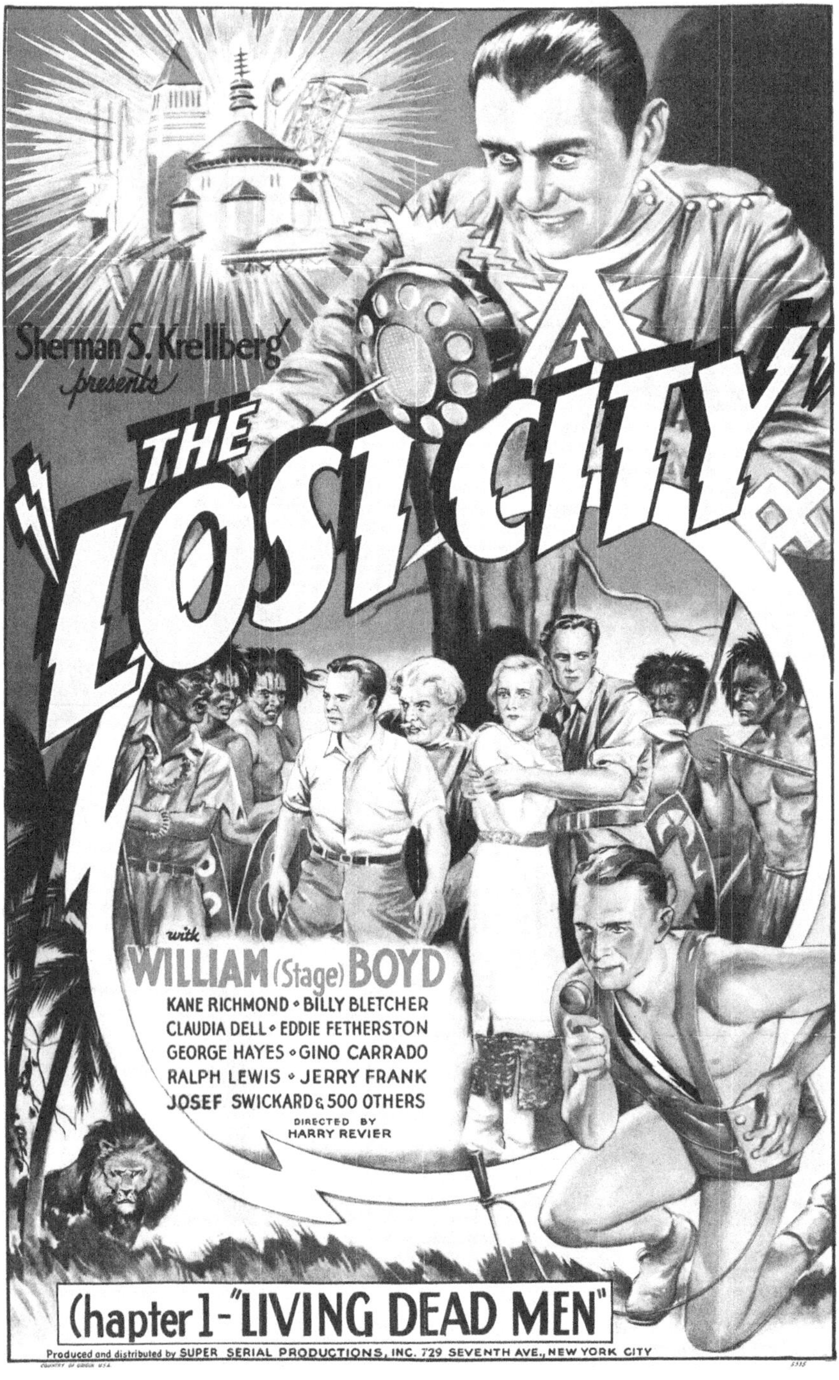
Sherman S. Krellberg
presents
THE
LOST CITY
with
WILLIAM (Stage) BOYD
KANE RICHMOND • BILLY BLETCHER
CLAUDIA DELL • EDDIE FETHERSTON
GEORGE HAYES • GINO CARRADO
RALPH LEWIS • JERRY FRANK
JOSEF SWICKARD & 500 OTHERS
DIRECTED BY
HARRY REVIER
Chapter 1-"LIVING DEAD MEN"
Produced and distributed by SUPER SERIAL PRODUCTIONS, INC. 729 SEVENTH AVE., NEW YORK CITY

Top: Bruce Gordon (Kane Richmond, right) and his friend Jerry Delaney (Eddie Fetherston, left) rescue Dr. Manyus (Josef Swickard) from a death trap and return him to grateful daughter Natcha (Claudia Dell). Bottom: Bruce and Natcha are captured by Arabs led by Shiek Ben Ali (Gino Corrado, grabbing Claudia Dell).

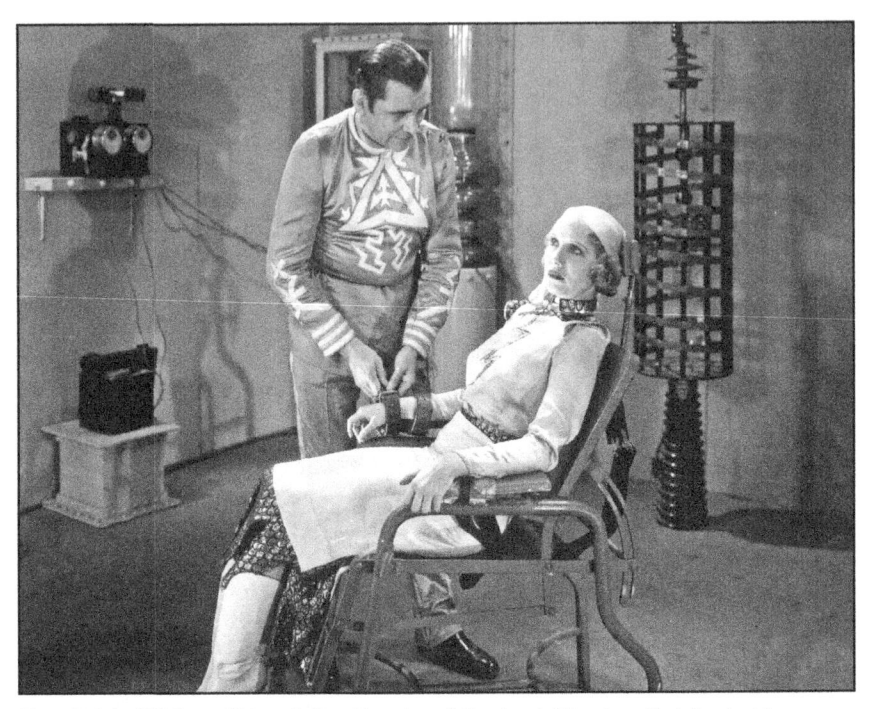

Top: Zolok (William "Stage" Boyd), ruler of the Lost City, has Natcha in his power. Bottom: Butterfield (George Hayes) mistreats one of the natives under his control.

Top: *Radio Patrol* begins with Tahata (Frank Lackteen, left) trying to purchase the formula for flexible steel from Adams (Harry Davenport), but arousing suspicion from the scientist's patron, Wellington (Montague Shaw, right). Bottom: Policeman Pat O'Hara (Grant Withers) find Harry Selkirk (Max Hoffman Jr) with Adams' body.

Top: Tahata and his henchmen believe Selkirk has the formula for flexible steel. Bottom: Pat catches two thugs who threatened Molly Selkirk (Catherine Hughes).

GALLERY 2 / 201

Top: Pat and Pinky Adams (Mickey Rentschler) at the mercy of Harrison's thugs.
Bottom: While on plainclothes duty, Pat attempts to capture a fleeing murderer.

Top: Thrown into a closet after being knocked out by hoods, Pat is freed by Molly. Bottom: *Red Barry* starred Buster Crabbe (right) as the police detective looking for stolen bonds, aided by pals Mississippi (Frances Robinson) and Hong Kong Cholly (Philip Ahn), who also were popular characters from the comic strip by Will Gould.

Top: Red and Inspector Scott (Wade Boteler, center) apprehend one of the crooks.
Bottom: A passing motorist (Gladden James) offers to help Red recover the bonds.

Top: Red Barry is locked in a life-or-death struggle with Gray (Tom Steele), one of Weaver's henchmen, in the Lyceum vaudeville theater. Bottom: The society sleuth Valentine Vane (Hugh Huntley) is being used for target practice by Captain Moy and his men, who are secretly working for Wing Fu in a bid to recover the bonds.

Hawk of the Wilderness

(1938, Republic Pictures Corporation)

OF THE MANY imitation Tarzans who paraded across the pages of pulp-fiction magazines in the wake of Edgar Rice Burroughs' success, only a few are remembered fondly by aficionados of rough-paper storytelling. And of those, only one followed ERB's immortal Ape Man to Hollywood: William L. Chester's Kioga, the Snow Hawk. His initial adventure, *Hawk of the Wilderness*, was serialized in seven issues of the pulp magazine *Blue Book* (from April to October 1935) before being issued in hard covers by Harper & Brothers the following year. Chester's yarn posited the existence of a volcanic island, north of the Bering Sea, with dense evergreen forests, a temperate climate, savage wilderness creatures, and a lost race from which the Native American is said to have derived. A white boy, christened "Kioga, the Snow Hawk," grows to maturity amongst the wild beasts. Never accepted by the island's indigenous people, he lived with his animal friends. Extremely well written, but not slavishly imitative of Burroughs, *Hawk of the Wilderness* was bound to attract the attention of filmmakers at one studio or another.

Republic Pictures entered into negotiation with Chester's representative in the late spring of 1936. A deal was formalized and the contract signed on July 7, 1936. The author received $1,000 in exchange for granting Republic one-time rights to make either a feature or serial, with no options for sequels. Chester insisted on a codicil requiring the studio to show the Harper & Brothers book cover on screen behind the main titles, presumably to enhance sales of the novel.

Oddly, Republic allowed the property to lay dormant for nearly a year before assigning Ridgeway "Reggie" Callow to write an adaptation, which he completed in June 1937. Callow's qualifications for this job were non-existent; at this time he was a Hollywood hanger-on, married to minor actress Peggy Watts. He later became an assistant director of some note (working on such major films as *Gone with the Wind*, *Watch on the Rhine*, *Seven Brides for Seven Brothers*, and *The Sound of Music*) but never received a single writing credit.

As *Hawk of the Wilderness* was being touted as a release for the upcoming 1937-38 season, the project suddenly took on urgency. Following the shelving of Callow's adaptation, head serial writer Barry Shipman and staffers Norman S. Hall and Rex Taylor were told to take a whack at Chester's story. They came up with an acceptable treatment that was filed on November 27, 1937. But actual production would have to wait for completion of *The Lone Ranger* (then just going before the cameras), *The Fighting Devil Dogs*, and *Dick Tracy Returns*. Hammering the treatment into a workable shooting script didn't begin until the end of May and lasted well into September.

In 1992 I met Shipman, conducting an in-person interview followed up by correspondence and several telephone calls. *Hawk of the Wilderness* was one of numerous Republic serials about which we spoke at some length. He was very forthcoming and not at all dismissive of or embarrassed by his serial work. Indeed, when I asked if he was surprised the old chapter plays had finally attained respectability in the eyes of film historians, he replied that it was long overdue.

"*Hawk of the Wilderness* was a tough one," Shipman confessed. "I liked the book, myself. But it was very densely plotted and there was a lot of material we couldn't use, including a long section about Kioga growing up. That was where the story most resembled the first Tarzan novel. It made great reading, but if we'd tried to get it into the serial we'd have used up half the chapters before getting to the main plot. Also, Kioga's Indian friend [Mokuyi] gets killed off during that section. We kept him alive all the way through.

"I remember we cut out a bunch of minor characters and combined a couple others. In the book the girl [Beth] has a brother; we did away with him and made her the daughter of the scientist [Munro] looking for Kioga's parents. And our heavy, the guy we made the lead pirate, doesn't last very long in the book. He gets killed off by one of the other pirates. There was also a big to-do about the lead Indian heavy [Yellow Weasel]. We cut some of that stuff too. And the bears—*Hawk of the Wilderness* had bears like *Tarzan* had apes. Kioga's sidekick was a bear cub. That wasn't feasible so we made it a dog.

"The big challenge you have, adapting a novel into a serial, is breaking it down into equal installments that each have a certain amount of action while driving the plot forward, and ending with that big moment of suspense. Most books don't divide up that conveniently, so you have to massage the plot to give each chapter the elements that audiences expect."

Shipman, Hall, and Taylor fleshed out their treatment. The "estimating script," a first draft given to studio department heads for purposes of compiling a budget, was gone over with a fine tooth comb to strip away non-essential or potentially costly sequences. Producer Robert Beche began the process of hiring actors while waiting for the final numbers.

Directors William Witney and John English, beginning their fifth serial as a team, were invited to participate in casting for the first time. They readily agreed on Herman Brix for Kioga; no other actor was seriously considered. Having recently worked with Brix on *The Lone Ranger* and *The Fighting Devil Dogs*, they knew his capabilities; beyond that, he had played Tarzan in a

1935 chapter play and was accustomed to leaping from trees, swimming in rivers, and dashing across rugged terrain. And a well-muscled physique guaranteed his favorable appearance in abbreviated garb.

Witney had "kept script" (ensured scene-to-scene continuity) on 1936's *Robinson Crusoe of Clipper Island* and thus already knew that serial's star, Ray Mala, who was deemed perfect for the role of Kias, Kioga's boyhood friend. Mala hailed from Alaska and worked in Hollywood as an assistant cameraman before being tapped by director W. S. Van Dyke to essay the lead in *Eskimo* (1933). Since then he had been cast as Inuits, Polynesians, and Native Americans. Of *Hawk*'s principal players only Mala could lay claim to authenticity of casting, coming from the general area in which the story took place.

The directors heartily endorsed the casting of former silent-era star Monte Blue and prolific character actor William Royle as the heavies Yellow Weasel and Manuel Solerno respectively, and they were delighted to secure screen veteran Noble Johnson for the key role of Mokuyi, Kioga's foster father.

In later years Witney could not recall having chosen Poverty Row ingenue Harley Wood for the ingenue part; he suspected that producer Robert Beche had hired her early on in the process. For her role in *Hawk of the Wilderness* Wood changed her name to Jill Martin in an apparent attempt to reboot her career. It didn't work, as she made only a few more films (uncredited in several of them) before retiring from the screen the following year. Interestingly, Martin achieved much greater success as a composer and songwriter, working in collaboration with her second husband, Sy Miller. They even owned a music publishing company together.

The final casting decision was rather unorthodox. It was for Kioga's canine companion Tawnee. Witney had briefly considered Buck, the Saint Bernard that first made an impression on movie-goers in *The Call of the Wild* (1935), later in *Robinson Crusoe of Clipper Island* (1936) and *Trigger Trio* (1937), Witney's first feature film. But Buck wasn't appropriate for the part and other trainers were invited to bring their dogs to the lot for auditioning. Among them was an Australian sheepdog named Tuffie. He belonged to a former South Dakota cowboy named Ger Orvedahl and had already appeared in several movies. Bill Witney described the "casting" in his 1996 autobiography:

> When they came into the office, Tuffie sat at the trainer's feet while we talked about what the dog had to do [in the serial]. In the same tone of voice he used with us in conversation, [Orvedahl] suddenly said, "Tuffie, it's dark in here. Turn on the light." We watched as the dog jumped up, searched the room, and spotted the light switch. He came to my chair, which was closest to the switch, and tried to pull it toward the switch. I stood up. He pulled the chair to the wall, jumped up on it, put his feet up on the wall, and with one paw turned the light on. Everybody in the room "saw the light." Tuffie got the job.

Witney and English had scouted just a few locations when they settled on Mammoth Lakes, a heavily forested area in the Eastern Sierra with an elevation of nearly 7,900 feet above sea level. Already a popular spot for filmmakers looking to replicate Canadian and Alaskan locations, Mammoth enjoyed warm, dry summers and long, snowy winters. *Hawk of the Wilderness* was scheduled to commence production in mid-September—a matter of days after final script revisions—and wrap in mid-October. The goal was to avoid being caught in pre-seasonal snowfalls, which were not unheard of.

There had been cost overruns of $14,000 on the previous serial, *Dick Tracy Returns*, and producer Beche was pressured to bring in *Hawk* for even less than originally anticipated. He shaved thousands of dollars off the budget, estimating a meager $118,000 in production costs. There was considerable reason to believe the chapter play could actually be completed for this amount. To begin with, unlike the typical outdoor-action serial (almost always a Western), *Hawk* did not require rentals of horses and other livestock that would need to be fed and stabled. Nor did it have any hydroplane chases, which required speedboat rentals and extra time spent in outfitting a camera boat. The action set in Mammoth had the actors on foot. Most of the scripted scenes were exteriors that could be shot sans electric lights and generators, with carefully positioned reflectors providing extra sunlight as needed for close-ups and medium shots. Sparse airplane traffic in the area meant fewer disruptions in sound recording, thus reducing the need for dubbing sessions back in the studio.

Cast and crew made the trip to Mammoth Lake on Sunday, September 18, with shooting to begin the following day. A few days into principal photography Beche received a phone call from Republic. Studio executives screening the first batch of rushes (brought down to Los Angeles by car every day) complained that the close-ups had too much "headroom," meaning that actors' faces were being squeezed into the bottom of shot compositions to allow more space for clouds and the tops of Mammoth's picturesque pine trees. The frame's bottom line was cutting them off at the chin.

Director of photography William Nobles, who made sure the scenes were properly lit and chose lens filters to make the clouds stand out, was puzzled until camera operator Eddie Lyons, an old serial-unit holdover from the Mascot days, sheepishly admitted to tilting the camera up to get more clouds into the frame. "I'm guilty, Bob," he told Beche, "but you'll have to admit that they're prettier than the actors."

As a compromise, Witney suggested Nobles use a one-inch (wide angle) lens in shooting close-ups. This allowed more room for the clouds, which added considerable visual allure to the exterior scenes. Everybody agreed that *Hawk* was probably the most beautifully photographed Republic serial to date.

Production ended on October 13, the 12 chapters having been committed to film in 22 working days. Cast and crew, tired but happy, made the trek back to Studio City. On the way home Witney and English reflected on the shoot, which had been a pleasant one. Everything had gone smoothly and they were confident the footage would cut together well. Pickup shots had been filmed at

Lake Sherwood, and an important sequence for the last chapter involving a plane was staged at Bronson Canyon at the south end of Griffith Park.

Yet there remained a bit of work to do. As Herman Brix explained in his exclusive 2002 interview with *Blood 'n' Thunder*:

"At the end of the shooting schedule, there were still a number of scenes—maybe 15 pages of script—that hadn't been filmed. Scenes with the Hawk doing things alone—running, climbing, swinging from trees, and whatnot. This stuff hadn't been shot when the production originally shut down. So [producer Beche] had me come back and we went back up to the location, just me and a camera crew. Well, we shot one whole day, that night, and into the next day—without stopping. Now, by that time the Screen Actors Guild regulations were [being enforced], and I was paid triple overtime. I got more money for those two long days and one night that I got for practically the whole film!"

The second-unit excursion back to Mammoth Lakes helped push *Hawk of the Wilderness* over budget by slightly more than three thousand dollars, but at a negative cost of $121,168 it was still a remarkably inexpensive production, but one looking and sounding like a film that cost three or four times as much.

Hawk of the Wilderness begins aboard the *Cherokee*, a schooner battered by storm-tossed Arctic waters. Famed scientist-explorer Lincoln Rand (Lane Chandler), his wife Helena (Ann Evers), and their Indian servant Mokuyi (Noble Johnson) have been searching for a long-lost island believed to be inhabited by a race of savages from whom descended the Native Americans. Realizing he is close to his destination but unlikely to see it, Rand writes a letter to his best friend and colleague, Dr. Edward Munro (Tom Chatterton), inscribing on it the island's latitude and longitude. He seals the note in a bottle and tosses it overboard, hoping someone will eventually find it. The *Cherokee* smashes to bits on the island's breakers and the Rands are killed, but Mokuyi makes it to shore with their infant son.

Some 23 years pass. Mokuyi has raised Lincoln Rand, Junior (Herman Brix) to manhood. They live in a mountain cave but give a wide berth to the natives, whose medicine man Yellow Weasel (Monte Blue) blames them for the last eruption of the island's volcano, which occurred when they escaped the doomed *Cherokee* and made landfall. The Indians refer to Rand as "Kioga," which means "hawk." His only friend in the tribe is Kias (Mala), a young cripple who alerts the Hawk to the tribe's activities.

The bottle cast overboard by Kioga's father is found by Manuel Solerno (William Royle), head of a criminal gang, who reads the message and mistakes Rand's reference to "great treasure" for the promise of wealth to be found on the island. He brings the letter to Munro, whose daughter Beth (Jill Martin, aka Harley Wood) and her fiance Allen Kendall (George Eldredge) agree to accompany him on an expedition to the lost island. Solerno cleverly gains Munro's confidence and persuades the scientist to hire his gang as sailors. They set sail on the schooner *Alberta*. Landing on the island shore, the party stumbles across a gold bar and Solerno, believing Munro knows the location of treasure hidden by Rand, demands to be cut in. During the ensuing mutiny the ship's captain and first mate are slain. Rand escapes into the wilderness with Beth, Kendall, their servant George (Snowflake, aka Fred Toones), and Professor William Williams (Patrick J. Kelly), an eccentric scientist fondly nicknamed Professor Bill-Bill.

Upon learning of the white people who have invaded his island, Yellow Weasel attempts to capture and kill them. Over the course of the remaining 11 chapters Kioga is pitted against two enemy bands: Solerno and his fellow pirates, and Yellow Weasel's incensed Indians. The gold turns out to have belonged to the Hawk's father. Mokuyi salvaged it from the wrecked *Cherokee* and buried it on shore. Solerno's repeated efforts to obtain Kioga's fortune result in his temporary alliance with Yellow Weasel, which puts the Munro party at even greater risk.

Per Republic's customary practice, half the serial had been edited when prints of the first chapter were sent to the company's 39 exchanges for distribution to first-run exhibitors, who played it during the first week of December. Trade reviews heaped praise on *Hawk*, with *Film Daily*'s anonymous critic sounding the most favorable note: "With fast action and a good plot disclosed in the opening episode of this new serial, it bids fair to rank with the best of the thrillers that Republic has turned out. Herman Brix, a powerful athlete and able actor, portrays the role of the Hawk naturally, and the supporting cast has been well chosen."

Theater owners were somewhat less enthusiastic, with the majority grading *Hawk* as reasonably entertaining fare but not up to the level established by *The Lone Ranger* and *Dick Tracy Returns*. The serial was profitable but hardly a runaway hit, and a sequel was never considered, obviating the need for further negotiation with author Chester.

There is much to recommend in *Hawk of the Wilderness*. Brix is perfect in the role, his athletic feats (augmented by those of stunt double Ted Mapes) calling to mind his prodigious work in *The New Adventures of Tarzan*. The action, most of it cut to the capture-and-rescue pattern to which most chapter plays adhered, is well staged and beautifully photographed. Kioga's encounters with the Indians become repetitious, but the chases and fights are so vigorous that one doesn't really object. A contributory asset is the musical score, a collection of stirring cues written for the serial by William Lava (who gets Musical Director credit for the first time), Cy Feuer, Alberto Colombo, and Joseph Nussbaum. As written, neither William Royle's Solerno nor Monte Blue's Yellow Weasel is the strong villain that pulls most serials together, but as a pair they provide more than adequate menace to the Hawk and his friends. Tuffie the dog also contributes his fair share of memorable moments to the film.

By the time *Hawk of the Wilderness* reached the screen, William L. Chester had written three sequels, all of them serialized in *Blue Book*: "Kioga of the Wilderness" (1936), "One Against a Wilderness" (1937), and "Kioga of the Unknown Land" (1968). Unlike the first novel, however, the follow-ups didn't see publication in hard covers. (They were, however, published in paperback decades later.)

Following completion of the final Kioga story, Chester abandoned the writing of fiction even though *Blue Book* editor Donald Kennicott urged him to submit more yarns and promised they would receive special consideration (which usually meant a sure sale). The author declined, giving himself up to other pursuits. During World War II he served with the Ski Troops headquartered at Camp Hale in Colorado. After the conflict he returned to civilian life, getting involved in the advertising business and writing numerous non-fiction articles. So little is known about this enigmatic but imaginative storyteller that the exact date of his death has never been established.

The Spider, Master of Men

(1938 and 1941, Columbia Pictures Corporation)

Hollywood has not always been kind to popular characters adapted from other media such as dime novels, comic strips, radio dramas, and pulp magazines. But it's hard to find a more faithful screen adaptation than *The Spider's Web*, a 1938 cliffhanger serial released by Columbia Pictures in 15 pulse-pounding episodes. And for this, those of us who revere pulpdom's Master of Men can thank one man: a long-forgotten movie producer named Jack Fier.

The July 31, 1937 issues of prominent movie-industry trade papers carried the story that Fier, formerly of Republic Pictures, had bolted to Harry Cohn's Columbia, where he was to oversee that organization's newly announced serial department. Still in the process of transitioning from Poverty Row independent to major Hollywood studio, Columbia at that time geared its mostly formulaic, inexpensive product to small-town exhibitors and big-city "neighborhood houses" (theaters located in outlying bedroom communities). These venues largely presented "B"-grade melodramas, Saturday-matinee Westerns, and other low-budget films. Fier was an old hand at the chapter-play game, having spent a full decade as the assistant of producer Nat Levine, who made episodic epics first under the auspices of his own company, Mascot Pictures, and later for Republic, of which he was a founding member.

In a separate deal, the Weiss brothers—Louis, Max, and Adrian, veteran independent producers and distributors—had been contracted to provide Columbia's first four serials, all scheduled for release during the 1937-38 "season." Cutting corners to fatten their own salaries, the siblings delivered chapter plays that stinted on production value and lacked the thrills that fans of the form had come to expect. The initial two, *Jungle Menace* and *The Mysterious Pilot*, were deemed failures. *The Secret of Treasure Island* was more palatable to audiences and exhibitors but still lacked the quality Columbia needed to compete with Universal and Republic, which dominated the market for episodic epics. The trades reported in late May that Columbia had suspended its contract with Louis Weiss and assumed responsibility for *The Great Adventures of Wild Bill Hickok*, fourth of the 1937-38 chapter plays. Fier was assigned to produce it himself.

Earlier that month—on May 4th, to be exact—*Film Daily* carried the news that Columbia had purchased rights to the Spider pulp and would produce a serial featuring the character. When Columbia announced its slate of serials for the upcoming 1938-39 season, *The Spider, Master of Men* occupied the coveted lead-off slot, to be followed by *Mandrake the Magician*, *The Great Adventures of Kit Carson*, and *Flying G-Men*.

The Spider was an inspired choice for adaptation to the serial screen because hero pulps and chapter plays primarily appealed to the same demographic: adolescent boys. The Popular Publications single-character pulps, however, skewed to a slightly older readership than those issued by Street & Smith and Standard's Thrilling Group, so the undertones of sex and sadism in the Spider's rough-paper adventures would need muting in translation to celluloid. In every other respect the property was tailor-made for a serial producer.

Fier delegated story-and-scripting chores to Columbia contract writer Robert E. Kent and hired long-time serial scribes Basil

Dickey and George H. Plympton to join him. With chapter-play experience going back to the Teens, Dickey and Plympton knew every trick in the book—and then some. Also pitching in was one Martie Ramson, about whom nothing is known. (*The Spider's Web* is the only motion picture on which he was credited in any capacity.) Working together, these scenarists crafted an exciting adventure that maintained unusual fidelity, in both letter and spirit, to the source material.

There *were* changes, of course, but relatively minor ones. Richard Wentworth's butler Jenkyns, an attenuated family retainer in the pulp yarns, shed several decades on screen so that he could be played by a much younger Columbia contractee. Commissioner Kirkpatrick's name was shortened to Kirk, presumably to facilitate rapid-fire dialogue delivery and minimize the risk of retakes. Also, the printed-page Spider typically ventured forth in fright wig, long cloak, and floppy hat, while outfitted with fangs and false hump. No doubt the screenwriters thought this get-up too cumbersome for the number of quick changes they envisioned Wentworth making over the course of 15 fast-paced episodes. So the serial Spider instead donned over his business suit a thin, flowing cape embroidered with a web pattern. He wore a hood of similar design and topped off the ensemble with a dark snap-brim Fedora.

Otherwise, the writers did a superb job of bringing the pulp Spider to celluloid life, perfectly replicating the kind of apocalyptic menace that animated most of the novels. They devised a cunning super-villain with an ambitious scheme to seize power by terrorizing a large city and controlling its key industries. They kept the Spider an outsider, hunted by police and criminals alike. They put his beloved Nita Van Sloan and his "three faithful musketeers"—Jackson, Jenkyns, and Ram Singh—in constant jeopardy. Danger was omnipresent; death lurked around every corner and behind every door. Each chapter's script offered more plot and action than most hour-long "B" pictures of the time.

Jack Fier had a lot riding on *The Spider, Master of Men*. The success of Columbia's youthful serial unit, which had nearly died stillborn as a result of the Weiss brothers' abortive early efforts, depended upon a successful launch to the new season. Chapterplay competition that autumn would be stiff: Universal was opening its season with *Red Barry*, starring Buster Crabbe and based on a popular comic strip, and Republic with *Dick Tracy Returns*, a sequel to its phenomenally profitable 1937 serial starring Ralph Byrd. Bearing this in mind, Fier apportioned extra money to *The Spider*'s budget, already larger than usual due to the high number of supporting players required.

Perfecting the screenplay required almost the entire summer. Norvell Page, who wrote most of the character's pulp adventures, was paid a token $50 to review the final scripts. Likely his input was restricted to relatively small matters such as having Wentworth call Ram Singh "warrior" and having Jackson address his employer as "Major"—minor details that enhanced the serial's faithfulness to its source. (One wonders if perhaps Page didn't also contribute some of Ram Singh's juiciest lines, such as the classic "Dog with a pig's face! If I had my knife, I'd carve my name in your heart!")

Leaving nothing to chance, Fier hired two silent-serial standbys to direct. Ray Taylor had been helming chapter plays for years at Universal, logging a list of solo hits and lending uncredited support to such blockbusters as *Tarzan the Mighty* (1928) and *Flash Gordon* (1936). Best known for his Laurel and Hardy comedies, James W. Horne was no stranger to cliffhanging action: in 1917 he ramrodded *Bull's Eye*, the initial starring vehicle of phenomenally popular Eddie Polo, and the following year he directed *Hands Up* (1918), the first major effort of serial queen Ruth Roland. Both men were eminently qualified to handle what promised to be a hectic shoot teeming with time-consuming action sequences.

In mid-August, with the script finally completed and pre-production planning well underway, Fier turned to casting. Several principal roles were assigned to Columbia contract players. Aristocratically beautiful Iris Meredith, regular leading lady in the firm's "B" Westerns featuring Charles Starrett, was the first and only choice for Nita. Richard Fiske, a young utilitarian actor who lacked leading-man qualities, took the role of Jackson. Scottish thespian Don Douglas played Jenkyns, whose name underwent a slight change to Jenkins. Forbes Murray, a freelance character actor regularly seen in Columbia movies as an authoritarian figure, was ideally cast as Commissioner Kirk. Various minor parts were doled out to familiar Columbia contractees, among them Marc Lawrence, Dick Curtis, Ann Doran, John Tyrrell, and Edward LeSaint (who frequently played Meredith's father in the Starrett Westerns). But Fier decided to go outside the studio for his star.

Initially cast as Richard Wentworth was John Trent, late of Paramount Pictures. Prior to being discovered by Paramount exec B. P. Schulberg, Trent had been an aviator, flying passenger planes for TWA and serving in the Army Air Corps Reserve. During his year at Paramount, Trent worked in five films alongside some major stars, but he failed to impress studio brass and was dropped in early 1938. Tall and well built, with square jaw and dimpled smile, the erstwhile pilot seemed like a pretty good match for the Wentworth depicted in illustrations by pulp artist John Fleming Gould. But while a passable actor, Trent lacked the charisma and dynamism crucial to an effective portrayal of the Spider. (Although it should be said he made a pretty fair Tailspin Tommy in four 1939 Monogram "B" pictures.) Did his shortcoming suddenly become apparent to Jack Fier? Did John Trent have eleventh-hour reservations about assuming the role? We'll probably never know.

Several trade papers denoted Thursday, August 25th, as the first day of shooting. But commencement of principal photography was delayed until Monday, August 29th, and when the camera finally began turning Warren Hull was playing the Spider. Handsome, personable Hull had previously been a Warner Brothers contractee specializing in bright young men of the "Tennis, anyone?" type. With breezy personality and pleasing baritone voice, he was most comfortable in comedies and musicals, and his action-film credentials were negligible. What Fier saw in the freelance actor—other than instant availability—is never been determined. But he guessed fast and he guessed right. Hull had to have been hired on the 25th or the 26th.

As it happens, the replacement of Trent with Hull guaranteed the chapter play's success. Viewing the first Spider serial today, it's hard to imagine any actor of Hull's stature—he was strictly a "B"-picture guy, and major stars like Gable or Cooper didn't work in serials—doing a better job of interpreting Richard Wentworth for thrill-hungry Saturday-matinee audiences. He brings appropriate levels of intensity and authoritativeness to the role. When he narrows his eyes and grits his teeth, you just *know* that Wentworth is about to make a daring move. There's nothing tentative about his movements or body language. And when adopting the guise of underworld habitué Blinky McQuade, Hull submerges himself into this persona with the undisguised joy of an actor who relishes kidding his audience. In his first transformation from Wentworth to Blinky, he mutters a couple lines of dialogue that could well have been ad-libbed. While adjusting his makeup, Hull as Wentworth stares into a pocket mirror and says, "Well, Blinky, it looks like you're due for some action." Then, adopting Blinky's gravelly voice, he replies to himself, "Dat's okay wit' me, boss."

Though possessing a muscular frame, Hull was not especially athletic and left strenuous or dangerous stunts to doubles George DeNormand and Dave O'Brien. But he convincingly wielded the Spider's deadly automatics, mowing down the villain's henchmen with unerring accuracy. In short, the last-minute replacement was more than up to every challenge the role presented.

Taylor and Horne made an effective directorial team. Neither was a particularly stylish filmmaker, but both realized the importance of maintaining a cyclonic pace. The serial's action was fast and furious, and it was captured on film with speed and efficiency. Iris Meredith later confessed she had no idea what her character was doing from one minute to the next, because her scenes were shot out of sequence and the breathless cast was hustled from one set to another, day after day, to complete principal photography on time. Most of the footage was taken on the studio lot. Standing facades on what was called "the Columbia ranch," located in Burbank not far from the Warner Brothers plant, were employed for exterior scenes. The pulp Wentworth's Manhattan townhouse became a roomy suburban home on the faux street also used in the "Blondie" movies. City streets erected on both the Columbia and Warner lots were pressed into service, as was the mansion facade built for Frank Capra's 1936 hit, *Mr. Deeds Goes to Town*. Fier's unit also commandeered interior sets built for recently finished Columbia "A" films such as *Holiday* and *You Can't Take It With You*.

Although publicity stills released during the early weeks of production were labeled *The Spider, Master of Men*, on September 24 the serial's title was changed to *The Spider's Web*. No reason was given. The following week, a squib in *Hollywood Reporter* claimed that production wrapped on September 29, but a later edition of the *Motion Picture Herald* stated that filming extended well into the next month. With film editors working long hours, Chapter One was released nationally on October 22nd, as promised, and played to capacity crowds in theaters that had booked the serial on a first-run basis. By then the trades were carrying full-page ads for *The Spider's Web* and promising it would break records. For once, a film lived up to the hyperbole in its ads.

The initial stanza gets underway in the secret sanctum of a hooded, white-robed villain known as the Octopus. His colorful cognomen derives from the false arm that dangles from one of his sleeves. This prosthesis enables the Octopus to keep his right arm hidden beneath the robe's folds, and in the unseen hand he habitually clutches a revolver that can be brought into play instantly if danger threatens.

This maniacal miscreant, who in regular meetings addresses his assembled henchmen from behind a voice-distorting microphone, is determined to control the city—and later the state, and maybe even the country—by first crippling and then seizing control of local industries and utilities. He employs violent terrorism to establish a reign of terror and makes the bus line of Alvin Roberts (Byron Foulger) his first target.

With the basic premise established, things start popping immediately. A pre-emptive strike against famed criminologist Richard Wentworth (Warren Hull) and his fiancee Nita Van Sloan

(Iris Meredith), thwarted with the help of Jackson (Richard Fiske) and Ram Singh (Kenne Duncan), results in the deaths of several Octopus henchmen. A quick phone call from Commissioner Kirk (Forbes Murray) brings Wentworth up to speed on the latest depredations of this emerging menace. Subsequently, Nita and Ram Singh narrowly evade death on a bridge that is dynamited. Then Wentworth and his Sikh bodyguard are captured by another group of henchmen and taken to one of many Octopus hideouts. Freed from his bonds, the wealthy criminologist disguises himself as underworld habitué Blinky McQuade and, slipping from the room in which he's been imprisoned, engages a henchman in conversation and learns about the plot to blow up a bus terminal packed with commuters.

Escaping from the hideout, Wentworth and Ram Singh race to the terminal, which the criminologist enters in the familiar webbed hood and cloak of the Spider. Knowing that most citizens believe his alter ego to be a vicious killer, Wentworth fires shots in the air to frighten people out of the building before the scheduled explosion, which is imminent. A dozen Octopus henchmen, waiting in the terminal to see that nothing goes awry at the last minute, open fire on their nemesis and a pitched gun-battle ensues as terrified civilians flee for the exits. With Ram Singh's help, the Spider shoots his way to the booby-trapped bus with seconds to spare. Leaping inside, he attempts to drive it away but is apparently caught in the explosion that rocks the terminal.

And that's just in Chapter One.

The next fourteen episodes of *The Spider's Web* unreel at the same frantic pace. The Master of Men (who, of course, escapes the bus explosion) continually matches wits with the Octopus, who wreaks considerable havoc in pursuit of his ambition. He attacks industries with wild abandon and deploys then-current weapons of mass destruction, even using a mobile death ray to bring down airplanes in flight. In his repeated attempts to keep Wentworth at bay, the degenerate kidnaps Nita, Jackson, Ram Singh, and Commissioner Kirk in turn. Finally realizing that it's the Spider who always shows up to rescue them, the arch-villain puts two and two together. But by now Wentworth has figured out that the Octopus is in reality a banker named Chase, between whose eyes he places a well-deserved bullet in the closing minutes of Chapter Fifteen.

Screenwriters Kent, Dickey, Plympton, and Ramson skillfully emulated the style and substance of Norvell Page's Spider novels. The principal characteristics of the best series entries—a grotesque mystery villain, a destructive campaign of near-apocalyptic proportions, a series of pitched battles with advantage seesawing from one side to the other—were there in abundance. About the only element missing from Page's repertoire was Wentworth's habitual bouts with despair and paranoia. Apparently, including those particular character tics was a bridge too far for Jack Fier.

Another facet of the pulp series—the hero's uncompromising lethality—was brought to the screen with gusto. The Spider killed 12 heavies in the first two stanzas alone, but with later chapters still being prepared for release, Columbia was chastised by the Hays Office, which in reviewing the serial claimed that it was much too bloodthirsty for kids. Film editors were forced to revise completed episodes, making strategic cuts of individual shots that showed bullet-riddled heavies slumping to the floor. Therefore, later chapters typically found the Spider, blazing gun in each hand, wading into a room populated with a half-dozen or so Octopus henchmen. A close-up would depict him firing multiple rounds toward the off-screen villains, and the subsequent cut pictured him striding across the room, now littered with corpses who had not been seen taking the Spider's bullets. Only by such editorial obfuscation was Columbia able to satisfy the Production Code's stricture forbidding excessive killing in kiddie-oriented movies.

Reviews stressed the character's potent appeal to youthful viewers. "Juveniles will relish each installment," said the *Motion Picture Herald*, "but adults may not unanimously accept the devices by which the hero is rescued from various death traps."

Film Daily said *The Spider's Web* "has all the thrills, chills and action that serial fans expect, and then some. There is murder in wholesale lots, fights all over the place, and a mysterious character called the Octopus who plots the overthrow of the government so that he himself may rule."

The *Motion Picture Exhibitor*'s appraisal: "The first two episodes reveal a smashing action serial with more thugs being killed in five reels than in most other complete serials. In addition to the blood, action, it has good production, fast pace, with Warren Hull a very convincing hero. It also has the type of story the kids go for: a gun-fighting crusade against the 'Octopus' (a mad degenerate) using the madman's own methods."

Early notices from exhibitors were equally enthusiastic. Pierce Parkhurst, manager of Torrington, Connecticut's State Theatre, was the first to report on *Spider's Web* and characterized it thusly: "A good serial which if given the proper exploitation should build up matinee business to considerable extent.... There is great opportunity here.... A swell little serial for the kids but a little bit too fantastic for the older folks."

Apparently *some* older folks enjoyed the serial, including patrons of Mayme P. Musselman's Princess Theatre in Lincoln, Kansas. "We have just run the ninth chapter," reported Musselman in the *Motion Picture Herald*'s "What the Picture Did for Me" column, "and are using it on bargain night to get [customers] back week after week. They make plenty of fun of this serial but go to see it on that account. Maybe they are right."

Claude Fismer, manager of Hamilton, Ohio's Lyric Theatre, penned an enthusiastic summation after screening the last episode for his patrons: "Wound up in a blaze of glory. One of the very best serials we have ever played. Final chapter brought us a very big weekend."

But Randolph Covi, owner of the Covi Theatre in Herminie, Pennsylvania, identified a serious screenplay flaw that escaped the notice of most critics. "*The Spider's Web*," he explained in the *Herald*, "features a mysterious character, the Octopus, whose identity is unknown. This formula of maintaining suspense and keeping patrons guessing until the last chapter as to the identity of the Octopus follows old traditions. The Columbia script writers forgot, however, the importance of having as the Octopus someone who participated actively in the play. Who is the Octopus? He is revealed as a character who appeared in a mob scene in the first episode; we got a back view of him in the fifth episode and another mob scene in the 13th chapter. This man, then, is the Octopus. Our audience really didn't care. The Octopus might just as well have been Charlie McCarthy...."

The Spider's Web was hugely successful and got Columbia's in-house serial unit off to a good start. The remaining 1938-39 entries—*Flying G-Men, Mandrake the Magician,* and *Overland with Kit Carson* (previously announced as *Great Adventures of Kit Carson*)—boasted equally impressive production values and provided fast-moving entertainment, but the studio lost interest in the production of high-quality serials very soon thereafter. Fier's approach clearly resulted in fine chapter plays, but Columbia still failed to dominate this limited, specialized market (serials regularly played in only a third of the nation's theaters) and the profits, while substantial, didn't justify the extra care and expenditure. As a result, production of the firm's subsequent serials were entrusted to independent filmmakers Larry Darmour and Sam Katzman, whose primary interest was chiseling extra money for themselves out of already shrunken budgets. Large chunks of future funds earmarked for Columbia's episodic thrillers went toward the purchase of screen rights to highly marketable characters from other media.

In all probability Jack Fier relinquished control of Columbia's serial program with no regret. He continued to oversee the company's "B"-Western output and personally produced dozens of low-budget movies through 1945. At that time he was demoted to production manager, working in that capacity on another 90 Columbia films, prestige pictures and undistinguished quickies alike.

Independent producer Larry Darmour, whose early successes included a series of comedy short subjects featuring the young Mickey Rooney, had been making cheap "B" Westerns for Columbia release. His stars included cowboy great Ken Maynard, contract player Bob Allen, and minor leading man Jack Luden. He'd recently completed a series of four horse operas with newcomer Gordon "Wild Bill" Elliott, who proved so popular that he was hired away by Columbia and put in Jack Fier's stable with Charles Starrett.

Darmour had a small, tightly knit production unit that included cinematographer James S. Brown Jr., associate producer Rudolph Flothow, assistant director Carl Hiecke, sound engineer Tom Lambert, and film editors Dwight Caldwell and Earl Turner. He even had his own plant, the old Berwilla Studio owned by silent-serial star and producer Ben Wilson.

While hardly exceptional, Darmour's "B" pictures satisfied the exhibitors who booked Columbia product. So when Columbia decided to cut serial budgets they entrusted chapter-play production to him. He was given a tight budget significantly smaller than those Fier had been granted. Like most outside producers working for bigger studios, Darmour was not a salaried employee but an independent contractor instead. The budgets included a producer's fee, but if Darmour brought in any serial for less than the allotted amount, he could keep the difference. Therefore, he had every incentive to chisel. A dollar saved, after all, was a dollar pocketed.

Based on his co-direction of *The Spider's Web* and *Flying G-Men*, arguably Jack Fier's best two serials, James W. Horne was signed to a contract making him Darmour's permanent chapter-play helmer. The first serial of the 1939-40 season, *The Shadow*, set the pattern for Darmour's chaptered product. Horne, an experienced comedy director with a keen eye for hokum, instructed his actors to play their scenes in an exaggerated manner: speaking loudly and emphatically, reacting with overblown "takes" (as in, "taking it big"), and rushing about as though their lives depended on it. Cognizant that serials were largely intended for kids, and perhaps sensitive to complaints about violence, Horne kept most of the action non-lethal, with lengthy fistfights substituting for gunplay and brutality.

Film historian William K. Everson summed up the Horne approach in his introduction to Alan G. Barbour's 1970 serial history, *Days of Thrills and Adventure*:

The Columbia serials directed by James W. Horne were clearly tongue-in-cheek, with exaggerated melodramatic gestures, derisive and sarcastic end-of-chapter narrations, and moments of truly lunatic comedy involving the villains. Serial purists understandably resented this and have never liked Horne's serials. Yet he was too good a director, too much a past master of great silent and sound comedy not to know precisely what he was doing. Undoubtedly he reasoned that to play the scripts straight, with their stereotyped stories and meager budgets, could only result in serials spectacularly inferior to the competitive ones issued by Republic and Universal. Playing them for comedy didn't make better, but it did keep them lively, distinctive, and different. Their speed and constant chances of pace, however, and their intermingling of melodrama and farce, to say nothing of their frequent elements of what we would now call black comedy, made them even more of a challenge for actors, who could do nothing but go along for the ride.

Since *The Spider's Web* had been so successful, Columbia was eager for a sequel. The studio renewed its license of the character and included *The Return of the Spider* in its 1940-41 serial release slate. Darmour assigned the property to a handful of writers: Morgan B. Cox, John Cutting, Harry Fraser, and Lawrence Taylor devised the original story, while the actual scriptwriting was delegated to Jesse Duffy and George H. Plympton. Cutting and Taylor were relative newcomers whose contributions may have been marginal at best.

Next, Darmour engaged Warren Hull to reprise his role as Richard Wentworth. Since completing *The Spider's Web* Hull had played Mandrake the Magician and the Green Hornet in serials. His film career had gone nowhere, though, and after the second Spider serial he appeared in one more film—an East Side Kids comedy for lowly Monogram Pictures—before quitting the picture business. He later became a popular quiz-show host.

Iris Meredith's Columbia contract had just expired and she left the studio embittered; Darmour would never get her to play Nita a second time. Instead he cast Mary Ainslee, a coarse "bottle blonde" of the type that played gum-smacking telephone operators or chorus girls. Giving Ainslee the part of Nita Van Sloan effectively doomed the project at the outset, although based on what the character was given to do, the outcome was predictable.

Kenne Duncan the Canadian returned as Ram Singh. Stephen Chase (also known as Alden Chase) played Jenkins, and personable Dave O'Brien portrayed Jackson. The role of Commissioner Kirk was taken by 70-year-old Joseph W. Girard, a veteran of serials going back to 1915. Production began early in 1941 and was completed in four weeks—perfectly typical of a Darmour chapter play but incredibly fast work. Uncomfortably so, for the actors. The title was changed to *The Spider Returns* while principal photography was still underway.

Chapter One, "The Stolen Plans," went into release on May 9, 1941. It begins with Richard Wentworth savoring his "retirement" and enjoying home life with Nita. His complacency is shattered by a sudden onslaught against local industries playing a vital role in the country's defense. The wave of sabotage forces Wentworth to revive the Spider. Kirk asks his old friend to join a committee of industrial tycoons trying to mobilize against the unknown malefactor, who presumably is working for a foreign government.

Wentworth learns that the culprit is a bizarrely garbed madman who calls himself "the Gargoyle." Eventually it becomes apparent that this demonic figure is one of the committee members. Even Nita's beloved uncle, Charles Van Sloan (Charles Miller) falls under suspicion.

The Gargoyle's gang is headed by a thug named Trigger (Anthony Warde), and Wentworth decides to cozy up to the henchmen in the guise of Blinky McQuade. He pretends to assist the gang while actually gathering information that will help him foil their plans as the Spider. In the end, the Gargoyle is revealed as McLeod, whose motivations are never clearly explained. Wentworth puts the Spider back in mothballs.

The Spider's Web was faithful to the pulp canon, but *The Spider Returns* is fundamentally different. As mentioned above, the most jarring difference is the characterization of Nita, who becomes a brassy, wise-cracking, over-emotional dame as interpreted by Mary Ainslee. Jackson, depicted in the first serial as a respectful subordinate, is played by Dave O'Brien as a jocular sidekick who treats Wentworth as a pal rather than an employer. Ram Singh doesn't do as much in *Returns* than he did in *Web*, but he also addresses Wentworth with less deference than the pulp character.

The Spider of *Returns* behaves in a manner wholly incomprehensible to anyone familiar not only with the character depicted in *Web* but also the one whose pulp-page adventures were written by Norvell Page. He engages heavies by the handful in bone-crunching fistfights but, even when the opportunity presents itself, refuses to shoot any of them. When overpowered he's either knocked out and left to perish in an explosion or some such trap, or he breaks away and fires his pistol—a snub-nosed revolver, by the way, not an automatic—into the floor to scatter his panicky sparring partners.

The serial's comedy element is pronounced and manifests itself without warning and in strange ways. Some humorous bits seem unscripted and improvisational, perhaps suggested by Horne on the set. For example, while Trigger lectures Blinky in an underground dive that doubles as the gang's hideout, two of the henchmen are seen dancing the Big Apple in the background. Other gags are more clearly defined and developed. In one chapter the Gargoyle and his eccentric mad-scientist assistant Stephen (Harry Harvey) train their X-ray television camera on Trigger's apartment. The gang members are seen cavorting with floozies, prompting the master villain to call his chief lieutenant and scream, "These wild parties must *cease!*"

Such silliness extends to the chapter-ending "tease" of scenes from the next episode, narrated by radio announcer Knox Manning. For one, showing Gargoyle henchmen running after and boarding a moving train, Manning asks: "Who are the two extra passengers? *Have they bought tickets?*" For another, showing Nita chased by thugs, he wonders, "Why do the Gargoyle's men want the girl? *We wish we knew!*"

This is not to say *The Spider Returns* isn't fun. On the contrary, the very qualities that make it such a travesty next to *The Spider's Web* also make it quite entertaining. The pace is fast and the action plentiful. Even with director Horne urging him to comedic excess, Warren Hull maintains his dignity. Blinky goes over the top frequently, but Richard Wentworth is more restrained than other protagonists in Horne serials.

The Spider Returns did not perform especially well at the nation's box-offices, so the character's Hollywood career ended with the conclusion of its theatrical engagements. But the first serial was so strong that we need not remember the second's weaknesses. Sadly, there were no further attempts to bring Richard Wentworth and company to the screen. In 1943 Popular Publications discontinued the *Spider* pulp magazine citing declining sales and wartime paper shortages as reason for the termination.

Adventures of Red Ryder

(1940, Republic Pictures Corporation)

TALL, LANKY COWPOKE "Red" Ryder, his nickname referring to the unruly thatch of flame-red hair that spilled out of a wide-brimmed Stetson hat, lived on the fictional Painted Valley Ranch located in the Blanco Basin near Colorado's San Juan Mountain Range. Riding on behalf of the ranch's owner—his aunt, known far and wide as the Duchess—Red was most frequently accompanied by a young Indian boy named Little Beaver and grizzled ranch hand Buckskin Blodgett. He made not-too-serious efforts to romance a young lady named Beth Wilder and constantly tangled with crooked gambler Ace Hanlon, whose Jackpot Bar in the crook's paradise of Devil's Hole played host to such vicious characters as One-Eye Chapin.

Red and his circle were invented by cartoonist Fred Harman, a real-life Westerner whose Colorado spread in Pagosa Springs was not far from Ryder's Painted Valley Ranch. The son of a homesteader, Harman learned to ride as a young boy and became familiar with ranch life. He barely got through grade school before dropping out. A wholly self-taught artist, he joined younger brother

Hugh in 1922 to partner with animator Walt Disney in Kansas City. Their joint venture failed before a year had passed and Fred returned to Colorado. (His brother and Disney, operating along separate but roughly parallel tracks, eventually became prominent figures in the animated-cartoon business.)

Throughout the 1920s Harman illustrated catalogs and produced advertising art in addition to supplying the occasional book frontispiece and selling a painting here and there. Western themes dominated his work in oils, and in 1927 he sold a piece featuring a red-haired cowboy to pay the hospital bill incurred by his son's birth. The Depression found Fred struggling to make a living—like millions of other Americans. In 1933 he moved to Los Angeles and launched a Western magazine that he edited, illustrated, pasted up, published, and distributed single-handed. Undercapitalized and competing in an over-saturated market, the sheet folded after just three issues.

At that point Harman, with nothing to lose, began developing a Western-action comic strip titled *Bronc Peeler*. Its eponymous hero was a two-fisted, straight-shooting, red-headed cowboy whose sidekick was an old desert hand named Coyote Pete. Harman's advertising work and other ventures had exposed him to various newspapers and he syndicated the colorful feature as a Sunday strip. The first installment appeared in selected papers on October 7, 1934.

Bronc Peeler failed to attract a significant readership and Fred struggled to keep it afloat. At his wife's suggestion, he replaced Coyote Pete with a much younger sidekick—an adopted Navajo boy named Little Beaver—in a bid to make the strip more relatable to young readers. But he continued to tread water until early 1938, when a meeting with former literary agent Stephen Slesinger changed the destinies of both men.

As an agent Slesinger had represented such popular Western authors as Zane Grey, Rex Beach, and Will James. In the interest of expanding their reader base he acquired secondary rights to their work, which in James' case included illustrations. He marketed the stories and art to newspapers directly and later forged an alliance with the Ohio-based Newspaper Enterprise Association syndicate. But Slesinger didn't stop there. He recognized the value in licensing popular properties to manufacturers of consumer products who might pay him for the right to brand their goods with the images of recognizable characters, thus enhancing sales prospects.

By the time he met Fred Harman, Slesinger had already made a small fortune representing A. A. Milne and Edgar Rice Burroughs, whose famous creations—Winnie the Pooh and Tarzan, respectively—had their images plastered all over toys, games, blankets, watches, penknives, and articles of clothing, not to mention Pop-Up Books, coloring books, Big Little Books and other forms of printed matter. He obtained for former client Zane Grey a lucrative deal as the supposed author of a King Features Syndicate comic strip, *King of the Royal Mounted*, actually written by Grey's son Romer under Slesinger's supervision.

Eager to achieve greater success with his struggling feature, Harman took all of Slesinger's suggestions. *Bronc Peeler* had a cartoony look that gradually evolved to something more closely resembling the realistic appearance of the better adventure strips. Fred added numerous supporting characters who would allow greater flexibility in plotting. Bronc himself underwent a metamorphosis, apparently gaining several years in the process. Finally the old strip faded away, replaced by *Red Ryder*. The new feature debuted as a Sunday page on November 6, 1938. It rapidly gained popularity, partially because no major Western strips had been introduced in some time. Slesinger entrusted its syndication to NEA, which added Harman's new brainchild to a lineup that already included such favorites as *Tarzan*, *Alley Oop*, and *Ripley's Believe It or Not*. The next year Harman added a daily version of the strip, increasing his workload but swelling Red's fan base.

Slesinger wasted no time pursuing licensing opportunities. He had first tasted Hollywood success in 1936 with the licensing of *King of the Royal Mounted* to independent producer Sol Lesser, then distributing his films through 20th Century-Fox. Lesser's feature, which retained the strip's title and starred Robert Kent as the intrepid Mountie, was rather weak and not particularly well received. Slesinger's deal with King Features allowed him to deal with studios for film rights to the Zane Grey strip, but regarding *Red Ryder* NEA assigned that right to the Orsatti brothers, the best-connected agents in Hollywood.

Herbert J. Yates' Republic Pictures, for whom Western features and serials was a specialty, saw the potential in *Red Ryder* and opened negotiations with the Orsattis in the spring of 1939. A deal was quickly struck, and the pact inked on June 14, 1939 by Republic's parent company, Consolidated Film Industries, granted the studio rights to Harman's strip for $12,500. Shortly thereafter Republic announced that *Adventures of Red Ryder* would be one of its "Streamline" serials (12 chapters as opposed to 15) on the 1939-40 release slate.

Serial-unit producer Hiram S. "Bunny" Brown Jr. put his writing staff—Franklin Adreon, Ronald Davidson, Norman S. Hall, Barney Sarecky, and Sol Shor—to work on *Red Ryder* in the winter of 1939-40, while production of the previous Republic chapter play, *Drums of Fu Manchu*, was racing toward completion. As per standard operating procedure with properties licensed from the funny pages, the writers poured over tearsheets of the strip supplied by NEA before deciding how to adapt the character. In typical Republic fashion they retained certain elements of Harman's concept while jettisoning others.

Meanwhile, Brown and his directors, William Witney and John English, occupied themselves with the important task of casting. Some roles were easy to fill; perennial villain Noah Beery had a few pounds on the strip's Ace Hanlon but otherwise resembled him quite closely, and the same could be said of hatchet-faced Bob Kortman's similarity to the vicious One-Eye. Maude Pierce Allen, one of the many stage performers who gravitated to Hollywood following the advent of talking pictures, was just a tad too much the dowager to make a thoroughly convincing Duchess, but she had the necessary acting chops.

For the ingenue, Beth Andrews (changed from the strip's Beth Wilder), Brown and his directors cast 20-year-old Earl Carroll showgirl, bit player, and occasional stunt performer Vivian Coe. Her husband, millionaire auto dealer Glenn Austin, was an avid polo player who owned his own horses. He taught Vivian to ride, a skill that was more important to Witney and English than her ability to deliver lines, of which there would be few. "I could sit a horse," Coe told interviewer Mike Fitzgerald in 1980, "which led to me doing my own stunts in Red Ryder. I could shoot to the back of me while horseback riding [and] did a lot of stunt work, even before the Ryder serial. Republic used me to great advantage as a result."

Nine-year-old Tommy Cook, already experienced in stage and radio work but a relative newcomer to film, was awarded the key role of Little Beaver, Red's young sidekick. As Cook recalled in a 2015 interview with me, he didn't formally audition for the part. Instead, he was invited out to Witney's home in Tarzana and given an impromptu riding lesson on a little black mare belonging to the director's wife, actress Maxine Doyle. Satisfied with Tommy's pluck and personality, Bill told Jack English and Bunny Brown they had their Little Beaver. Witney invited Tommy and his parents back to his small ranch for several more riding lessons before production commenced.

The principal characters had all been cast save one: the lead. As Fred Harman drew him, Red Ryder stood well over six feet and was decidedly lanky, with high cheekbones and a square jaw. Brown and the directors interviewed a couple dozen likely candidates and screen-tested at least a handful. They couldn't seem to find one with the right combination of acting ability, athletic skill, and resemblance to the comic-strip Red. Serious consideration was given Ted Mapes, a stuntman and bit player who had double Herman Brix in *Hawk of the Wilderness* and, more recently, *Daredevils of the Red Circle*.

In early March, with the script nearly complete and the budget set at approximately $145,000, Brown received a call from the front office. The problem was solved, he was told; Red Ryder would be played by recently hired contract player Donald Barry. Born in Houston on January 11, 1912, Barry (whose real last name is given in some sources as Poinboeuf and in others as De Acosta) was a college football player who developed a yen for acting and did some stage work before moving to Hollywood in 1933. Without representation, he wangled small roles in such major films as *Dead End* (1937) and *Only Angels Have Wings* (1938) and played a young interne in several of M-G-M's early Dr. Kildare movies.

Discovered by director George Sherman, he made a strong impression as a sympathetic cattle thief in *Wyoming Outlaw* (1939), one of the final Three Mesquiteers films starring John Wayne. Don was equally effective in two 1939 Roy Rogers pictures, *Saga of Death Valley* and *Days of Jesse James*, and took top billing for the first time that same year in a non-Western Republic "B," *Calling All Marines*. At five-foot-five (on tiptoes), round-faced Barry packed a lot of talent—and an outsized personality—into his small frame. The feisty Texan sensed he might do better as a big fish in one of Hollywood's smaller ponds and lobbied Republic executives for more starring roles.

Around this time, late in 1939, the front office decided to add another Western series to its 1940-41 schedule. Sherman, who had been helming the Mesquiteers pictures since 1937, would transition out of that long-running series to direct *and* produce the new one, comprised of eight releases per season. The search for a leading man began in December of '39. Rather than sign an established cowboy star at a big salary, Republic president Herbert Yates and his assistant William Saal wanted to hire a virtual unknown for peanuts. Sherman suggested Barry, and after screening the bantam actor's most recent work for the studio Yates became interested. A face-to-face meeting clinched the deal, and a February 13, 1940 studio announcement named Donald Barry as Republic's latest Western star. Not announced was Barry's salary, a paltry $150 per week.

Exhibitors would have to book their 1940-41 offerings, so to introduce Barry properly Sherman rushed him into a first starring feature, *Ghost Valley Raiders*, shot between February 15 and February 22 and released nationally on March 26. No great shakes, it revealed Don Barry as a suitable Western lead. But Yates wanted to build a national following for his new "discovery" to bolster the series' chance of success. What better way, then, but to star him in a serial, which would give him 12 straight weeks of exposure to the same Saturday-matinee audiences to which exhibitors would be marketing his features? With a Western serial already in preparation, the front office had the perfect vehicle for this plan.

Barry knew he was all wrong for Red Ryder, and beyond that he resented being shunted into a lowly chapter play. (Although Republic's serials by that time were tops in the industry and quite profitable to boot, they were considered to be the least prestigious films in which an actor could star.) In later years he was fond of repeating a story that may have been apocryphal, although he always told it the same way.

According to Barry, upon learning of the decision to star him in *Adventures of Red Ryder*, stormed into Herbert Yates' office—interrupting a meeting of studio executives in the process—marched up to the prexy's desk, and yelled: "I just heard you want me to play Red Ryder. I'm not right for the part and I won't do it!"

Supposedly Yates replied, "Fine, I won't pay you."

To which Barry supposedly shot back, "I'll do it!"

Brown, Witney, and English introduced themselves to Barry, whose cockiness alienated them immediately. In his 1996 autobiography Witney recalled that first encounter tersely: "After we met Don we all decided that he was too short to play the role and his brain matched his size. The only thing he had that was big was his ego." The serial makers decided to confront Yates directly but Republic's head man had just left for New York and would not be back on the lot before *Red Ryder* went into production. They scheduled a meeting with William Saal, who explained their boss's rationale for using Barry in the upcoming chapter play. Saal claimed Yates believed Don could be another Jimmy Cagney and was determined to make the brash young actor a star.

In our lengthy 1991 interview Witney told me that back then, with principal photography beginning in just a few days, a resigned Bunny Brown met privately with his two directors and told them (as Witney remembered the speech): "Look, the old man's made up his mind. We're stuck with Don and we've got to make the best of it. If the serial is a flop we'll get the blame. So we've got to do our best to make the guy look good."

Making Barry look good in Red Ryder garb proved challenging, to say the least. The height issue was addressed by giving the actor custom-made boots with four-inch lifts and six-inch heels. Don later said he wobbled too much in them and feared he might lose his footing while running or fighting. With that option gone, the costume designer resorted to illusory tactics. Wardrobe man Ted Towey tailored a shirt with padded shoulders to make the star's waist seem narrow, in keeping with the comic-strip Red. To make his face look thinner, Barry wore a specially made hat with small flat crown and ultra-wide brim. It looked silly. And for a reason no one remembered later he was told to wear his chaps inside out. Bill Witney later recalled that his heart sank the first time he saw Barry in full Ryder regalia. Not a frame of film had been exposed, but he was already convinced the serial would be a stinker.

Cameras rolled on March 27 as scheduled. The oft-used Iverson's Ranch near Chatsworth had been chosen for exteriors, but for variety's sake Brown had the *Red Ryder* company shoot on what was called Upper Iverson's, the less-frequently-seen area of the ranch north of what today is the Simi Valley Freeway. Other sequences were lensed on nearby Burro Flats. Working on these locations, less than an hour's drive from the studio, enabled cast and crew to go home every night and kept the film's budget low. But producer and directors were committed to putting every penny up on the screen and spent wisely.

Adventures of Red Ryder was crammed with action, staged for the most part by the incomparable Dave Sharpe, taking the job of stunt ramrod for the second consecutive Republic serial. The ramrod selected other stunt performers for the picture and coordinated the staging of action sequences with the directors. Sharpe also doubled Don Barry and performed other spectacular feats as needed. Bill Witney, who had come to respect Dave immensely and rely on him heavily, wrote about one such "gag" in his 1996 autobiography:

There was one stunt in the picture that has stuck in my memory. There was a fight between Red Ryder and a heavy on top of a running stagecoach. One man is knocked off the top. We were working at a location called Burro Flats in the north end of the San Fernando Valley. The location later became the testing grounds for the rockets that sent a man to the moon.

Dave Sharpe, who doubled Don Barry throughout the picture, was to do the fall from the top of the stagecoach. Davy and I walked down a dirt road to see if we could find a good spot to do the fall. There was a steeply cut bank on one side and a hill on the other. We came to the cut bank and stopped. No stuntman likes to do a fall on flat ground. If there is a hill to roll down after they hit the ground, they can give you a more spectacular fall. Dave looked at me and nodded, "This will be fine with me if it's okay with you." I was kidding him when I said, "Dave, that big sandy hill looks like a big feather bed. You should be able to do a flip or two in the air before you tumble down the hill." Dave didn't laugh. He studied the hill, took a couple puffs on his cigar, and asked, "Will you settle for one?"

Later that day the stagecoach with six horses pulling it came roaring down the road. Dave and another stuntman were standing on top trading punches. When they came to the proper spot, the stuntman hit him. Dave fell off the top of the stage, turned over in the air, hit the ground halfway down the hill and rolled to the bottom where the camera was set up. When I said "Cut," Dave got up, picked his cigar up from the rock he had carefully laid it on a few before, and took a puff. He said, "How was it?"

A simple miscalculation nearly proved Sharpe's undoing while shooting a sequence for Chapter Five. As scripted, Red Ryder was to rescue Little Beaver from the hayloft of a barn to which the Indian boy had been brought by Hanlon's men. After defeating the henchmen in a fistfight Red, with the lad hanging from his neck, escaped from the loft by sliding down a rope hanging outside the barn.

Normally the stuntman would have a lightweight dummy wrapped around his neck, but the prop department didn't have one as small as Tommy Cook, so in the interest of saving time and money Dave opted to do the stunt with the child actor clinging to him. However, as he began the 20-foot slide, the boy's weight arched his back. The pressure caused him to release the grip his feet had on the rope. Without this method of braking his speed, Dave was forced to grip the rope tighter; the resulting friction burned through his cowhide gloves, searing his palms. Had he let go of the rope and dropped to the ground, Cook likely would have fallen under him and been seriously injured. After applying salve and bandages to his hands and getting another pair of gloves, Sharpe did the stunt over. This time he compensated properly for Cook's weight and the gag proceeded without incident.

It never ceased to amaze Bill Witney that Sharpe consistently provided extra thrills to the stunts as scripted without seriously injuring himself. Moreover, Dave proved readily adaptable to the director's notion of choreographing lengthy fight sequences like elaborate dance numbers in Busby Berkeley musicals. He worked with a hand-picked group of stunt performers that included vaudeville acrobats as well as former cowboys and ex-football stars. Ken Terrell, Jimmy Fawcett, Ted Mapes, Post Park, Bud Geary, Art Dillard, Duke Green, and Duke Taylor were among the stunters on *Red Ryder*, as were brothers Joe and Bill Yrigoyen. The latter was badly hurt while shooting a stunt on April 10, but his was the only significant injury logged during filming.

The big problem for Witney and English was Don Barry, who proved to be their least cooperative leading man since John Carroll in *Zorro Rides Again*. He argued with them constantly, mostly about how to play his scenes but also about small production details clearly outside his purview. At the time Bill Witney believed Barry was deliberately challenging the directors' dominance on the set. But in a 1979 interview with me Don claimed otherwise. "I was obnoxious, no doubt about that," he admitted. "But you have to understand, this picture meant a lot to me. I didn't want to do it, but old man Yates stuck me with it and told me to make good or else. He promised it would make me a star. To Bill Witney and Jack English it was just another serial. To me it was everything I'd worked for.

"Looking back, would I have done things differently? You bet I would. Those guys, that whole serial crew, they knew what they were doing. I didn't. I was still learning, and I didn't want them to realize how much I *didn't* know. So I threw my weight around, trying to make sure the picture turned out the way I needed it to turn out. My mistake was in not trusting those guys."

Barry's anxiety and insecurity, which he masked with egotistical behavior and periodic outbursts, made the 24-day shoot an unpleasant one for all concerned. Interviewed a few months after the star's untimely death in 1980, Vivian Coe had scant praise for the erstwhile Red Ryder. "He had such a temper!" she confessed to Mike Fitzgerald. "He would walk off the set—often—stopping production just because he disagreed with Bill Witney, or somebody, about some minor thing. I don't like saying negative things about the departed, but he wasn't a very nice fellow when we worked together."

In our 2015 conversation Tommy Cook was more diplomatic. "Let's just say I got along okay with Don," he told me. "I enjoyed working with Tom Neal [on the 1941 Republic serial Jungle Girl] a lot more, and he treated me better when we were between scenes. But I didn't have any particular problems with Don."

Production concluded on April 25. It had not been a pleasant shoot and producer Brown chose to skip the customary wrap party. Witney and English, retiring to their favorite Ventura Boulevard watering hole for a "good riddance" toast, expressed pity for George Sherman and whichever other directors who might work with Barry in the future. Ironically, within the next three years each man would direct the bantam star in Westerns when Sherman was promoted to "straight" feature films. Witney never lost his disdain for Don and still referred to him as "the midget" in the last years of his life.

Editors William Thompson and Edward Todd had already begun a rough assembly of the serial when the two directors joined them in the cutting room to massage the rough spots and use pieces of various takes to shape Barry's performance. Witney and English were well aware that they would be blamed if the newly minted star was perceived to be deficient in any way.

Although Republic's serial makers were familiar with Production Code standards and seldom ran afoul of the Breen office, they occasionally went too far with a scene and had to be reined in. Chapter Eleven had Red Ryder, eager to avenge the killing of Cherokee Sims, catching up with One-Eye Chapin and killing him fair and square in a gun duel. The scripted version, calling for Red to approach the corpse and pump three additional bullets into it, was shot as written. But the Code administrators found this sequence unnecessarily brutal and insisted Republic re-edit to show Red Ryder downing One-Eye with his first shot and leaving it at that.

The serial's climax in Chapter Twelve was altered for reasons not clear, becoming more confusing in the bargain. As originally scripted, Red Ryder chases and apprehends the chapter play's chief villain, banker Calvin Drake (played by Harry Worth). In the ensuing hand-to-hand fight, Drake falls on his own knife and is killed. This ending was also incorporated into a synopsis written for the pressbook. On screen, however, Red is seen pursuing Drake to the high country and catching up with him at a suspension bridge spanning a deep chasm. The banker is sawing at the rope with his knife when Red leaps on him. The fight carries them back on the weakened bridge, which collapses beneath their combined weight and plunges both men into the abyss. Fade Out.

The next sequence opens with the Circle R in mourning. One character refers to finding Drake's body, but not Red's. As this point, Red Ryder—one arm in a sling—rides up to the ranch. An ecstatic Little Beaver runs out to greet his pal, who swings the boy up behind him on the saddle. "Everybody think you dead!" the boy cries. "Well," Red says, "that's one time we fooled 'em, sprout!" They ride off.

This makes no sense. Revised script pages, however, indicate that both men fell into a river, not a chasm, and that a stunned Red floated downstream and was washed ashore. Drake apparently drowned and his body got caught in rocks at the water's edge, enabling the search party to find him. The omission of these scenes, and any explanation of them, renders the serial's denouement incomprehensible. Without knowing anything about a river below the suspension bridge, viewers are left to assume that Red survived a high fall onto rocky ground—a fall that killed his adversary—with nothing more than a sprained or broken arm. This rare editorial misstep mars what is otherwise regarded as one of Republic's best Western serials.

A text title at the beginning of Chapter One pinpoints the date as 1870 and the story's primary location as Mesquite, Arizona. A band of outlaws headed by One-Eye Chapin (Robert Kortman), acting on the orders of saloon owner Ace Hanlon (Noah Beery), has been brutalizing local ranchers and running them off their property. The land is then scooped up by local banker Calvin Drake (Harry Worth), who already holds mortgages on some of it and buys the rest for pennies on the dollar. Drake is the secret mastermind behind this campaign of terror. He has learned the Western Pacific plans to build its railroad through the territory, and by obtaining the land he can force the line to pay him a fortune for their right-of-way. Only Ace Hanlon, his unscrupulous partner, shares this secret.

Colonel Tom Ryder (William Farnum) decides to form a vigilante committee with the consent of local Sheriff Luke Andrews (Lloyd Ingraham), and he consults Drake, who's considered a trusted member of the community. The banker warns Hanlon to nip this insurgence in the bud, and Ace dispatches three hired killers to murder Ryder and Andrews. They are seen by Andrews' daughter Beth (Vivian Coe), who identifies them to the Colonel's son Red (Don Barry). Bent on vengeance, he strides boldly into the saloon to which the assassins have returned. In the shootout that follows, Red kills two of the trio and captures the third, a man named Shark (Ray Teal).

Worried that Shark will talk, Ace and crooked new sheriff Dade (Carleton Young) fake an escape. Beth Andrews, on her way to the Circle R, sees her dad's murderer boarding a stagecoach and kidnapped by him. Little Beaver (Tommy Cook), a witness to the hostage-taking, races to the ranch and informs Red, who overtakes the stage. The driver is thrown from his perch, and while Red is slugging it out with Shark inside, the runaway coach hurtles over a cliff and plunges into a lake far below. Thus ends the first episode, "Murder on the Santa Fe Trail."

In Chapter Two, the recaptured Shark is shot by another Hanlon henchman, who gets trampled by a posse's horses after being bulldogged by Red. The next several installments deals with the consequences of mortgaging the Circle R, which Red's aunt, the Duchess, does willingly to raise money for her displaced neighbors. Seeing an opportunity to gain control of the ranch, Drake orders Hanlon to prevent the Duchess from repaying the loan. The available water supply is poisoned and when Red attempts to drive his herd to another creek the pass is dynamited. (This cliffhanger is the only one in which Vivian Coe's Beth figures.)

Other subplots involve Red being framed for murder and his entry into a stagecoach race, winning a $5,000 purse that enables him to pay off the mortgage a matter of seconds before the note comes due. Drake has previously claimed to have sold the Circle R mortgage to something called "the S & S Land Company." With the aid of a county official Red learns that the S & S is a shell company backed by Ace Hanlon. This revelation sets into motion a chain of events that span the final three chapters.

A federal official, Commissioner Treadway (Hooper Atchley), arrives in Mesquite to check on the recent shady land deals. Red's pal Cherokee Sims (Hal Taliferro) is slain by One-Eye, whom Red subsequently captures and kills in a fair fight. Ace Hanlon is exposed and tries to escape with Cal Drake, who holds the valuable document he needs to deal with the railroad. But the crooked banker condemns his erstwhile partner as a bungler and shoots him down in cold blood, precipitating the chase in which Red eventually stops him at the suspension bridge.

There was nothing new or novel about the script for *Adventures of Red Ryder*. Virtually every situation included in the 12 chapters had been used before, in some cases dozens of times. The serial was devised as an all-action vehicle to establish Don Barry as a "B"-Western star, and from that standpoint it succeeded admirably. Even the much-lauded and over-praised *Daredevils of the West* can't compare with *Red Ryder* in terms of the variety of stuntwork. *Daredevils* has the set-destroying fistfights Republic fans love, but Dave Sharpe's acrobatic feats and the all-around splendid horse work in *Red Ryder* definitely give the earlier serial the edge in my book.

In 1940 Republic Pictures enjoyed a well-deserved reputation as the movie industry's top purveyor of fast-action Westerns turned out on low budgets. Its crews were equally well schooled in studio and location filmmaking, moving quickly and efficiently, anticipating the needs and wants of skillful directors with whom they worked frequently. For a sterling example of their flawless coordination one need look no further than the last 300 feet of *Red Ryder*'s first episode. The stagecoach pursuit and fight ranks among the most thrilling sequences of its kind. Direction, stunting, editing, scoring, location photography, process-screen work—you will rarely see such a polished, exhilarating three minutes in a production of this budgetary class. To execute a sequence of that length and complexity today—assuming one could still find experienced people to do it—would take a week or more. Bill Witney and his Republic crew did it in less than a day.

Despite the bad taste it left in the mouths of directors Witney and English, *Adventures of Red Ryder* succeeded in its purpose. Billed as Don "Red" Barry, the troublesome leading man became the star Herbert Yates anticipated. He made 29 "B" Westerns for Republic between 1940 and 1944, guest-starring in several more and appearing in non-Westerns as well. He quit the studio in 1948 and was off the screen for almost a full year. Although Don worked right up until the time of his tragic death in 1980, his career never regained the momentum it had at Republic and he rarely had a lead role after 1950.

Stephen Slesinger acquired the Red Ryder movie rights from Victor Orsatti in 1943 and wasted no time negotiating another, more lucrative deal with Republic. Herbert Yates' studio produced and distributed 23 feature films using Fred Harman's comic-strip characters first starring Bill Elliott and then Allan Lane. Constant motion-picture visibility for the property helped Slesinger close multiple deals for licensed product. But his most profitable and culturally significant transaction came to fruition in the spring of 1940, just as Republic's serial was being readied for national release. That's when the Daisy Manufacturing Company introduced its Red Ryder BB gun, a lever-action, spring-piston air rifle coveted by three generations of young boys and immortalized in the 1983 film *A Christmas Story* ("You'll shoot your eye out!").

Never officially re-released, *Adventures of Red Ryder* for several decades was considered a "lost" serial. It resurfaced in the late Seventies and was licensed by The Nostalgia Merchant for distribution in 16mm and on video tape. Now available on DVD as well, it continues to win new adherents. But it still has old fans, including a very special one. Tommy Cook, the screen's original Little Beaver, still remembers seeing the serial complete, one chapter at a time, during its first-run theatrical release. Every Saturday his father drove him and his friends to their local movie house, the Granada Theatre in Inglewood, a suburb of Los Angeles. Tommy says he whooped and hollered at the screen like all the other kids. Moreover, as a spry 87-year-old, he looks back on his time making serials for Republic as "the happiest days of my life."

Anatomy of a Serial: The Making of Spy Smasher

(1942, Republic Pictures Corporation)

REPUBLIC'S *Adventures of Captain Marvel* had not yet completed its first-run engagements when Fawcett Publications, delighted with the serial, inaugurated new negotiations with the studio to license its other comic-book characters. In June of 1941 Republic offered Fawcett $1,500 for screen rights to Bulletman and Spy Smasher, only to rethink the offer when DC Comics sued its top competitor, claiming that Captain Marvel infringed upon their copyrighted character Superman. Republic was named as a co-defendant in the suit, which would drag on for 12 years. As a result, studio brass determined that it would be unwise to make a Bulletman film: since that character (which debuted in a 1940 issue of Fawcett's *Nickel Comics*) had the ability to fly, he could be taken for another Superman knockoff. Therefore, the agreement was rewritten to license Spy Smasher alone for $750.

The 42-page contract, signed on August 28, 1941 by Republic Assistant Secretary Gordon Schaefer and Fawcett vice president Roger Fawcett, obligated the studio to use Spy Smasher's name in the film's title and faithfully replicate the character's costume but otherwise placed no restrictions on Republic's treatment of the character. Additionally, it granted Herbert J. Yates' studio a ten-year exclusive option of producing a sequel.

Based on Fawcett's verbal acceptance of the terms in June, Republic included the proposed chapter play, simply titled *Spy Smasher*, in its 1941-42 campaign book formally announcing the upcoming season's product slate. The lead-off serial was *King of the Texas Rangers*, followed by *Dick Tracy's Revenge* (ultimately released as *Dick Tracy vs. Crime Inc.*), *Spy Smasher*, and *Perils of Nyoka*, with Frances Gifford said to be reprising the role that she created in *Jungle Girl*. By this time the latter commenced production in early 1942, however, Gifford was unavailable and Kay Aldridge would take the role.

In the summer of 1941 Hiram S. "Bunny" Brown still held the position of serial producer and on August 8 hired Harrison Carter to adapt *Spy Smasher* from printed page to silver screen. Paid a weekly salary of $100, Carter spent five weeks on a 15,000-word treatment that would be fleshed out by the staff writers under the supervision of Norman S. Hall.

Introduced along with Captain Marvel in *Whiz Comics* #2 (February 1940)—the first number was a non-circulating issue prepared solely for copyright-registration purposes—Spy Smasher fought Fifth Columnists and foreign agents intent on undermining America's defense buildup for a possible entry in World War II. In reality one Alan Armstrong, "wealthy Virginia sportsman," the self-appointed scourge of espionage agents in the U. S. abandoned his pose of languorous fop and donned his unique costume (initially khaki jodhpurs and tunic, aviator's helmet and goggles, and flowing red cape) to do battle with spies and saboteurs. His most handy accessory was the Gyrosub, a combination of automobile, autogyro, and submarine.

Armstrong had a fianceé, lovely blonde Eve Corby, whose father was an admiral in U. S. Naval Intelligence and therefore privy to actionable threats facing the homeland. At first Spy Smasher traded upon knowledge gleaned from contact with Admiral Corby, but within a year or so of being introduced he accepted assignments from government agencies, although his connection with the Feds became official following the declaration of war. His earliest and most implacable foe was The Mask, a German diplomat who hid his identity prior to America's entrance into the war.

Either Carter or the serial unit's staff writers came up with the brilliant idea of making Alan Armstrong a foreign correspondent who adopted the Spy Smasher persona after being thought killed in France while covering the conflict. They also gave him an identical twin brother named Jack, who worked for Admiral Corby and was engaged to Eve. Someone realized Republic's target audience—kids who attended Saturday matinees—would already be aware of one Jack Armstrong, an All-American Boy whose exploits were broadcast on a popular radio serial. For that reason, neither Alan nor Jack was ever addressed by his surname; the former routinely appeared in Spy Smasher garb and the latter was referred to by the Mask's henchmen as "Corby's man."

According to Republic, the Mask was a German naval officer just beginning his American activities as the story got underway. This, of course, left him with no reason for wearing the protective face covering: Nobody in the U. S. would know who he was. Yet he wore it anyway, at least part of the time, to keep faith with the comic book's loyal followers.

Hall and his collaborators—Ronald Davidson, William Lively, Joseph O'Donnell, and Joseph F. Poland—worked diligently on the 12-chapter screenplay throughout the fall of 1941, completing what Republic called an "estimating script," circulated to studio department heads for purposes of compiling a budget.

Even before finishing *King of the Texas Rangers*, Bunny Brown rocked the serial unit by announcing he had accepted a commission in the Army Signal Corps and would be leaving Republic's employ immediately. The news hit unit directors William Witney and John English especially hard; they had come to respect Brown and enjoyed working for him despite the minuscule budgets and difficult working conditions to which the makers of chapter plays were typically subjected. Bill Witney, especially, disliked change and dreaded the prospect of "breaking in" a new producer.

With preparation of *Dick Tracy vs. Crime Inc.* already underway, Brown's replacement was not long in coming. Promoted from within the studio ranks, it was William J. O'Sullivan, a 29-year-old New Yorker who had worked at the old Biograph studio and Yates' Consolidated Film laboratory before relocating to Hollywood in 1939. Starting at Republic as an assistant director, he quickly moved up to unit manager and was rumored to be a pet of Yates. A fastidious dresser whose every pomaded hair was always in place, O'Sullivan habitually exuded the air of one "to the manner born." Bunny Brown had been warm and friendly; the dapper Irishman, cool and aloof, made a bad first impression.

After finishing *Dick Tracy vs. Crime Inc.*, John English asked to transfer out of the serial unit. For months he had been itching to direct feature films, although Witney in his 1996 autobiography pegged his partner's decision to the arrival of O'Sullivan. After screening the last of *Crime Inc.*'s dailies with the remaining director, the new producer asked Witney what *his* intentions were. Although Bill believed that America would soon be drawn in the war and he would go into military service, he vowed to stay with the serial unit as long as possible.

Up to this time Republic serials had always been directed by two men alternate work; while one shot, his partner would prepare for the next day's scenes. In this way the unit worked like the proverbial well-oiled machine. Occasionally the routine varied, especially when inclement weather affected tightly scheduled location jaunts, but it had been standard operating procedure dating back to the Mascot days.

Replying to O'Sullivan's request for the name of other directors he thought likely replacements for English, Witney opined that he could helm chapter plays solo provided that he got "close cooperation" from the producer—and, by extension, the unit managers and assistant directors. O'Sullivan took him up on the offer and promised to cooperate any way he could, given time and budget constraints.

Spy Smasher's estimating script was complete by December 1. Witney was not impressed. "When I read the script," he wrote in his autobiography, "I found that the writers hadn't left out anything. They even had the kitchen sink and had added the toilet. There was so much flag waving and propaganda that I thought the whole thing stunk."

The scripters had written into Chapter One an introductory sequence to have been delivered by FBI director J. Edgar Hoover. The nation's top cop would stress the importance of ordinary Americans remaining vigilant, and congratulate men like Spy Smasher for holding the line against Fifth Columnists attempting to subvert the national defense effort. Republic went as far as to schedule the filming of Hoover's introduction at the NBC radio station in Washington, D. C.

Then came December 7 and the Japanese sneak attack on Pearl Harbor. Suddenly, the idea of Hoover importuning ordinary Americans to be vigilant seemed rather superfluous. It was no longer enough to monitor subversive activities. The nation, finally, was at war with the Axis. The battle for democracy's future had officially been joined.

No one could be certain—at least, not yet—how the war would affect priorities in Hollywood. At Republic, preparation of *Spy Smasher* continued with alacrity. The writers were almost done with final shooting scripts, but O'Sullivan had them revise Chapter Nine, which involved the hijacking of a gold train by the Mask's men. In the early days of the war, many people believed the government would nationalize the railroad industry. Since such a move would inevitably disrupt the plans of filmmakers, the episode was rewritten to have heavies steal a gold-bearing armored car.

Republic typically submitted estimating scripts to the Production Code Administration so that potentially censorable scenes could be adjusted. The Breen office suggested deleting a Chapter Two shot that would have shown a German soldier accidentally hanged during a fight scene, and a Chapter Three glimpse of Spy Smasher pointing a machine gun at the camera. Incorporating these minor changes, as well as others dictated by budgetary concerns, the writing staff completed the final shooting script on December 9.

That same day O'Sullivan called Witney into his office to report that the front office had okayed a budget of $153,682, more than 20 percent of which was allotted to what studio bean counters called "non-productive salaries and expenses"—clerical costs, liability and unemployment insurance, and studio overhead (more than a sixth of the total amount). An additional $4,000 was set aside as a "reserve for contingencies." This left approximately $120,000 for actual production.

Principal photography was scheduled to consume four weeks, at that time the Republic average for a 12-chapter serial. But with shooting set to begin on Monday, December 22, Witney realized he would have to absorb time lost to observance of the Christmas and New Year's holidays. "That was the moment I began to regret telling O'Sullivan I could handle the serial by myself," the director admitted to me in 1991. "It would have been a tough schedule to meet in any event, but I remember going home that day and saying to Maxine [his wife, actress Maxine Doyle], 'What the hell did I get myself into?' " He would earn every penny of his weekly salary, at that time $175.

Casting director Robert Webb and his assistant Nate Edwards had already drafted a list of candidates for the principal roles. Witney and O'Sullivan agreed on handsome, square-jawed Kane Richmond, a former Fox contractee who had previously starred in two 1935 serials, *The Lost City* and *Adventures of Rex and Rinty*. A good actor, and an athletically gifted one to boot, Richmond looked like a comic-book hero come to life. He was officially signed on December 16 for $450 weekly, with a four-week guarantee.

Witney chose shapely brunette Marguerite Chapman to play Eve Corby; she was a former telephone switchboard operator who broke into modeling as a Powers Girl before crashing Hollywood in 1939. After brief stints at 20th Century-Fox and Warner Brothers (neither very productive), she was freelancing when she tested for *Spy Smasher*. Chapman, in her first female lead, was paid $225 for one week's work. The same deal went to Italian actor Franco Corsaro, who would appear as French army officer Pierre Durand.

Tris Coffin had played uncredited bit roles in two Witney-English serials, *Dick Tracy's G-Men* (1939) and *Mysterious Doctor Satan* (1940). He was Witney's choice for the part of Drake, The Mask's chief American operative, earning $650. Sam Flint got $400 to play Admiral Corby. Paul Bryar, Tom London, and John James were picked as other heavies. The Mask himself, German-born stage actor Hans Schumm, was paid just $300 for his work in the serial, despite being the villain of the piece and getting fourth billing on the list of principal players. James Dale, whose uncanny resemblance to Kane Richmond made him a perfect stand-in for either brother when both appeared on screen together, earned more than twice Schumm's salary—$625 with overtime factored in—without speaking dialogue or receiving billing.

The incomparable David Sharpe, stuntman extraordinaire, was the first full-time "ramrod" employed by Republic's serial unit and had held that position since late 1939. In this capacity he not only doubled a serial's leading man but also chose the other stunt performers to be used. Sharpe relied heavily on a group of stuntmen known informally as "the Cousins," including former circus and vaudeville acrobats along with expert drivers and semi-professional athletes. Among them were Jimmy Fawcett, Carey Loftin, Eddie Parker, Loren Riebe, Tom Steele, Ken Terrill, Louis Tomei, and Bud Wolfe. Of this brotherhood, only Eddie Parker would be absent for *Spy Smasher*, being otherwise occupied doubling the leading man in a Columbia serial that was filming at the same time.

Due to the tremendous amount of scripted action sequences in the serial, Sharpe also hired stuntmen Tommy Coats, John Daheim (who doubled Spy Smasher's brother Jack in fight sequences featuring both men), Duke Green, Jerry Jerome, Bert LeBaron, Gil Perkins, Charles Regan, Buddy Roosevelt, Cy Slocum, Duke Taylor, Sid Troy, and Bill Wilkus. Previously, that job had been undertaken by the studio's casting department, but the ramrod would know better whom to hire based on the script's requirements. Making his final serial appearance as a bit player doing stunt work was the legendary Yakima Canutt, who would soon transition to stunt coordinator, then second-unit director, and eventually full director. Sharpe earned $1,375 for his work on *Spy Smasher*, the other stunters were paid an aggregate of $4,440—a staggering amount for any production in this budgetary class.

The whole cast's final cost, including overtime, would come to $15,056.

Spy Smasher continued the Republic-serial trend—inaugurated by producer O'Sullivan in the previous chapter play, *Dick Tracy vs. Crime Inc.*—of utilizing the entire studio, not just the back lot or standing sets, for the staging of lengthy or elaborate sequences. The writers were specifically instructed to do so, partly as a way to stretch budgets and later because of wartime travel restrictions. The Mill Building, standing next to the Art Department on the lot's southeast corner, was where sets and miniatures were constructed, but it became the scene of a major fight sequence in the middle of Chapter Four. The Transportation Department garage, normally used for vehicle repair and maintenance, substituted for a rental-car depot in Chapter Six. The addition of two small, strategically placed signs transformed the studio lumberyard into the Atlas Lumber Company, site of a Chapter Seven chase ad fight. Stage 10, one of the lot's two largest, appeared in Chapter Eight as a warehouse.

Chapters Two and Three, unfolding largely on the Vichy French island of Martinidad, made good use of the back lot's "Old Mexico" section: Hacienda Square, Spanish Street, and Cantina Street. (The adobe-style building with their tile roofs are unmistakable.) A barn employed by counterfeiters is the one built for Gene Autry's *Melody Ranch* (1940). The Chapter Three scene of it being blown up, frequently seen in Republic serials and Westerns of the Forties and Fifties, was originally shot for *Dick Tracy vs. Crime Inc.*

A camera shop figuring prominently in Chapter Six was among a group of building facades comprising New York Square, erected behind New York Street and Western Street. The side entrance onto Carpenter Street, bordering the south end of the Republic lot, was also used briefly. And, of course, the familiar cave set was revised considerably for service in the Chapter One climax.

O'Sullivan was fortunate in being able to commandeer a large mansion set recently built for *Yokel Boy*, a rube comedy starring Eddie Foy Jr. It consisted of a spacious living room and adjacent foyer with a winding staircase and second-floor balcony. Initially seen at the beginning of Chapter One as the inside of Gestapo headquarters in Paris, the living room was redressed with different props and furniture to become part of the Corby home. The foyer and staircase could be glimpsed in later episodes when the living-room door was open but were not otherwise used again.

Other interiors required the consumption of more resources than O'Sullivan would have liked. Some $16,000 was allotted to building of sets, which was supervised by long-time Republic construction boss Ralph Oberg, a dour, burly Swede who designed them all himself prior to establishment of the studio Art Department in 1937. The construction budget included $2,825 for miniatures to be crafted by sibling specialists Howard and Theodore Lydecker, by that time turning out models every bit as good as (and often better than) those produced at the major studios.

Working closely with studio production manager Max Schoenberg and serial unit manager Mack D'Agostino, director Witney spent weeks preparing for what he would later call "one of the roughest schedules I had ever tried to meet." December 22 finally rolled around and principal photography began. Serial casts and crews in those days normally assembled in the studio at 6 a.m. each morning, Monday through Saturday. Grips, prop men, and electricians prepared the set: arranging props and furniture, moving light stands into place, stringing cables where they wouldn't be tripped over, and so on. In spare moments they gulped coffee and wolfed down a donut. Typically, the process consumed an hour. While it was going on, cast members were having makeup applied and wardrobes adjusted if necessary.

By seven a.m., Witney was on the set ready to go. Thanks to Republic's famous production board, developed by unit manager George Webster and refined by assistant director Louis Germonprez, he knew exactly which players would be working that day and how many "set-ups" (changes in lighting and camera position) he was expected to get through. Jack Mathis, chronicler of the studio's history, described this innovative production aid in his 1999 book *Republic Confidential: Volume 1—The Studio*:

> Sized in relatively large portable panels for features and enormous ones for serials that covered much of an entire Production office wall, the crosshatched scheduling boards were overlaid with a clear acetate sheet and fitted with movable vertical plastic strips to isolate any sector. Information entered into the grid-pattern cells by the unit manager and first assistant director using an erasable red grease pencil profiled every single scripted role scene-by-scene and day-by-day as to where, when, and with whom each sequence was to be shot. Plotted in this easily read and revisable manner, each board depicted an entire production in timetable form that kept efficient track of all talent—especially the day players and stunt people—permitting completion of their parts as expediently and hence as economically as possible.

Witney, O'Sullivan, and the writers had all worked with one goal: to make *Spy Smasher* seem like its four-colored counterpart come to life. And since comic-book heroes subdued their adversaries with fists rather than guns—in acknowledgment that their readers were mostly children—the serial was designed with a heretofore unparalleled emphasis on lengthy brawls with as many daring leaps, falls, and athletic stunts as Dave Sharpe and his crew could cram into their fight routines.

Doubling Spy Smasher, Sharpe relied not only on his own prodigious, preternatural athletic ability but also something he learned from Douglas Fairbanks, with whom he worked as a teenaged tumbler on *The Thief of Bagdad* (1924). Fairbanks too was a superbly trained athlete, but he enhanced the effect of his screen stunts by having sets designed to accommodate the limits of his abilities. In other words, if he could leap a distance of 15 feet by straining, but 12 feet without appearing to strain, he made certain that sets and props were arranged at the lesser distance to make his feats seem graceful and effortless. Sharpe did much the same throughout the serial—indeed, throughout his career. Over the course of 12 chapters Spy Smasher never walked around a desk his stunt double couldn't leap over.

Spy Smasher's fast-moving fight sequences took several hours to choreograph, rehearse, and shoot. In a 1973 film-festival panel discussion moderated by serial historian Alan G. Barbour, Sharpe was asked how the donnybrooks were staged.

> Our pattern was this. Bill [Witney], when he was breaking down his script and was cognizant of each and every step there would be in the action, would check the set with the art director, see how many windows were in it, establish how the set would be decorated, and would put in the furniture he wanted to have wrecked. Maybe he'd want a staircase or balcony. Then he'd check the location of the windows and exits. With the architectural and geographic locations fixed in his mind, he would lay out just how he wanted the action to start and finish.
>
> Invariably, Bill would call me in and explain what he desired, where we'd begin, what characters were involved, what incident precipitated the action. He would give me a script, which was unusual, but Billy was like that, and it points up a difference between Republic and other studios: everyone knew exactly what was happening at all times.
>
> We would discuss [the fight] and, from his predetermined patterns and my suggestions after I'd analyze the sequence, would evolve a routine. Then we'd get the best men available to double the principals involved. At other studios the system was different. We'd come to the studio, they'd hire us and talk to us for about five minutes, and turn us loose. The cameras would grind away and we'd fight until we couldn't go on any more. Of course, everyone was exhausted. When you go for three or four minutes in a fight, your timing and coordination are way off.

Bill's invention was to pre-determine the entire routine as I've just explained, and then break it down into segments where we would do only two or three punches or falls. It was just a matter of "taking" 10 or 15 seconds, but they would be done superbly. This is one of the things I've been asked about so much; the answer to why there was such a fluidity of movement, why [a Republic serial fight] never lost its tempo. It was because of Billy's way of shooting. He'd only shoot a small segment but in his master optical picture of [the whole sequence]. But that segment would be perfection. Everyone would be at his best. When a man had to do a stunt, say a fight had to go up a staircase and a fellow had to come through a railing, he didn't have to do that if he'd already fought for two minutes and was so exhausted he couldn't even push through the railing. There would only be two or three punches exchanged before he'd actually do the stunt—just enough to make it overlay and meld well. That was Billy's idea and it was a great one.

The collaboration of director Witney and stunt coordinator Sharpe resulted in the best fights ever filmed for a Republic serial. Segmenting the brawls and inserting close-ups of principals to fill the gaps wasn't new; by 1941 it was standard operating procedure on Witney-English chapter plays. But *Spy Smasher* took the practice to a higher level; both the frequency and intensity of fistic encounters in this episodic thriller inspired heavy Tom London in later years to refer to it as "a real stuntman's serial" that "kept us on the run" with its action quotient.

Nearly half of *Spy Smasher* had been filmed when the company made its only significant location jaunt. Early on Thursday, January 15, cast and crew arrived in beautiful Lake Elsinore, about 70 miles southeast of Los Angeles, to begin four 16-hour days of shooting. Location Manager John Bourke, one of Republic's earliest employees in the Production Department, had analyzed the script and found spots near Elsinore that could be used for at least a half-dozen major sequences.

The first stop was a water tower needed for the second reel of Chapter Seven. It would be blown up (in miniature, of course) at episode's end, with Spy Smasher escaping the blast by leaping from the structure's top onto a tarpaulin-covered truck parked below. Scaling the tower's winding staircase, Dave Sharpe noted the presence of wind and feared the character's cape might billow enough to create a parasail effect that could cause him to miss the truck. Wardrobe man Ted Towey, who always accompanied the serial unit on location to address costume mishaps, quickly sewed the cape to Sharpe's tunic and trousers. This last-minute solution to an unanticipated problem proved adequate and the stunt was completed without incident.

The unit then proceeded to the lake for motorboat sequences, working on the water as long as sunlight allowed. Remaining scenes with the rented Chris-Craft boats were completed the following morning. Later that day saw a flurry of activity on the Showboat, a unique lakeshore restaurant built to resemble a showboat with its own pier. Built in the Twenties, it was 200 feet long and weighed 200 tons. The Showboat was mounted on wheels atop steel rails that extended into the water, enabling management to roll the entire structure into the lake. It had previously been used in the Republic serials *Mysterious Doctor Satan* (1940) and *Dick Tracy vs. Crime Inc.* (1941); in *Spy Smasher* it was the scene of a dramatic last-chapter confrontation between the hero and the Mask's lieutenant Drake. A violent fight (filmed previously in a cabin set erected on a Republic soundstage) ends with Spy Smasher dangling from the top deck as the heavy pulls away in a motorboat to rendezvous with the Mask's submarine.

The script called for Our Hero to regain his balance and dive into the water just as Drake's boat pulled away from the dock. Catching hold of a mooring rope trailing behind the craft, the hero pulled himself toward the boat hand over hand, eventually reaching it and clambering aboard to engage the heavy in another fistic battle. Sharpe timed the stunt perfectly but had failed to account for the strength of the backwash. As Bill Witney described the scene in his autobiography:

I yelled to the boat driver to hit the throttle, and soon Davy was planing over the water. I yelled cut, and as the boat made a circle to pick him up, I realized he was in trouble. When we came along beside him I reached down and grabbed his arm. One of the grips helped me pull him aboard [the camera boat]. He was as white as a sheet. I rolled him on his stomach and pounded his back. He spit up about a gallon of Lake Elsinore. I helped him sit up, and he coughed. "You son of a bitch, you tried to drown me!" I swatted him on the back [and said], "Why didn't you let go?" Another cough. "Because I thought I could pull myself up to the boat." Years later we were at a film festival and Davy told the audience, pointing at me, "Did I ever tell you about the time he tried to drown me?"

The sequence was completed by splitting the scripted action into several shots. A view from the boat's stern pictured Sharpe pulling himself hand over hand toward it. The shot was slightly undercranked, which made the backwash seem more rapid and violent. The next cut, with Spy Smasher climbing into the boat, was shot back at the studio on Stage 5, where Bud Thackery's Process Department did rear-screen photography.

The next two days, Saturday and Sunday, were spent in and around the Los Angeles Brick & Clay Products Company at Alberhill, six miles north of Lake Elsinore. By scheduling Republic's visit for the weekend, therefore not disrupting the plant's business, Bourke had been able to rent the facility for a mere $200. All told, including location rentals along with food and lodging for cast and crew, the Elsinore trip cost just $3,541, not counting $366 for boat rentals and the overtime paid out for work on Sunday.

Closer to home, the *Spy Smasher* company filmed scenes at the Van Nuys police station and the Consumers Rock & Gravel Company in North Hollywood. Nearby Studio City landmarks, including Ventura Boulevard, can be spotted in car chases. Iverson's Ranch near Chatsworth, a familiar site to fans of Republic serials and Westerns, hosted the serial unit for a major Chapter Four sequence involving the Mask's new "batplane" (a variation on Spy Smasher's gyrosub, which did not appear in the serial).

The Lydeckers' miniature batplane had bomb-bay doors that could be opened by either a small electrical charge or a hook at the end of piano wire pulled taut when the craft's ascent reached a certain point. The wobbly but otherwise convincing full-size version consisted of sheet metal stretched over a wooden frame.

The model built for Chapter Seven's water-tower explosion was so solidly put together Howard Lydecker feared it wouldn't topple after the relatively small charge was set off, so one of his technicians fastened a tug-wire that could be pulled when the blast occurred.

Reaching back to a technique they pioneered in *Daredevils of the Red Circle* (1939), the Lydeckers constructed an underground tunnel that would be flooded with burning high-test fuel instead of sea water. The Chapter One climax called for Spy Smasher to pump a railroad handcar down a track just ahead of the flames. Kane Richmond performed the action on a stationary handcar raised a few inches off the floor on Stage 5, where all scenes involving rear-projection were photographed by Bud Thackery's Process Department. For the last shot in the episode, in which a wall of flame rises in front of Spy Smasher (to simulate the torrent of fire having overtaken him), technicians placed a small butane gas jet between the actor and the camera.

By far the most complex challenge facing the Lydeckers on this serial was the fiery and explosive climax to Chapter Twelve, which had the Mask torpedoing an American munitions terminal before going to a watery grave when his submarine hit one of the harbor's underwater mines. The Miniatures Department created an entire waterfront—wharves, warehouses, gasoline storage tanks, assorted vehicles, even tiny fuel drums—at a scale measuring three quarters of an inch to one foot. This sizable diorama was placed at the edge of a water tank in the back lot. Since the sequence was set *and* shot at night, the miniature buildings were equipped with small light bulbs whose illumination was visible through the tiny windows.

Special-effects cinematographers Bud Thackery and William Bradford filmed the sequence from a rowboat held steady by crew members in the tank. Wire-mesh screens separated personnel from the diorama—a precaution against flying debris from the explosions. Technicians prepared squibs filled with black powder and flash powder, packed tightly with percussion caps. Inside the miniature gas storage tanks were toy balloons filled with high-octane gasoline along with the squibs; these provided fireballs when the charges were touched off. Underneath the diorama was planted a network of perforated pipes through which natural gas flowed for ignition simulating the wharf's eruption into flames.

As technicians detonated the charges one by one, the scene was filmed at 64 frames per second (producing slow motion) for maximum realism. For the shot in which the Mask's submarine surfaced in a burning sea, a mixture of crude oil and natural gas, piped into the tank just beneath the water line, blazed merrily while the model sub was towed by thin cables. This sequence was the most elaborate of its kind produced by the Lydeckers for a serial up to this time.

Production ended on Thursday, January 29. *Spy Smasher* finished one day over schedule, with 1,773 scripted scenes filmed in 32 working days of 12 to 16 hours each. That worked out to 55 scenes per day. Cast and crew were thoroughly exhausted. Years later, Kane Richmond told Alan Barbour that Spy Smasher was the most physically demanding role he had in his entire career. The *two* most demanding, actually. Alan quoted the actor as saying, "It wasn't just all those goddamned fights. It was doing everything twice in scenes with the brother. I'd have to go through all the moves in the Spy Smasher outfit, then change into the suit and do everything in the same scene as the brother. And I was damn lucky whenever I got more than three minutes to change!"

In 1991 Witney told me Richmond worked harder than any other leading man he'd directed up to that point. "Even when we had Davy or the stand-in [James Dale] in a scene, Kane would still be there as the other brother, in or out of costume. It was a punishing job, but he was a pretty tough guy. He held up well under the schedule and didn't complain. I had a lot of respect for him."

The *Spy Smasher* company officially wrapped on the 29th with dinner served on an empty sound stage. As per serial-unit custom, many members of cast and crew followed the meal with drinks at the nearby Little Bohemia watering hole on Ventura Boulevard. Witney made a mildly disparaging remark about their producer, who had not joined the party. This angered construction boss and O'Sullivan partisan Ralph Oberg, whose long-simmering feud with the director was about to erupt. As Witney got up to visit the men's room, the big Swede grabbed him from behind, swung him around, and pasted him in the face. Kane Richmond, perhaps having portrayed Spy Smasher a bit too long, jumped up and hit Oberg on the chin "with a punch I can still hear," as Witney wrote in his memoir. Several crew members grabbed the drunken construction boss and literally threw him out of the bar onto Ventura Boulevard. (The director claimed he later confronted Oberg when both men were sober, and the Swede backed down.)

Film editors Edward Todd and Tony Martinelli were still finishing the last chapters of *Dick Tracy vs. Crime Inc.* when the final dailies were printed. They began work on the new chapter play in mid-February. *Spy Smasher*'s release print—12 chapters, with the first episode coming in at three reels, the remainder at two reels—would total roughly 20,000 feet. Witney and company (including process and miniature photographers) had exposed 120,000 feet.

During 1942, the interior chapter length was standardized at approximately 16 minutes and 40 seconds. That worked out to exactly 1,500 feet, given the sound-era projection speed of 90 feet per minute. Chapters occasionally went long or short by 20, 30, or even 50 feet, but rarely more. Republic, it should be remembered, was the brainchild of Herbert J. Yates, owner of Consolidated Film Enterprises, the laboratory for a big chunk of the movie industry. Having serial episodes of uniform length made it easy to calculate print costs; measuring total footage in round numbers made it easier to do the math.

As Todd and Martinelli began assembly of raw footage into chapter form, the optical effects department at Consolidated's

Hollywood plant produced the credits used for each chapter's beginning and ending. Republic's Art Department forwarded sketches with the desired effect: an animated "wipe" of searchlights above a cityscape, forming a "V" that the musical scoring sounded out in the first four notes of Beethoven's Fifth Symphony, while showing that letter's equivalent in Morse Code: dot-dot-dot-*dash*. The crossing searchlight beams wiped title cards onto the screen in one of Republic's most innovative serial openings. The composite images were expertly rendered by Consolidated's state-of-the-art optical printer. Main and end titles were produced for $1,016; additional titles and inserts (also prepared by CFI) cost $1,276. The Hollywood lab charged Republic $1,349 more for such optical effects as fades and lap dissolves.

The dramatic rendition of Beethoven's Fifth was adapted and orchestrated by musical director Mort Glickman with help from Cy Feuer and Raoul Kraushaar. The remainder of the serial's musical score was composed by Glickman, Paul Sawtell, and Arnold Schwarzwald. Together they wrote 23 pieces of music, many titled as chapters were ("America Beware," "Iron Coffin," "Stratosphere Invaders," et al). The "Spy Smasher Theme" used those first four notes of Beethoven's Fifth as a motif. Among the last Republic serials to have a totally original score, *Spy Smasher* benefitted enormously from Glickman's work. Interestingly, several of its musical cues were reused in a 1944 serial, *Haunted Harbor*, which also starred Kane Richmond.

The editing was completed by Todd and Martinelli for a flat $3,000. Total laboratory expenses incurred during this process, up to conforming of the final negative, amounted to another $8,448. This brought the serial's negative cost to $156,431, a meager 2 percent over budget. As per Republic policy, prints of the chapter play's first half—six chapters—had been struck and were shipped to the firm's 39 national exchanges by Saturday, April 4, when first-run exhibitors showed the opening episode to audiences.

Republic's top executives habitually screened the first two or three episodes of every serial and opined on them freely. The reports on *Spy Smasher* were unanimously favorable, the consensus view being that it was the best chapter play yet produced by the company. Oddly, several major trade papers (including *Variety* and *Motion Picture Herald*) didn't review it, but those that did seemed impressed. *Film Daily*'s anonymous critic wrote, "While this serial stretches the imagination almost to the breaking point, it packs a big punch and a world of action, if the initial chapter is at all representative."

Showmen's Trade Review characterized *Spy Smasher* as "exciting" in its notice's headline. "Based on a plot as up to the minute as tomorrow's newspaper," wrote the *Review*'s critic, "this serial gets off to a fast start with plenty of excitement crammed into the first chapter. . . . The kids in your town should surely go for this subject, which caters to their love for action and at the same time strikes a patriotic note."

As it did for *Adventures of Captain Marvel*, the entire Fawcett publishing organization—30 or so field men and 700 distributors throughout the country—agreed to cooperate with exhibitors who booked *Spy Smasher* for their theaters. The big promotional campaign included full-page ads for the serial in all Fawcett comic books; these ads contained coupons that readers were asked to fill out and return to the publisher, naming their local theater if it wasn't playing *Spy Smasher*. These coupons were sent to Republic, which in turn forwarded them to its salesmen in the appropriate territories, This enabled the sales force to make targeted visits to recalcitrant showmen, explaining that local patrons had requested the serial.

In some cases, the publishing company's field operatives addressed groups of exhibitors to explain various cross-promotional opportunities. Fawcett's New York-based promotion manager Max Wolff convened a meeting of Warner Brothers' New Jersey district theater managers and local independent exhibitors at which he outlined in detail the *Spy Smasher* promotional campaign. As a direct result of this confab, nine Warners houses booked the serial immediately and others promised to follow suit.

Republic reciprocated by producing a special trailer for the chapter play which showed the latest *Spy Smasher* comic book on screen and urged viewers to purchase it from local vendors. One of the most successful examples of promotion at the neighborhood level was supplied by Louis Stein, manager of the Stanley Theatre in Newark, New Jersey. Working closely with Fawcett's Newark representative, Sam Nichols, the independent exhibitor plugged the arrival of Chapter One two weeks before its scheduled playdate.

For the next 13 days the back page of the Stanley's daily program brochure was given over entirely to advertising the first episode and announcing items that would be given away free to patrons who showed up for the initial chapter. All children in attendance would be presented with both a four-color photo and pinback button of Spy Smasher, along with a copy of Fawcett's *Whiz Comics*. To promote the *Spy Smasher* comic book Stein ran the special trailer every day during the run-up to Chapter One. Additionally, he posted a 40x60 color display in the theater lobby. Three hundred one-sheet posters with "Stanley Theatre" snipes pasted on their fronts were distributed to all local newsstands and candy stores that sold Fawcett comic books.

Manager Stein's dedication to successfully launching *Spy Smasher* paid off handsomely when nearly 2,000 people showed up at the Stanley for the two Saturday programs featuring the first episode. All got photos and buttons but Fawcett had given Stein just 1,500 copies of *Whiz Comics*, thinking that would be more than enough.

Like most Republic serials of this period, *Spy Smasher* was rented to exhibitors for an average of $5.00 per chapter, although big-city chains might pay twice as much and small rural houses half as much. Salesmen working out of Republic exchanges had considerable leeway, with some even offering serials free to owners of big theater chains booking the studio's entire yearly output. *Spy Smasher*'s earnings are not available, but the serial is known to have been profitable. But Republic chose not to exercise its option for a sequel, which indicates that the studio collected less in rentals than on such big hits as *Dick Tracy* (1937) and *The Lone Ranger* (1938).

William Witney completed two more serials for O'Sullivan, *Perils of Nyoka* and *King of the Mounties*, and was nearly finished with a third, *G-Men vs. the Black Dragon*, when he was inducted into the Marine Corps. He served with distinction and returned to Republic after being mustered out in 1946, directing one more serial, *The Crimson Ghost*, before joining the Roy Rogers unit as main director. Witney remained at Republic for the duration of its existence as a production entity. Between 1937 and 1956 he helmed 11 "straight" feature films, 24 serials, and 39 Westerns. Of all the studio's contract directors, only Joe Kane wielded the megaphone more times.

In later years Witney guested at numerous film festivals, including the 1991 Hollywood Cinecon at which I was privileged to host a 50th anniversary *Captain Marvel* reunion featuring Frank Coghlan Jr., Louise Currie, and William Benedict in addition to Bill. Although I had chatted with him on previous occasions, we spoke for several hours prior to the reunion. Some of his remarks to me on that occasion have been included here and in other essays in this book. He died in 2002, several years after suffering a debilitating stroke. He was two months shy of celebrating his 87th birthday.

William J. O'Sullivan adapted the *Spy Smasher* formula to his subsequent chapter plays, including *King of the Mounties*, *G-Men vs. the Black Dragon*, *Secret Service in Darkest Africa*, *The Masked Marvel*, and *Captain America*. Even his one Western serial, *Daredevils of the West*, boasted a reliance on set-demolishing fights and constant explosions. The sudden retirement of Herbert Yates' longtime number two man Moe Siegel in early 1944 prompted a shift in management that saw O'Sullivan promoted from Associate Producer to Executive Producer in charge of Westerns and serials. The move doubled his weekly salary from $100 to $200 and entitled him to stock options. Head writer Ronald Davidson was temporarily named Associate Producer of the studio's chapter plays, answering directly to O'Sullivan. The dapper Irishman, who in later years evinced little interest in revisiting his days as Republic serial producer, passed away in 1994 at 81.

Kane Richmond made several more serials—the aforementioned *Haunted Harbor* for Republic, then *Jungle Raiders* (1945) and *Brick Bradford* (1947) for Columbia—and a number of "B" pictures for Republic and Monogram (including three as The Shadow) before quitting show business in 1948. He had been acting in motion pictures since 1930 without gaining much career traction, and at 42 years of age was convinced stardom had passed him by. Richmond entered the women's fashion business, beginning as a salesman. While headed to an oppointment with sample kit in hand, he suffered the indignity of passing a Los Angeles movie theater just as a showing of his final film, *Stage Struck*, ended and the audience exited. Richmond was instantly recognized and mobbed for autographs, making him late for his appointment. At one time, he later told film historian Sam Sherman, he would have been happy to mingle with fans. But in 1948, faced with the necessity of finding steady work, he regarded it as a humiliating nuisance. Kane Richmond ultimately succeeded in the business he adopted as a middle-aged man. He died in 1973 at 66.

Secret Service in Darkest Africa

(1943, Republic Pictures Corporation)

REPUBLIC'S PRODUCT LINEUP for the 1942-43 movie season included four serials, named in the company's "campaign book" (a lavishly designed brochure sent to exhibitors as an inducement to pre-order films released during the upcoming year) as *King of the Royal Mounted Strikes Again*, *G-Men vs. the Black Dragon*, *Daredevils of the West*, and *Samba in Darkest Africa*. The last-named listing was accompanied by an illustration of a knife-wielding Tarzan clone rescuing a scantily-clad Jane clone from wild animals.

The firm's initial chapter play for 1942-43 was retitled *King of the Mounties*. The second, *G-Men vs. the Black Dragon*, pitted Federal agent Rex Bennett against Japanese saboteurs working within the homeland. It was the last serial directed by William Witney for the duration; he entered the Marines shortly before principal photography ended. *Daredevils of the West* saw the temporary return of director John English to episodic thrillers, but he was determined to keep helming features. Serial-unit producer William J. O'Sullivan would need to find a replacement for the season's fourth and final entry. But that wasn't the only problem.

At some point very early in 1943, Republic brass made the determination that serial fans were not exactly clamoring for another Tarzan simulacrum. Fast-paced yarns with intrepid heroes battling Axis enemies were much in demand. Yet exhibitors had been promised a chapter play taking place in "darkest Africa." In late 1942 the Allies had invaded French North Africa, a campaign in which Morocco's port of Casablanca was one of the targets. This cosmopolitan city—fully half its residents were Europeans—had also made news in January as the site of an important and highly publicized conference attended by American president Franklin D. Roosevelt, British prime minister Winston Churchill, and Free French general Charles de Gaulle. Serendipitously, the Warner Brothers film *Casablanca* had been released the same day that the conference ended.

To capitalize on current events, *Samba in Darkest Africa* was retitled *Secret Service in Darkest Africa* and O'Sullivan instructed to make it a thriller with a wartime background, with Allied agents pitted against Nazi operatives in and around Casablanca.

With Ronald Davidson heading a team of writers that included Royal K. Cole, Basil Dickey, Jesse Duffy, Joseph O'Donnell, and Joseph F. Poland—experienced serial hands all—a treatment and the first four episodes had already been scripted by March 8, when freelance actor Rod Cameron was signed to play the lead. The hero was intended to be one Lance Hamilton, an autonomous U.S. government agent thought to have been killed while working with Russians during the siege of Stalingrad. With Cameron back in harness, producer O'Sullivan elected to have the lanky star reprise his *G-Men vs. the Black Dragon* role of Rex Bennett.

Born in Alberta, Canada on December 7, 1910, Nathan Roderick Cox was an athletic boy who played basketball and ice hockey in high school and later took a shot at semi-professional football. As a young man he tried to enlist in the Royal Canadian Mounted Police but, amazingly, failed the physical exam. Moving to Hollywood, he did stunts and played bit parts for a year or two before landing a contract with Paramount Pictures, where he won meatier roles and worked as a stand-in for Fred MacMurray. Now billed as Rod

Cameron, the six-foot-four Canadian in 1942 declined to re-up at Paramount and began searching for leading roles. *Black Dragon* had earned him top billing for the first time.

The female lead went to pert and petite Joan Marsh, the daughter of Oscar-winning cinematographer Charles Rosher, a former child actress, and a popular freelance player who had bounced around the major studios since the beginning of talkies without achieving stardom. Of late she had been mired in thankless supporting roles; her turn as feisty war correspondent Janet Blake would prove the last substantive part she received before retiring from the business in 1944.

Duncan Renaldo, a Republic regular who had already appeared in five of the studio's serials and been one of the Three Mesquiteers (in the 1939-40 season), earned third billing as Free French Captain Pierre La Salle, whose Casablanca office served as headquarters for Rex Bennett once he reached Casablanca. Practically all the other characters were Nazis, played by actors from Poland, Germany, and Austria-Hungary.

O'Sullivan's director problem was solved when he signed industry veteran Spencer Gordon Bennet, whose roots in the picture business stretched back to *The Perils of Pauline* (1914), in which he performed stunts. A protégé of pioneering serial writer-director George B. Seitz, Bennet worked on Pathé chapter plays almost exclusively for the next 15 years, with time out for service in the first World War. He was Seitz's assistant for years, finally becoming a solo director in 1925. Bennet's second serial as chief helmer, *The Green Archer* (1925), was both a critical and commercial success; it was followed by such episodic epics as *The House Without a Key* (1926, the first Charlie Chan film), *Hawk of the Hills* (1927), and *The Man Without a Face* (1928), to name just a few.

When Pathé in 1929 was absorbed into RKO and abandoned serials, Bennet took whatever assignments he could find. His reputation for turning out quality product on low budgets and short schedules followed him throughout the sound era, and during the Thirties he labored mainly for Poverty Row producers such as Larry Darmour and the Weiss Brothers.

Bennet had recently finished directing two serials produced by Rudy Flothow for Columbia release—*The Secret Code* and *Valley of Vanishing Men*—when William O'Sullivan lured him to Republic with the promise of a lucrative long-term contract. Signing with the studio in early 1943, he directed the first film in a brand new "B"-Western series, *Calling Wild Bill Elliott*, while the scenarios for *Secret Service* were being completed. The 15-chapter serial was budgeted at $174,536, a significant increase over the recent Republic chapter plays. (*G-Men vs. the Black Dragon*, another 15-episode thriller, came in just slightly over budget at a negative cost of $156,600.) A lot was riding on Bennet's first chapter play for his new employer.

Early on, O'Sullivan recalled in 1992, it became apparent that *Secret Service* costs would surpass the estimate. A record number of new sets were required, straining the resources of the studio's Art Department. Russell Kimball and his associate Fred Ritter were tasked to design, construct, and furnish expansive sets replicating the Moorish architecture American moviegoers associated with films set in Arabian countries. This extended not only to the interiors but exteriors as well, requiring designers and carpenters to add Moorish trappings to buildings on the back lot's Spanish Street, Cantina Street, and Hacienda Square. In truth, of course, the Casablanca of 1943 was largely a modern city, its architecture reflecting French rather than Moorish influence.

Dressing the sets required more props of Arab character than John McCarthy's Prop Department had in stock, necessitating more rentals and purchases than typically required for serials. On top of all this, wartime material shortages had driven up costs in general. O'Sullivan had no choice but to allot more money to production appurtenances and hope he could save a few dollars elsewhere.

Shooting began on Monday, April 12. Early in production the *Secret Service* unit traveled to Lake Elsinore, which stood in for both the Atlantic Ocean and an unnamed river near Casablanca. Along with scenes requiring motorboat chases, Spencer Bennet shot extensively at various shorefront locations scouted and rented by Locations Manager John Bourke. The Lakeland Showboat, so prominently used in earlier Republic serials, was once more pressed into service for major sequences. Returning from Elsinore, the unit completed exterior shooting on familiar turf: Iverson's Ranch in Chatsworth.

Secret Service in Darkest Africa, following the formula established in *Spy Smasher* and then refined in *King of the Mounties* and *G-Men vs. the Black Dragon*, eschewed linear plotting in favor of multiple sub-plots, all of them resolved in a chapter or two. Each new situation was simply a peg on which to hang action sequences, and the second Rex Bennett opus had a surfeit of them. Twenty-six major fight scenes were spread out among the 15 episodes; many chapters ended with a fistic encounter that was recapped in the following stanza, so some installments had three donnybrooks in their two reels. This is addition to numerous one- or two-punch skirmishes, not to mention car chases, horse chases, gun battles, and exploding miniatures. Producer O'Sullivan, the proponent of this formula, was exploiting it to the hilt.

Stunt ramrod Tom Steele, who doubled Cameron just as he had in *Black Dragon*, assembled a small but extremely able team for the fights and chases. Duke Green handled the action for secondary villain Frederic Brunn and played seven other heavies with changes in wardrobe and makeup. In addition to doubling Duncan Renaldo, Ken Terrell appeared in eight other roles calling for action. Other stunt performers used in minor parts included Joe Yrigoyen, Eddie Parker, George Magrill, John Daheim, Carey Loftin, Bud Geary, and George DeNormand.

The fights in *Secret Service* set a new record for destruction, with so many props being smashed that Steele and his crew were reduced to filching breakaway chairs, tables, and crockery from the sets of other productions on the Republic lot. These grueling exhibitions of fistic prowess usually took an entire morning or afternoon to block, rehearse, and shoot. After consulting the script for details of each encounter, Steele would walk through the routine with his comrades and director Bennet, who would suggest certain "gags" they could incorporate into the sequence. He was fond, for example, of having one combatant throw a fist (or maybe a chair) *toward* the camera lens, that cutting to a reaction shot of the blow's recipient falling backward *away* from the camera. Although this meant using two close-ups where one medium shot would normally suffice, the gimmick always elicited favorable responses from Saturday-matinee moviegoers—who, it should be remembered, were seeing these donnybrooks on theater screens as much as 30 feet high. A giant fist hurtling toward the camera had quite an impact on goggle-eyed viewers.

In a 1971 interview with film historian Jon Tuska, Bennet expounded upon his method of shooting those bone-crunching battles for which the mid-Forties Republic chapter plays are so fondly remembered.

> When I went over to Republic, the other directors [and] the stuntmen told me I must shoot a full panorama of a fight routine. They would knock everything down and break everything, then stop and set everything up again so that we could get close-ups [of principal players]. I knew how to match shots better than that. I would say to the stuntman, "Now, I want you to start from here. It's going to take a minute . . . say, a minute and eight seconds to do that. But I want it done well." So I would set them up and they fought in a corner. Then I would cut in my principals, right while I could remember their positions, and we wouldn't have to set up all the props again. Now I would match shots and bring my principals out of it and take them right into the next routine, cut, put in the doubles, and go on. All the editor had to do was assemble the footage. The other way, fights took twice as long.

Principal photography was finished on Thursday, May 27, after 40 working days. Thanks to Bennet's cutting-in-the-camera approach, film editors Wallace Grissell and Tim Malloy had no trouble preparing the first seven chapters for shipping to Republic exchanges in plenty of time for the chapter play's July 24 national release date. Negative cost amounted to more than $210,000, an overrun of fully 20 percent, making *Secret Service* both the most expensive Republic serial to date and the one to run the most over budget.

Chapter One opens with the arrival of Sultan Abou Ben Ali (played by Lionel Royce) at Casablanca's Hotel Internationale, where he has rented a lavish suite and conference room to entertain North Africa's Arab sheiks. They are debating whether to support the Axis or the newly formed United Nations. Unbeknownst to the Sultan, his German-born secretary Ernst Muller (Kurt Kreuger) is a Nazi agent working for Baron von Rommler (also Lionel Royce), whom plastic surgery has turned into an exact duplicate of Ben Ali. Von Rommler has been sent to Casablanca to impersonate the Sultan in an attempt to sway the sheiks to Germany's side. To this end the Gestapo has stolen a priceless religious artifact, the Dagger of Solomon, and replicated the ancient scroll buried in the tomb of Kubla el Baida. The forged document urges Arab chieftains to follow the sign of the Swastika.

In short order Abou Ben Ali is kidnapped and imprisoned in a dungeon constructed below his hotel suite and reached via a false floor section that slides into the fireplace at the touch of a button. Von Rommler dons the Sultan's clothes and begins his masquerade by convening a meeting of the local sheiks. The dagger and scroll are being flown from Berlin to facilitate the Nazi plan.

American secret agent Rex Bennett (Rod Cameron), operating undercover in Germany, impersonates a Gestapo agent and gains control of the religious artifacts. His identity is discovered, but he fights his way out of the country and flies to Casablanca, where he immediately contacts Captain Pierre La Salle (Duncan Renaldo) in the city's French Diplomatic Headquarters. Aided by the Captain and Janet Blake (Joan Marsh), a World Press Organization reporter assigned to cover the North African conflict, Bennett recovers the dagger and scroll after they are stolen by von Rommler's henchman Wolfe (Frederic Brunn). He presents them to the assembled sheiks, who realize the scroll must be a fake because otherwise it would still be in the tomb.

This initial gambit runs its course in the first two chapters, leaving 13 installments in which the phony Sultan uses inside knowledge to interfere with the Allied war effort in North Africa. Troop convoys are sunk by a submarine wolf pack; an attempt is made to destroy food and medical supplies; a United Nations courier is targeted for assassination; a large quantity of ordnance is earmarked for destruction with a "munitions disintegrator." Some episodes revolve around the rescues of Janet and La Salle when they fall into enemy hands. And one of Von Rommler's operatives frames Bennett for the murder of a sheik whose signature is needed to ratify an agreement between the Arab tribes.

When mounting evidence indicates that the Sultan is behind the recent outrages, the Baron heartlessly kills Muller and blames his dead secretary for the many leaks of sensitive information. Rex sees the flaw in von Rommler's story, rescues the real Sultan, and kills the Nazi mastermind before he can escape with recently acquired plans for the Allied campaign in North Africa.

From a production standpoint, *Secret Service in Darkest Africa* represents a high-water mark for Republic serials. Its many spacious and well-appointed sets (invariably reduced to rubble during fight scenes), lavish miniatures, extravagantly staged action, and glossy photography by William Bradford (a veteran cinematographer of the studio's Westerns, shooting his one and only serial), the second Rex Bennett adventure far surpasses its predecessor. The musical score—credited to Mort Glickman but also employing cues written by Paul Sawtell, Walter Scharf, Marlin Skiles, and Arnold Schwarzwald—is largely original but incorporates selected pieces from *Spy Smasher* and *Perils of Nyoka*. The latter serial also took place in North Africa, so the music cues borrowed from it are of similar character.

But, of course, it's those breathlessly staged fight sequences that most fans vividly remember. These elaborate fistic encounters, which more than anything else distinguish Republic's episodic thrillers from those produced at the same time for Universal and Columbia, are undercranked to a fare-thee-well. Rod Cameron throws a convincing punch and Tom Steele is an effective double for him; the daring leaps of Duke Green and the acrobatic feats of Ken Terrell complement his flat-footed brawling style. There's also a surprising reliance on lethal action: Bennett and La Salle frequently shoot adversaries they've just bested in a fight when the miscreants keep trying to kill them. Even Janet Blake proves surprisingly bloodthirsty, fatally shooting a handful of Arab henchmen, one of them in the back.

I discussed *Secret Service in Darkest Africa* with Cameron during an interview conducted at the 1983 Western Film Fair in Charlotte, North Carolina. Although he put up a brave front, the star was losing his several-year battle with cancer and would be dead before year's end. But he still cut a tall, imposing figure and was extremely open to questions from fans. He told me: "The Rex Bennett things were important to my career. Up to that time I'd mostly been doing bits at Paramount. Serials weren't considered prestigious, but I finally got a *lead*. And they helped sell me to Universal [where Cameron wound up under contract in 1944].

"What I couldn't understand, though, was why they kept giving me these short guys to fight. The guy who played Wolfe [Frederic Brunn] couldn't have been more than five-five. I was constantly trying to hunch down, you know, hunch my shoulders while I was fighting them. Sometimes I let them get me on my knees so I wouldn't tower over them. I remember saying, 'Jesus, Spence, it's going to look like I'm tossing rag dolls around the set.' He just said, 'Don't worry about it. The odds are always going to be two to one, and we'll be moving so fast the kids will never notice.'

"Spence was a great director for action, nobody else like him in the business. But if you expected him to coach you on your acting, boy, were *you* in for a surprise! He was one of these guys [who would say], 'Okay, you pause when you're coming through the door, then run over to the desk and grab the phone.' That was about as much directing as you got from a performance point of view. Every now and then he might say, "Look like you're mad" or something like that. To him it was all about doing one run-through, then one take. Unless it was bad for camera or sound, he was already moving on to the next set-up."

In later years, when asked to name the best serial he directed, Spencer Bennet would routinely choose *The Green Archer* (1925), the second chapter play he made for Pathé. But if limited to episodic thrills of the sound era, he would pick *Secret Service in Darkest Africa*. In a 1971 interview with film historian Jon Tuska, he said it "was a fine production . . . and had good actors," adding: "I thought I worked out the fights better than usual."

During his four-year Republic tenure, Bennet directed another 12 serials (including such favorites as *The Masked Marvel, The Tiger Woman, Haunted Harbor,* and *Manhunt of Mystery Island*) and eight "B" Westerns, including the first Red Ryder feature, *Tucson Raiders* (1944). In 1947 he went to work for legendarily penny-pinching producer Sam Katzman, then making chapter plays for Columbia release. Always chiseling on budgetary expenditures so he could pocket extra cash, Katzman was able to crank out his serials on the cheap because, for the most part, they were based on characters that were licensed from other media (mostly comic books) and had built-in followings. Therefore, the film's actual quality was strictly secondary.

At first, Sam worried that his new director wasn't shooting enough film. He wasn't aware of Bennet's ability to cut in the caera, but Spence soon clued him in:

> When I first worked for Katzman [on Columbia serials], I sent him my first week's dailies—I was up in Kernville—and he said, "You're not getting enough picture . . . you're not getting enough picture . . . we're going to be short." I tried to convince him on the phone that he would have more than he needed. He was so used to all this repetitious stuff, to all this repeating; do it in a long shot, then do a close-up, dialogue and everything. He would get this tremendous amount of dailies [and] be there for two or three hours looking at all that, and only about a third would end up in the picture. I didn't have any waste, and finally when he got the first few episodes cut, he had plenty of film. Not only did I save time, but I saved him money on

his lab bill. I always said to Katzman, "You aren't paying me anything on these pictures. I'm saving you my salary on the lab bill." And I did.

Bennet's Columbia chapter plays included the two *Superman* serials with Kirk Alyn (1948 and 1950), *Batman and Robin, Congo Bill, Bruce Gentry, Brick Bradford, Captain Video, Blackhawk,* and others—21 in all. Ironically, he was the only craftsman associated with American chapter-play production from beginning to end, working as a stunt double on the third serial (1914's *Perils of Pauline*) and wielding the megaphone on *Blazing the Overland Trail* (1956), the last episodic thriller produced in the United States for theatrical distribution.

That's Warren Hull behind the mask as the two-gun hero of *The Spider's Web*.

Top: Wentworth and Nita (Iris Meredith, right) help Kate Sands (Beatrice Curtis), a crime victim. Bottom: Jackson (Richard Fiske) and Ram Singh (Kenne Duncan).

Top: The Spider holds Octopus henchmen at bay as they storm the powerhouse.
Bottom: Nita is rescued while the Spider uses a henchmen's corpse as a shield.

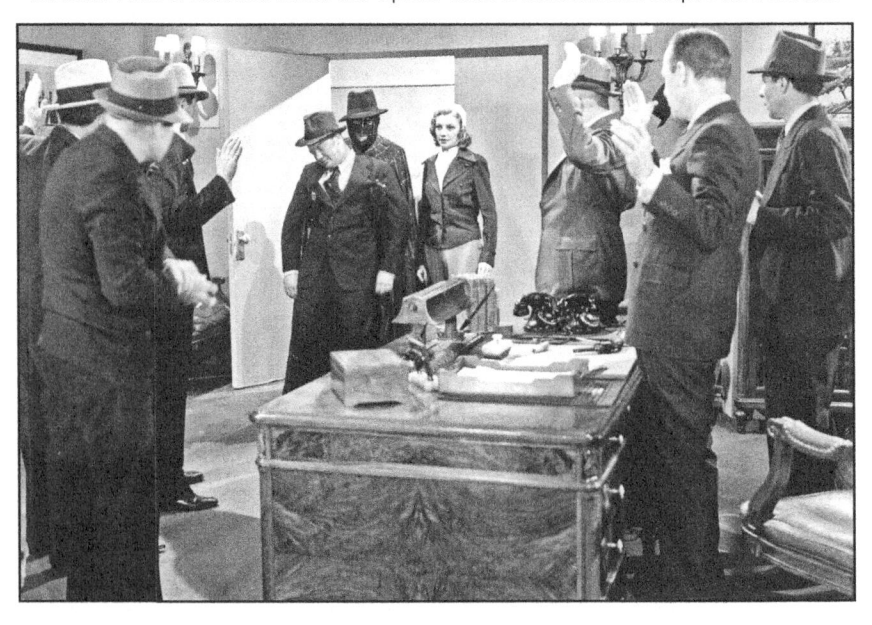

GALLERY 3 / 283

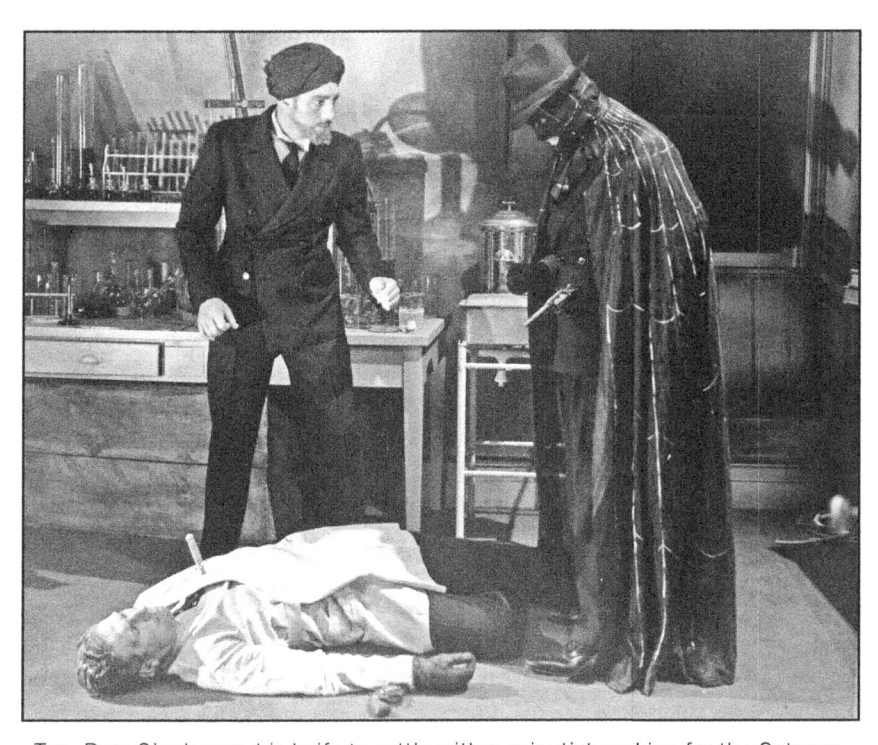

Top: Ram Singh uses his knife to settle with a scientist working for the Octopus.
Bottom: The original 1940 trade-paper ad for what became *The Spider Returns*.

Top: (L to R) Kenne Duncan, Mary Ainslee, Stephen Chase, Warren Hull, and Dave O'Brien in *The Spider Returns*. Bottom: The Gargoyle seems taken aback!

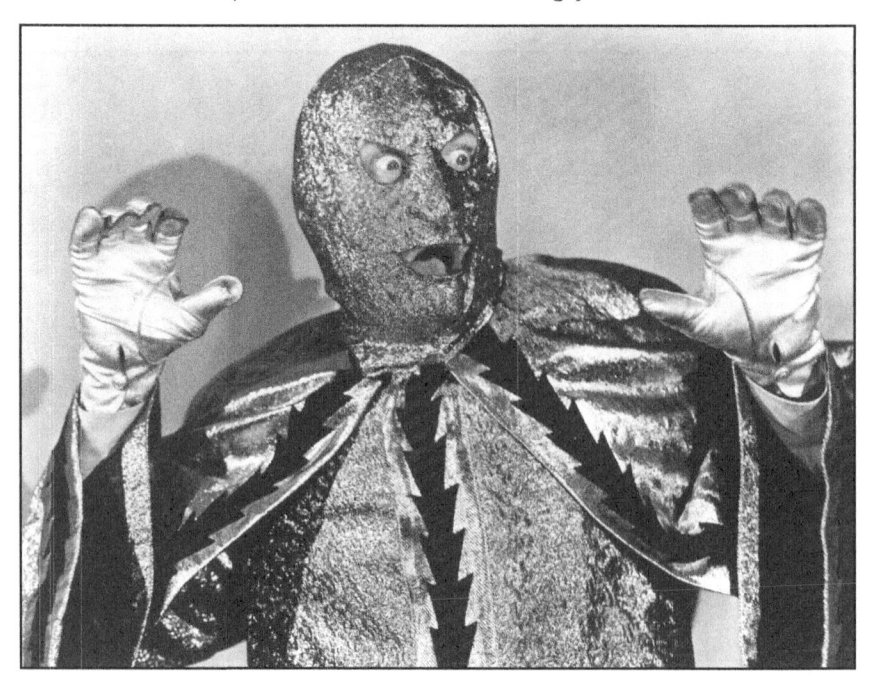

Top: The Spider infiltrates one of the Gargoyle's hideouts. Heavies (L to R) include Dale Van Sickel (standing), Chuck Hamilton, Michael Vallon, and Charles Sullivan. Bottom: Herman Brix as Kioga in this publicity shot from *Hawk of the Wilderness*.

Top: Kioga takes a brief history lesson from his mentor, Mokuyi (Noble Johnson). Bottom: Yellow Weasel (Monte Blue, center) and his men have captured the Hawk.

Top: Kioga gets some important information from his friend, Kias (Ray Mala).
Bottom: The Hawk attempts to get Beth Munro (Jill Martin) away from pirates.

288 / Blood 'n' Thunder's Cliffhanger Classics 2

Top: Kioga nearly falls victim to a deadly trap. Bottom: A warning signal seen by Kioga, the pirate Solerno (William Royle), and Allan Kendall (George Eldredge).

The Chapter Six one-sheet poster for *Adventures of Red Ryder* (1940).

Top: Red Ryder (Don "Red" Barry) comes to the aid of Beth Andrews (Vivian Coe).
Bottom: Red settles with the Apache Kid (Joe De La Cruz), one of his dad's killers.

Top: Red and the ranchers confront banker Calvin Drake (Harry Worth, in suit). Bottom: Ace Hanlon (Noah Beery, pointing) accuses Red of some skullduggery.

Top: Drake hesitates to give the Duchess (Maude Pierce Allen) her mortgage back. Bottom: One-Eye (Bob Kortman) and his henchmen hold Red at their hideout.

Gallery 3 / 293

Spy Smasher was already a popular comic-book character when Republic brought him to the screen in a 1942 serial that set new records for non-stop action.

Spy Smasher had a twin brother who sacrificed himself in the penultimate chapter. Kane Richmond played both, although stand-in James Dale is the dead one below.

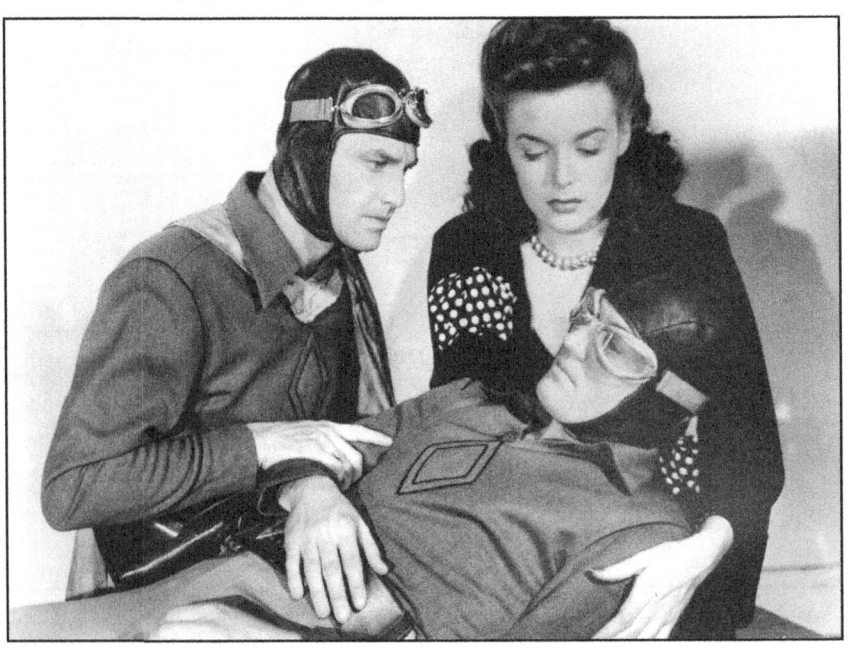

One-sheet poster for the last chapter, with a portrait of Richmond and Chapman.

Top: Admiral Corby (Sam Flint) and Eve are robbed at home by The Mask's men. Bottom: The disguised Baron von Rommler (Lionel Royce) reviews plans with his ruthless henchmen Wolfe (Frederic Brunn, center) and Muller (Kurt Kreuger).

Interestingly, neither hero nor heroine appears on this Chapter One poster.

Top: Rex Bennett (Rod Cameron, right) crosses swords with a Gestapo officer. Bottom: Rex struggles to rescue his comrade Pierre Durand (Duncan Renaldo).

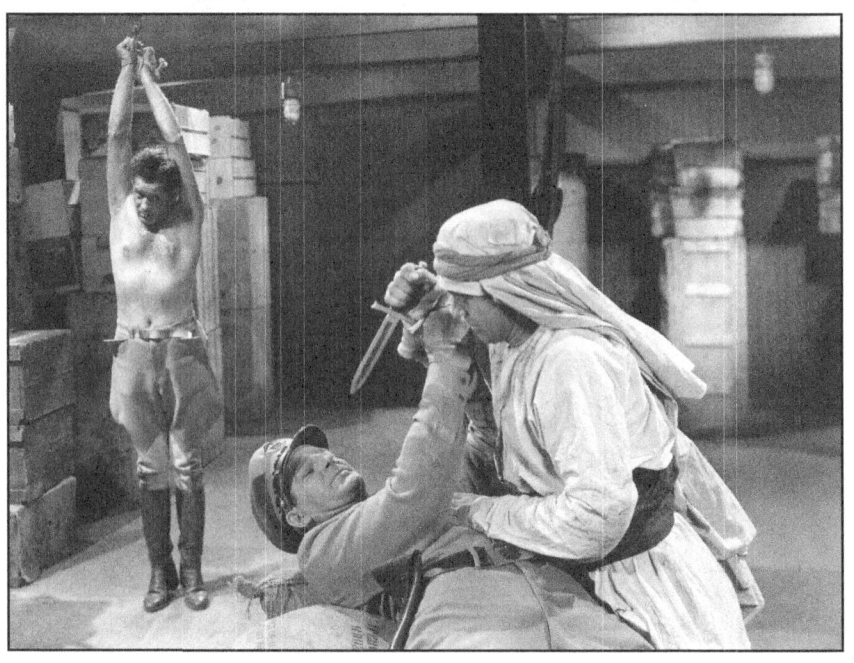

GALLERY 3 / 299

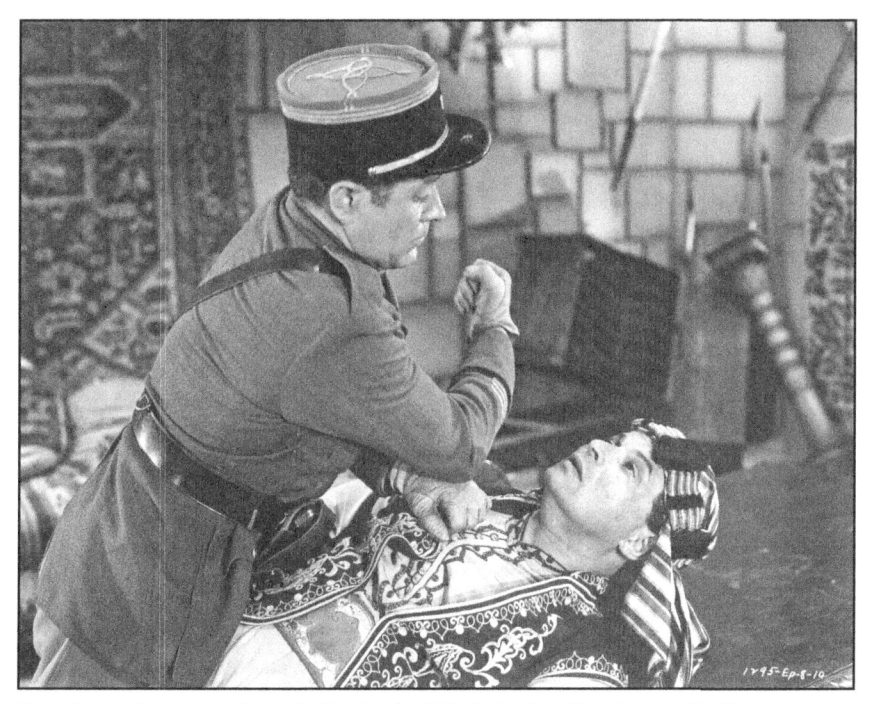

Top: Durand temporarily gets the best of Wolfe in the Moorish castle Nazi hideout.
Bottom: Posing as Sultan Abou Ben Ali, von Rommler has Rex fooled—for now.

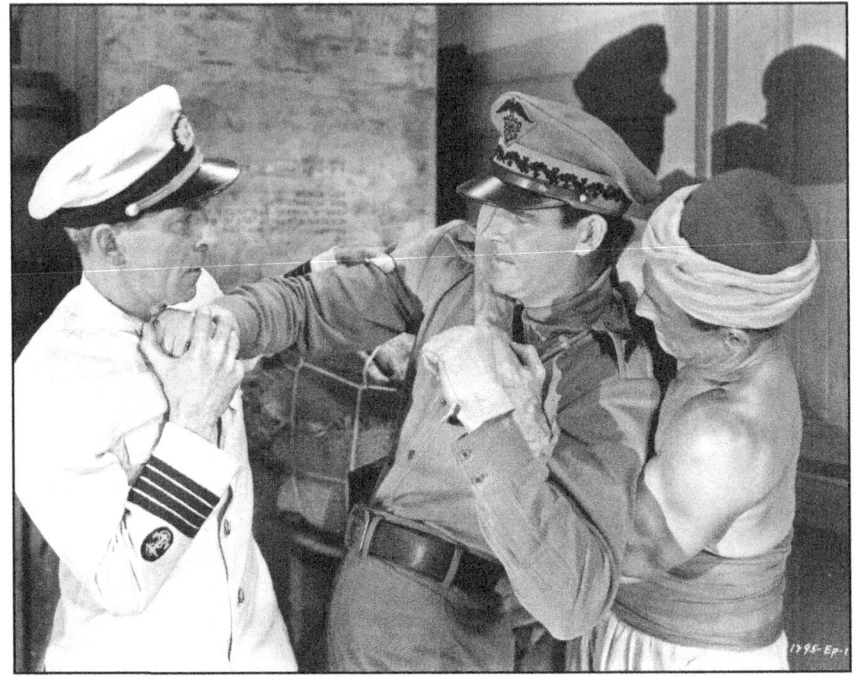

Top: Rex battles the riverboat captain (Ralf Harolde) for the dagger and scroll. Bottom: Boschert (William Vaughn) stops Wolfe from striking Janet (Joan Marsh).

Made in the USA
Las Vegas, NV
23 June 2023